THE CREATION OF POLITICAL NEWS

For
Fleur, Peter and Di

The Creation of
Political News

Television and British Party Political Conferences

JAMES STANYER

sussex
ACADEMIC
PRESS

BRIGHTON • PORTLAND

2 4 6 8 10 9 7 5 3 1

First published 2001
in Great Britain by
SUSSEX ACADEMIC PRESS
PO Box 2950
Brighton BN2 5SP

and in the United States of America by
SUSSEX ACADEMIC PRESS
5824 N.E. Hassalo St.
Portland, Oregon 97213-3644

British Library Cataloguing in Publication Data
A CIP catalogue record for this book is available from the British Library.

Library of Congress Cataloging-in-Publication Data has been applied for.

ISBN h/c 1 902210 76 X   ISBN p/b 1 902210 77 8

Typeset and designed by G&G Editorial, Brighton
Printed by TJ International, Padstow, Cornwall
This book is printed on acid-free paper

Contents

Acknowledgements

The research for this book could not have been completed without the assistance of numerous people and organizations. I would like to thank the Liberal Democrat Party, the Labour Party and the Conservative Party for granting me access to their annual autumn conferences. I am particularly indebted to various party sources, who cannot all be named, and to the journalists, editors and planners at the BBC, ITN and Sky, not forgetting Roy Graham, who spoke to me and answered my questions in letters. I would like to thank them all.

This research was only made possible by a research grant from the Economic and Social Research Council, aided by additional funds from the London School of Economics and the Reeves Foundation. I am grateful for the help of: the LSE Audio Visual Unit for recording the news, the LSE Methodology Institute for running a series of useful courses, Robert Moore, Paul Chipchase, Tony Grahame, Editorial Director at Sussex Academic Press, and colleagues at CMCR. Finally, I would like to thank the following friends and colleagues. Tom Nossiter, for first seeing the potential of the project. Maggie Scammell, whose initial idea it was to examine the party conferences and for her support over the years. Pat Dunleavy, for his drive and support, and his ability to see through the complex problems that arose in writing and without whom the project would not have been finished. Colin Seymour-Ure and Sonia Livingstone for their helpful comments on an earlier draft of the work. Raymond Kuhn, Ralph Negrine and John B. Thompson for their encouragement.

A special thanks goes to my friends, Richard Heffernan, Andy Chadwick and Oliver James, without whose constant encouragement and helpful insights this project would not have been completed. Last, but most importantly, I owe a special debt of gratitude to my parents, Peter and Di, for their enormous help and to Fleur, for her unwavering belief in me and her constant support throughout the period. Any errors are of course my responsibility alone.

The Creation of *Political* News

Television and British Party
Political Conferences

Introduction: The News from Blackpool, Bournemouth and Brighton

Anyone watching a television news bulletin or reading a newspaper in early autumn would be hard pressed to avoid reports on the party conferences. These annual gatherings of the three main political parties routinely receive not only a relatively large amount of news coverage but also live coverage. In fact they have been covered live by the BBC since 1954, five years prior to the first televised election campaign.[1] In recent years, each conference has had websites dedicated to them as well. In the light of the almost saturation coverage they receive it is not surprising therefore that party conferences have been described as 'media events'.[2] Each party accordingly has sought to take advantage of the opportunity afforded them to promote their leading personalities and policies to a national audience beyond the conference hall.

This book through examining the construction of television conference news seeks to show first, how party elites manage news coverage of their conference and the problems they face in trying to do this. And second, it seeks to show the way in which the news broadcasters mediate conferences. In doing this, the book builds upon existing studies on news production and news management in the field of political communication, and contributes to existing research on the formation of political news agendas.

Television news and the modern publicity process

In Britain, campaigning by parties is no longer confined to the period of general elections, but is an almost permanent feature of political life. This so-called 'permanent campaign' (Blumenthal, 1982) is particularly news media centred. The news media are the main conduit through which competing political advocates seek to reach the public on a daily basis. Broadcast news is possibly the most important source of exposure for political parties, keen to gain as much 'positive' publicity as possible (see Blumler *et al.*, 1989; Swanson and Mancini, 1996; Tiffen, 1989). This is because of its impartiality – press coverage is often deliberately hostile to publicity initiatives from parties they oppose. It is also due to its reach: news coverage, particularly in the evening, attracts an audience of millions, one much larger than for the live coverage of political events. News coverage is also seen as 'less manufactured than [political] advertisements [or party websites] and, as such, may be thought to carry more legitimacy and credibility [with the audience]'.[3]

Between elections, parties and politicians are involved in an almost continuous struggle to ensure that their views, rather than those of their rivals, dominate the broadcast news agenda and shape public opinion. The battle pitches campaign teams against each other in an attempt to secure the most beneficial coverage. This process of hyper-competition has been termed the 'modern publicity process' (Blumler, 1990). The consequences of this process are well documented (see Blumler, 1990).[4] It has led to all main political parties allocating greater resources to news management activity. There has been a well-documented rise in the number of media specialists within party ranks (Panebianco, 1988; Scammell, 1995; Shaw, 1994). Communication professionals are now a permanent fixture at party headquarters. In addition every minister and their shadow now has a 'special advisor'. These so-called spin doctors[5] have regular access to leadership actors and in many cases are an integral part of the leadership cadre (Heffernan and Stanyer, 1997). These communication professionals have in turn made news management a central weapon in achieving the leadership's publicity goals. Greater attention is paid to how announcements will play in the news media. A lot of emphasis is placed on communication strategies to aid agenda dominance and also kill off any rival's attempt at determining the news agenda (Blumler, 1990; Jones 1997). It has also led to party leaderships placing greater emphasis on discipline amongst party members (Franklin, 1994; Rosenbaum, 1997; Shaw, 1994) in an attempt to avoid negative publicity which may do damage to their party's image and electoral fortunes.

The struggle for agenda supremacy inevitably impacts upon the broadcasters. Journalists are subjected to almost continuous attempts to influence the way they frame political events (Jones, 1995, 1997). The broadcasters' reactions to the public relations onslaught have been documented in several studies (see Blumler *et al.*, 1989; Semetko *et al.*, 1991). These have noted an increasing disdain, even cynicism, towards the agenda-setting ploys of political parties. Disdaining commentary, in particular, is becoming a common feature of British campaign reporting (Nossiter *et al.*, 1995). The broadcast organizations have also instituted procedures to deal with the barrage of complaints and accusations of bias they receive from party spin doctors (Franklin, 1994). Journalists in the face of a 'spin' blizzard seem to be determined to reassert their autonomy and their contribution to shaping news output.

Conferences and agenda-setting competition

For each party elite, conferences represent a unique opportunity to set the news agenda.[6] Conference time is the only period in the year where each party is in a one-on-one relationship with the news broadcasters. The sole focus of the news broadcasters' attention is the party that hosts the conference – the other parties are relegated to the coverage sidelines. While interaction between political parties and the news media professionals is often intense throughout the period of each conference, competition between the parties is significantly less or virtually non-existent compared to a general election period. With their rivals momentarily relegated to the sidelines, conference coverage provides an opportunity to promote the best possible image of a party's policies and organization to the viewers beyond the conference hall, un-challenged by political opponents. The main parties have sought to exploit this opportunity and the lengths to which they have gone to do this has been documented by media and political professionals (Bruce, 1992; Cockerell, 1989; Grice, 1996, 1998; Jones, 1995, 1997 and 1999; Landale, 1996; Thomas, 1989; Wintour, 1990, 1995b), and by academics (Kavanagh, 1996; Rosenbaum, 1997; Scammell, 1995; Shaw, 1994). Some critics (for example, Blumler *et al.*, 1996; McNair, 1995) have suggested that the modern publicity process has changed the function of con-ferences over the last twenty years; from forums for intra-party debate to 'pseudo events' (Boorstin, 1961)[7] stage-managed to ensure that the television audience receives a favourable impression. In other words the dominance of this media-centred competition has reduced the distinctiveness of all party conferences.

Each conference also provides the news broadcasters with a series of opportunities not available in their 'run-of-the-mill' coverage of Westminster – an opportunity to focus on policy development and the launch of new policy initiatives. However, the news broadcasters are not at the conferences simply to mirror leadership publicity initiatives. As a gathering of the whole party, the conferences also allow greater access not only to the parliamentary party and leadership but also to the activists. They represent an opportunity to examine debate within the parties, test activists' opinions and capture party divisions; and if gaffes, mishaps and unforeseen events occur, they are covered too. Being under the continual 'gaze'[8] of news hungry broadcasters is a source of anxiety for the party leadership as well. The news agenda can shift easily, overshadowing planned events. It is not surprising therefore, in the competitive political communication environment, that each party elite goes to great lengths to ensure that their conference achieves the requisite positive publicity and avoids any negative or damaging events.

The news production process

Television news is co-produced (Bennett *et al.*, 1985; Blumler and Gurevitch, 1995; Blumler *et al.*, 1986, 1989, 1995; Semetko *et al.*, 1991). While the parties are the originators of the information, the broadcast journalists repackage the material for the viewing audience. Television news is also the product of different interrelated stages (Gans, 1979; Golding and Elliott, 1979). Conference news is no different in this respect; it is jointly constructed by both the parties and the news broadcasters and encompasses different stages. The production of conference news involves both parties and broadcasters in: advance planning for the conferences; and in the gathering, selection and presentation of news stories. The activities at each stage are routine, organized and interconnected with the next stage. Planning by the broadcasters and parties is a fundamental prerequisite for later news dissemination and gathering of information. The essential logistical elements of conference coverage have to be in place prior to the start of conference. These elements make the next stage possible.

Each stage involves frequent interaction between actors with working relationships and multiple inter-dependencies. Party and broadcast administrators are heavily interdependent during the planning stage. They engage in negotiation over the prerequisites for television coverage such as the position of the cameras, the lighting and sound arrangements, and the broadcast booths looking on to the main arena. Once conferences begin, interaction occurs between various political actors in the party hierarchy and its bureaucracy, and the correspondents, political editors and producers. These actors are in constant contact with each other throughout the conference week, in effect engaging in the well acknowledged exchange of information for publicity (Blumler and Gurevitch, 1995; Tunstall, 1970). As actors at Westminster some of them have pre-existing exchange relationships. For this group of actors, conferences are an extension of Lobby relations but in a different location.

The broadcast journalists finally package the day's events into a series of two-and-a-half to three-minute reports. These are a condensed montage of the main issues raised in debates and speeches and the reactions from party actors – bound together by a narrative. They also seek to expand upon the issues raised by producing a series of additional news items. These take the form of interviews with the main protagonists at conference, usually leadership actors, additional news reports and live question and answer sessions between the anchor and the journalist at conference. The questions often encourage speculation about, and explanation of, the significant events of the day.

Shared and divergent interests

Despite the dyadic interdependence which exists, party and broadcaster interests are not always identical. They share an interest in the conferences attracting high audience viewing figures; indeed in the planning stages both organizational bureaucracies want the event to run smoothly, so that the operation looks slick and professionally produced to the viewing audience. Interests also diverge over what issues should be the main focus of news reports, and how these issues are framed. The broadcasters attending conference, and the journalists who work for them, are happy to reflect the issues raised in key events such as the leader's speech and other newsworthy speeches but are generally reluctant to be passive relayers of information – a conduit for every politician's gambit – and do not always reflect the pre-planned conference agenda. The broadcasters reserve the right to focus on the issues they see as important and inform their audience as they see fit.

Important decisions on coverage are made on a daily basis independent of party elites. These decisions are influenced by attitudes. Studies on parliamentary broadcasting by Blumler and Gurevitch (1995) and on general elections with Nossiter (1986, 1989, 1995) show that the broadcasters' approach to political events is clearly attitudinal. The broadcasters approach each conference with a particular attitude. While motivated by a duty to responsibly inform their audiences of debates, announcements and decisions and cover the leader's speech, they are also driven by news values. News values are increasingly important in helping decide what events will be covered, which sources will be included and which excluded, the amount of coverage an event receives and its prominence. The 'stopwatch' is much less of a consideration in allocating coverage, as the normal 'bi-partisan' conventions of political balance under which the broadcasters operate outside conferences, do not apply. The significance of news values is reinforced by the fact that both the BBC's and ITN's main bulletins are engaged in ratings-driven competition with each other and with rivals such as *Sky News*. They want to make sure that their conference coverage is not a 'turn-off' and does not adversely affect their audience share. Even the longer more 'serious' bulletins, *Channel Four News* and *Newsnight*, have to cater for and maintain their audiences. The content of all reports has to fulfil certain audience criteria, even if the audience might be 'a concept more than a real force';[9] it has not only to inform but increasingly grab audience attention. One area of divergence with party leaderships surrounds the coverage of intra-party conflict. While party elites prefer it not to be covered, all broadcasters find it particularly newsworthy. Whether it is vocal opposition to party policy, or the criticisms of disaffected former ministers, such conflict is given a high priority in bulletin running orders.

Managing conference news

For the leaderships and their teams of spin doctors the desired coverage is achieved by minimizing any existing and potential differences of interest between the broadcasters and themselves. Each leadership cadre achieves this in two ways. First, by managing the conference timetable and agenda, and second, through a systematic adaptation of party communicative activity to the news broadcasters' needs.

The leaderships and their spin doctors realize that the broadcasters find overt conflict on policy issues particularly newsworthy. Their solution is to minimize such sources of distraction. Through the agenda committees they are able to have some influence on the selection and positioning of debates, either blocking them because the issues they raise are deemed controversial, or placing them in a position in the conference timetable where it is judged that they will receive less attention from journalists. Indeed this process of manipulation has been well documented (Kavanagh, 1996; Kelly, 1989; Minkin, 1978). Even though delegates are allowed to debate balloted motions, these are rarely on issues which are considered controversial and the leadership through the platform are still able to influence which delegates speak.

While minimizing one form of newsworthy occurrence the communication professionals, working on behalf of the leadership, increasingly seek to provide broadcasters with another. They produce 'safe' newsworthy information. Senior party members are encouraged – particularly when in government – to take account of news values when making speeches and use them to deliver the newsworthy policy announcements journalists repeatedly want.[10] Policy announcements are often saved for the leader's speech, to ensure they gain maximum exposure. The delivery of this information takes the broadcasters' deadlines seriously. Speeches are usually synchronized to the bulletin schedules, so that every aspect can be covered. Gathering the information is made easier and quicker for journalists with the provision of 'information subsidies' (Gandy, 1982). These are informal briefings and formal press releases, factual information such as policy statements, and transcripts of speeches. The broadcasters are supplied with opportunities to gain fresh visual material to supplement existing footage. All three parties allow cameras on the floor of the main hall during debates to gather more interesting angle shots. They also provide regular photo-opportunities essential as 'visual fills' for television news reports.

It is also considered important that the conference set generates the right impression on television. The design of the main platform has changed greatly over the last twenty years, to take advantage of the cameras. Particular attention is paid to its colour, its shape, the logo, the platform seating arrangements and the position of the rostrum. The parties hire specialists to design the main platform. The specialists over the years have adapted their designs in response to specific technical realities raised during discussions with the BBC and ITN through to the general demands of the medium based on experience from previous events.

As well as adapting to the broadcasters' needs, communication teams also take advantage of the competition between journalists and news outlets. Certain senior journalists are regularly offered exclusive information in advance of a speech to increase the publicity that policy announcements attract. The spin doctors are aware that news reports are heavily influenced by the availability of particular key sources (Bruce, 1992; Jones, 1995, 1997 and 1999) and offer the broadcasters exclusive access to senior party actors for interviews, but on their terms. In sum, a belief persists amongst communication professionals that the desired coverage can be achieved through tight party management and by adjusting to the broadcasters' news values, deadlines, and easing the cost of gathering of information and visuals – in short adopting a 'media logic' (Altheide and Snow, 1979). This is an on-going process not limited to the conference period that involves a continual reassessment of existing strategies and practices with the view to improvement.

The unmanageable and the unforeseen

However, such strategic management of conference is never completely successful. First, it does not eradicate dissent or conflict but displaces it from the main hall on to the fringe of each conference where it can be picked up by journalists. Second, because each event is well managed, gaffes by leadership actors, leaks from senior politicians' memoirs or opposition spoiling tactics, when they do occur, are considered all the more newsworthy.

While many journalists complain that debates in the main hall have lost the cut-and-thrust of old, dissent is increasingly vocalized at fringe meetings. Although the traditional method of getting issues on to the conference agenda through the submission of motions or resolutions is heavily managed, the media presence on the fringe opens up new opportunities for critical 'claim-makers' (Spector and Kitsuse, 1987) to gain coverage. For those who oppose official party policy this is often a unique opportunity to gain national publicity for their views. While they do not command the same resources or have the same contacts as the leaderships, they improvise. They often print and distribute press releases for journalists (Heffernan and Marqusee, 1992; Minkin, 1978) and use the assortment of party newspapers and the Internet to advertise their views. They take advantage of broadcasters' presence, inviting them to fringe meetings in the hope that the meetings will be included in their final report.

In addition television programmes act as a forum for the further discussion of issues on the conference agenda and broader issues such as the electoral fortunes of the party. BBC *Conference Live* not only captures the debate in the main hall, but also brings together antagonists on certain issues, allowing them further space to air their views. In addition programmes such as *Breakfast with Frost*, the *Dimbleby Programme*, *On the Record* on Sundays and the daily *Conference Talk* often provide an opening for disaffected ministers and former ministers to express their criticisms – the contents of which are given further publicity in news reports.

The journalists, for their part, juxtapose the statements of the different protagonists in various locations around the conference venue and package them in a report (also see Paletz and Elson, 1976). They further frame the content and highlight the significance of these debates for the viewer. The reports are bound together by a narrative about intra-party disagreement and often speculate about the negative electoral consequences of such conflict. This speculation is taken further in live link-ups between the anchor and the correspondent in which a further series of questions are asked.

A determination not to be used, along with the conventionally journalistic instinct for a 'new angle' on the news, means that the communication teams cannot force any agenda upon the news bulletins or prevent other agendas arising despite planning. They can do little to prevent the broadcasters reporting intra-party conflict or shining a light on and amplifying gaffes that media managers prefer to remain unseen.

The only thing the spin doctors can do is try to keep planned speeches newsworthy and to enact a reactive news management strategy. This strategy of damage limitation seeks to minimize the distraction such events cause by providing an interpretation of events friendly to the leadership. If the circumstances require, the reactions of senior party actors are mobilized to condemn a particular actor, and their views or complaints are made against the broadcasters' reporting of events. While journalists expect interaction to be strategically guided to a certain extent, they resent attempts at editorial interference – particularly complaints.

Reassessing the formation of television news agendas

Television news occupies a central role in British politics (Semetko, 1989). However while there have been numerous studies of the news coverage and British general elections (Blumler *et al.*, 1986, 1989, 1995; Goddard *et al.*, 1998; Harrison, 1992, 1997; Norris *et al.*, 1999; Nossiter *et al.*, 1995; Semetko *et al.*, 1991) the period in between general elections has been largely ignored in political communication literature – although there are notable exceptions (Franklin, 1992; Jones, 1995, 1999; Negrine, 1996, 1998; Scammell, 1995; Tracey, 1977). Despite academic recognition of the importance of the television news in British politics, and of the conferences as key political events, the production of party conference news has not so far been specifically analysed in a full-length study. The party conferences raise some important questions about the underlying assumptions contained within the existing news agenda formation literature.

Existing analyses of news agenda formation (Blumler, 1990; Blumler and Gurevitch, 1995; Norris, 1998; Norris *et al.*, 1999; Scammell and Semetko, 1998; Semetko and Canel, 1997; Semetko *et al.*, 1991) almost universally see relationships between parties and the broadcasters in a triadic way, with party A competing with party B to shape news coverage. Based on encounters in the Westminster lobby and elections, they focus on the relationship between the different political parties and the news media, but always within the expectation that media–party relations are permanently located within a framework of inter-party competition. However, news coverage of the party conferences presents this model with certain problems which this book seeks to address. Party conference television news agendas are the product of interaction between the party actors and the broadcasters with inter-party competition having little or no impact. This means that each party for the duration of their conference is in the unique position of being able to promote policies and actors without the intervention of their rivals.

However, saying that each party faces little competition from its rivals in contributing to the news agenda at its own conference, adds only partially to our understanding of the formation of conference news agendas. What the party conferences raise is the importance of an intra-party dimension in the construction of news agendas. There is no denying that party elites and their communication teams play a dominant role in influencing the conference news agenda, but they are not 'the party'. The main political parties are heterogeneous organizations made up formally of different sections and divided on numerous issues. There is a tendency for agenda-formation literature – because of its inter-party slant – to focus on the communicative activities of the campaign professionals and leadership actors, and to ignore the activities of others, although there are extensive survey-based studies of party members' attitudes (Seyd and Whiteley, 1992; Whiteley *et al.*, 1994; Wilson, 1977) and studies of party interest groups (Barnes, 1994; Kelly, 1989; Minkin, 1978; Sowemimo, 1996) and their campaigning activity (Minkin, 1986; Tiffen, 1989; Wring, 1998). To fully understand the creation of conference news agendas the communicative activity of non-leadership actors also has to be taken into account. While the leadership enjoys certain advantages, this is not a fixed state of affairs. Factions, groups and actors opposed to the leadership-endorsed policy also seek to set the television news agenda. Therefore each leadership, on certain issues, faces competition from inside the party to set the news broadcasters' agenda.

The broadcasters play an important role in the construction of conference news agendas. They shape, amplify and reflect issues, packaging them for audience consumption (Blumler and Gurevitch, 1995). Their approach to conferences is shaped by well documented attitudes. In today's competitive news environment news values are one of the main arbiters in determining the formation of party conference news agendas. It is not necessarily the case, as some of the literature argues, that 'journalism-steered-by-news-values converts all too readily in practice into news-management-for-politicians'.[11] At the conferences 'journalism-steered-by-news-values' can convert into a publicity headache or nightmare for each leadership. The broadcasters can help dissident voices achieve national exposure, by-passing formal management mechanisms instituted by the leadership. In this respect the broadcasters go some way to counter-balancing the resource advantages and management strategies of the leadership. One can go further and also argue that journalists, in such an obviously managed news environment, try to 'reassert . . . the significance of their own contributions'[12] by focusing on dissent. In some ways this is a form of disdain (Semetko *et al.*, 1991), for it opens up the viewers' eyes to internecine warfare behind the show of unity in the main hall.

Structure of the book

This book focuses on news production at the three main political parties' annual conferences (Labour, Liberal Democrats and the Conservatives). It examines each step of the production process, concentrating first on the planning process, followed by dissemination and gathering, and finally the packaging of the actual reports. Within this framework it examines the issues raised in this introductory chapter.

Chapter 1 focuses on the co-ordination of conference planning by each leadership and argues that in order to avoid embarrassment and promote themselves and their policies, the leadership galvanizes committees and the bureaucracy into promotional planning to take full advantage of the presence of the broadcasters. Planning across the party is focused on publicity opportunities provided by the conferences, and on the risks. The planning goal of the party professionals and committees is to maximize the use of the broadcasters in promotional terms while simultaneously minimizing potential risks. The chapter focuses on the parties' organizational structure, the planning of the agenda and timetable, communications strategies and the stage set.

Chapter 2 examines the joint planning of conference coverage. It focuses on the co-operation between the two broadcasters (BBC and ITN) and the political parties. It also looks at the discussions and negotiations that occur on coverage matters. It notes that both the broadcasters and the parties are able to affect certain key coverage decisions made during a process of negotiation.

The analysis then moves on in chapter 3 to news gathering at the conferences. This chapter focuses on the structure of the news teams, the influences on the gathering process, broadcasters' attitudes towards speeches and debates, competition between journalists and interaction between journalists and spin doctors, and existing relationships between them.

Chapter 4 focuses on conference management. It examines the strategies used to manage the party throughout conference week. It provides a detailed examination of communication strategies implemented by party spin doctors. Such strategies are used in order to make sure that the broadcasters' news agenda corresponds to the planned agenda in the main hall. This chapter provides a case study of the implementation of communication strategies and the response of the broadcasters.

Chapter 5 examines in detail the management and reporting of one of the highlights of each conference week, the leader's speech, by six evening news bulletins (ITN's *News at 5.40* p.m. on ITV, BBC *Six O'clock News*, ITN's *Channel Four News* at seven o'clock, BBC *Nine O'clock News*, ITN's *News at Ten* at ten o'clock on ITV and the BBC's *Newsnight* at 10.30 p.m.).[13] It focuses in detail on the leader's speech at the Liberal Democrat, Labour and Conservative conferences in 1995. It shows the packaging process, the selection of passages, the contextualization of the passages and the contextualization of the speech overall, and the broadcasters' expansion of the news agenda through the production of additional news items.

Chapter 6 looks at competition to set the news agenda within political parties, often manifest during conferences, and at mistakes and gaffes by the party leadership. It focuses in particular on the response of conference managers to dissent and to gaffes and other mishaps.

Chapter 7 examines the spinning and framing of conflict-laden debates by the same six evening news bulletins. It focuses on debates at the 1994 Liberal Democrat conference, the 1994 Labour conference and the 1993 and 1994 Conservative conferences. It highlights in detail how journalists recreate and contextualize these events for their audience.

The insight this book provides into television news production and spin is of particular relevance in light of modern political parties' obsession with setting the media agenda. Its findings are important for all those interested in the future development of the autumn party conferences in Britain's media democracy.

1

Creating the 'Good' Conference

For the leadership of each party, the ultimate aim of conference is to generate a positive image of the party and get the planned policy agenda across to the public. A 'good conference'[1] is now almost solely defined in publicity terms, as a conference whose news coverage does not show 'unseemly divisions',[2] and promotes the party and its policies to as wide an audience as possible. Such a goal is not taken for granted and involves a substantial amount of planning. There is a concerted and centrally co-ordinated effort by each party leadership to galvanize different actors and committees to achieve this presentational goal. The planners are allocated different promotional tasks including: the planning of conference communication strategies, the broad agenda and timetable, and the aesthetics of designing the main stage and the conference hall. Promotional-oriented planning is an on-going process throughout the year in which little is left to chance. The planners continually seek new ways to improve presentation, taking account of failures or perceived defects in the previous year's conference publicity. This chapter examines the management of the agenda and timetable; and the advance planning of communication strategies and the conference platform.

The conference planning network

Conference planning is controlled and directed, with final decisions resting with the leadership and confidants. Each party's planning effort is centrally co-ordinated by at least one member of the leadership inner circle, usually a senior party actor (the Director of Strategy and Planning for the Liberal Democrats, the General Secretary for Labour, and the Party Chairman for the Conservatives) who liaises with the various committees and department heads. In each party, this actor regularly takes decisions on behalf of the leader and reports back to the leadership on important issues; he or she provides a strong link to the leader's office and the rest of the party throughout the planning process.

Organizational and logistical matters to do with coverage are the responsibility of the so-called 'machine bureaucracy' (Mintzberg, 1983), housed at party headquarters. Decisions about agenda, timetable and communication strategies are made by a series of task forces or committees – the 'adhocracy' (Mintzberg, 1983). The machine bureaucracy and the adhocracy in each party exist to service the leadership in carrying out numerous specific planning goals.

The professional administrators at each party's headquarters are part of a hierarchy centrally co-ordinated by directors. They are given routine organizational and logistical planning goals to achieve. The number of professional bureaucrats planning for each party varies. For the Liberal Democrats, logistical planning is conducted by the Press and Broadcasting office and by a small team of three in the Conference and Exhibitions Office.[3] In the other two parties aspects of logistical planning are spread between a greater number of individuals. At the Labour party it involves the Campaigns Office, the Conference Office, the Exhibitions and Events Office and the Press and Broadcasting Office. At the Conservative party the Conference Unit, Press and Broadcasting Office, the set designers and the board of the National Conservative Convention are all involved.[4] The number of administrators involved increases and the departments' activity becomes more conference-oriented nearer the start of each conference. Each party uses a specialist organization to design the main conference set.

In each party the conference agenda and timetable are the responsibility of a formally institutionalized committee. These committees sort through and select the motions for debate – the Liberal Democrats had the Federal Conference Committee (FCC), Labour the Conference Arrangements Committee (CAC) and the Conservatives the Conference Agenda Subcommittee (CAS).[5] The responsibility for planning conference communication strategies belongs to the communication departments (the Communications Office at the Liberal Democrats, the Press and Broadcasting Department for Labour and the Communications Department for the Conservatives) and to informal teams. The teams draw flexibly on experts from inside or outside party ranks in order to complete key tasks – people such as media experts, heads of departments, an advertising agency or campaign teams, and pollsters. The exact mix of actors varies between parties. In the Liberal Democrats, the Communications Committee is an informal advisory group formed by the Leader's Office and run by the party's Director of Strategy and Planning since 1994. The Committee consists of the Director, Head of Communications, Director of Organization and Events, party press officers, the leader's press officer and other outside specialists. The Committee's aim is to plan the promotional aspect of the motions that have been put forward by the agenda committee. In the Labour party conference communication strategies are planned by the Campaigns, Elections and Media Department, in liaison with the General Secretary and key actors in the Leader's Office. The Campaign Department's planning is given the final approval by the General Secretary. One source gave an example of the decision-making process:

> The campaigns people would come up with these propositions and you would have to say yes or no to them. It's a decision every year if you'd sing 'The Red Flag' or not. There was even one year where we had to make a serious decision whether to sing 'Auld Lang Syne' or 'Jerusalem'. John Smith didn't like 'Jerusalem' because it referred to England's mountains green. So there are some decisions which are trivial [and some] which can only be taken by the General Secretary because people get so upset by them.[6]

In each party these teams are more 'sensitized' to the presence of the news broadcasters, and much less concerned with internal party organization or conference housekeeping – so long as these areas do not threaten to impact on media reporting of the conference. The teams undertake: active promotional planning well in advance of the conference; take full advantage of the presence of the broadcasters; create positive publicity opportunities; convey a key sense of strategy; and plan ahead for potential risks and methods for combating them.

The different committees and departments do not plan in isolation but are interconnected and interact during the planning process. They are joined through their members sitting on other, usually more senior, committees and by overlapping links with departments. Together they form an interlinked planning network. Certain key actors, particularly those who are part of the leadership circle of each party, have an input on several committees, whereas others are confined purely to their own department or to one committee. There is often a complex relationship between the committees and departments. While departments are essentially the domain of professional managers, department managers often sit on committees where their expertise is needed. Through placing actors on these committees, the party's leadership (usually the party leader and advisors) manage and monitor the adhocracy's planning progress.

Fixing the conference agenda and timetable

Each party's agenda committee acts as the planning conduit through which the promotional desires of the leaderships are realized. The presentational wishes of the leadership and communication specialists are largely accommodated where feasible. Whether the agenda committee is elected or appointed they are all amenable to the opinions and views of senior actors within each party.

Reducing uncertainty

There is a concern amongst the party leadership, in part based on past experience, that coverage of dissent on policy and other party matters on the floor of conference generates an image of an ill-disciplined and divided party. With the presence of the cameras always in the back of their minds, agenda committees are increasingly publicity conscious when selecting issues for debate and determining their position in the timetable. The agenda committees seek to minimize controversy in the planning stages through managing the contribution from party activists, either by rejecting motions or manipulating their position within the timetable to reduce their coverage.

This fear of the broadcasters' 'gaze' is deeply ingrained in the Labour government; there is an apprehension that dissent will attract sensational and damaging coverage as it did in the 1970s and early 1980s.[7] An official party document recently noted: 'The more controversial or significant the debates . . . the more they attract sensational press [and television] attention. Gladiatorial contests and deeply divisive conflicts particularly capture attention, irrespective of their true significance; and the alleged power and influence of key individuals, unions or groups are emphasized.'[8] There is a concerted effort during planning to prevent awkward debates being timetabled. At the Labour conference 'all disciplinary issues have been effectively taken away from conference'.[9] Delegates are now only allowed one balloted debate. Also all debates perceived as potentially controversial are scheduled at an appropriate time. Often this is before live coverage comes on air or after it goes off air. Another gambit is to position controversial items before or on the same day as the leader's speech in order to prevent the conference being overshadowed by them and broadcasters being distracted from other planned events.[10] An agenda committee source suggested:

> [The CAC are] not eunuchs: they understand what it is all about. My motto was get the blood off the floor by Monday night. I didn't want

controversial things hanging over beyond the leader's speech and if there was anything highly controversial and which had been hyped by the media at the weekend then we knew beforehand that the idea was to get it over and done with on the Monday. Hopefully the leader [in his Tuesday speech] would then set the tone that carries you through.[11]

Another agenda committee source suggested: 'we put things in front of the leader's [speech] in the half past nine [a.m.] slot. This year [1995] it was Clause Four and the NUM messing around, because [at that time] the media are doing interviews and the delegates aren't awake.'[12] Another source concurred: 'You also take unpopular stuff immediately after the leader's speech because [on TV] there will be a review of the leader's speech. They [broadcasters] will have taken it [the conference session] all off-camera, and half the delegates will have walked out the hall.'[13] Recently Labour has gone as far as to exclude the cameras from question and answer sessions between the delegates and ministers, including Tony Blair, in case there were any hostile exchanges. One party source, in reference to the exclusion of cameras from the main conference hall, suggested: 'The aim is to encourage debate, not prevent it . . . we want people to ask questions they really want to ask, without feeling constrained by an outside presence. We don't want them to feel they have to toe the party line.'[14]

Sources on the Liberal Democrats' agenda committee professed to be relaxed about dissent on the conference floor, but this is not true for conferences immediately before general elections. A source noted:

There is a sort of rule for the first couple of conferences after an election: you let it hang out a bit. And part of the role of conference is to enable people to move on and enable people to come forward with new ideas. But the nearer you get to an election it does become more serious.[15]

Another source also suggested that potentially unpopular issues are unlikely to find their way on to the conference agenda immediately prior to an election:

Now you could take some other issue where we could potentially as a party take a very unpopular view, like gypsies for instance, where anything vaguely supportive of gypsies is an [electorally] unpopular view. And I think you'd find that would not find its way onto the agenda if the truth be told six months or eighteen months before a general election . . . And we said: 'We are not going to take this before a general election. We don't think it would be in the party's interest. Put it into the conference after the general election and it will have a very good chance of being taken'.[16]

At the conferences prior to general elections similar risk management tactics are used in the planning of the conference timetable. 'The media are interested in seeing debates – the more hassle the better, of course, for the media. And sometimes we think "Yes" and sometimes we think "No" because very often you know what the headline is going to be.'[17] The agenda committee often take advice from communication specialists in the party, on the communications aspect of their planning. As a Liberal Democrat source noted: 'Members of our media team would suggest X debate could be iffy in the media and the [agenda committee] will say "I'm sorry, no it has got to go in that spot" or the FCC will say "Maybe we could fit that one there and that one there" . . . '[18] One possible tactic open to the Liberal Democrats' agenda committee is to place awkward motions for debate in the Liberal Democrats' spring conference instead of the autumn conference, which receives far more media attention. A source suggested that this can be done, but added it is difficult to always 'juggle things to that extent'.[19]

Similar practices emerge in the planning of the Conservatives' conference timetable. With practical time limits in mind and no power to composite motions, only a tiny fraction of the motions that are submitted are called for debate. In 1995, of the 1250 motions submitted, only sixteen were debated. The subject areas for debate were pre-fixed by the National Union (now the National Conservative Convention) taking into account the leadership's views, with some subject areas always being debated and others intermittently so. Within the preordained subject areas it is generally accepted that the motions selected will be as general as possible in order to facilitate debate (Davies, 1995). As Kelly noted: 'the committee chooses ones that will give an opportunity for discussion and criticism where necessary.'[20] A Conservative source concurred:

> We'll look at all of the motions that have come in on the conference and we will come up with one that we believe is not so narrow that it's blinkered and will have a limit on the sort of debate that you can hold. So we do tend to have fairly bland motions in the main, but simply because we want to make it all-embracing.[21]

These general motions are also more importantly non-controversial in nature. Ball (1996) argues that many critical motions, from associations, very often do not get the required support of the Area Offices 'for fear of being tarred with the brush of disloyalty. Supportive motions have an easier ride especially if they are being "pushed" by the professional section of the party'.[22] He further suggests that the main 'cause of exclusion is the charge that the motion is unhelpful to the government's [i.e. the leadership's] position, particularly where it is made in sensitive areas of policies.'[23] When asked whether potentially embarrassing motions, however broadly worded, are passed over because of the presence of the broadcasters, a Conservative source suggested:

> If you're trying to put on a conference for whoever and you get a motion that says that "This government has got to bring back the death penalty tomorrow" or else "This conference has got to hold a referendum on Europe", are you going to urge everyone to put that in to the agenda knowing the sort of publicity the press would give it? Or do you want to steer away from it? If there is going to be any bad publicity, well, we'll leave it to the Labour party to try and hit us with it rather than go and give the media the luxury of getting it on a plate. We don't actually want motions that are pure back-slapping, they need to be constructive, but to be constructive they have got to be reasonably supportive in the first place, we just don't want the country to have the impression that the Conservative party is at each other's throats on every subject. So we end up just saying "No, we won't go for the difficult ones".[24]

Promoting policy

The agenda committees in each party not only perform their traditional function but also see their role as enabling the leadership to achieve the maximum positive exposure for party policy and personalities. In this respect scheduled debates are seen as an ideal promotional platform.

In each party slots in the timetable are allotted to a series of subject areas, on the economy, health, education, foreign affairs etc. In each slot preference is given to policy motions that originate from policy committees, government departments and policy units – rather than from activists or affiliated members.[25] The Conservatives' agenda committee gives preference to such policy motions. Labour's agenda committee gives priority to motions coming from the National Policy Forum[26] and to motions which 'the NEC or particular Shadow Cabinet members want[ed] to put through conference, which [were] decided to be of political importance'.[27] The Liberal Democrats' agenda committee gives preference to motions from the Federal Policy Committee (FPC), the main policy forum, and in many cases asks for motions and advice. One source suggested:

> We will certainly take a policy motion [and] we would normally take an ordinary motion from the FPC. We can suggest things to them as well, for instance, economics – any economic issue is difficult for a local party to draft. So what one wants to say in those circumstances to the policy committee is: "Look we have got a problem here, we want a decent motion on this subject. We haven't got one at the preliminary agenda stage, so we

will reserve a slot here on the agenda". So if we find we need a particular topic on the agenda we have the facility at the preliminary agenda stage to reserve a slot for a topical motion.[28]

Advice from the Communications Committee is readily accepted by the Federal Conference Committee (FCC). One source noted that the communications department were important 'in bringing together the various strands . . . If they say they are going to launch a campaign on homelessness we will have a motion on housing. It may not be the one they wanted for the campaign but in most cases it will be. But there will be a peg on which they can hang their campaign.'[29] Party business is discussed on days when there is no television coverage, usually the Sunday of conference. As one source suggested: 'There are certain things which are pretty boring to be on television – business motions, report of the FCC, report of the Federal Executive.'[30] This latitude provides more time and space for the presentation of policy motions during the week.

The aim of the committees is to provide a coherent, easily reportable package of policies on an issue rather than a series of unrelated speeches. In effect debates are themed around predetermined issues. As a Labour source pointed out:

> Instead of having the structure of debates determined by the number of resolutions . . . , there was a structure put on it. So we had an overall link in the debates . . . So instead of having umpteen mini debates we had an economic debate, an international debate which was put in an overall context by a major presentation of our . . . stance at the beginning of that debate. I think that has changed and improved the coherence of conference to a large extent.[31]

Asked about the use of themes, a Liberal Democrat source suggested: 'That is something we have not historically done but we have begun to do . . . I think it has been generally appreciated that it has worked reasonably well.'[32] Themes also take precedence in the planning of the Conservatives' conference agenda.[33] The themes for each day of conference are already decided upon and the meetings seek to slot ministerial speeches into these themes. These slots in the timetable are those that provide maximum television coverage: 'The agenda gets organized timetable-wise more for the media than in the past',[34] commented one party actor.

Personalities

Speeches by key individuals are used to deliver party policy announcements to the news broadcasters. These individuals are usually recognizable party actors, part of the leadership cadre. Communication professionals realize that the attention paid to announcements is related to the individuals delivering them. All conference debates feature speeches by ministers (Kelly, 1989) and by party spokespersons; prior to general elections more time is allotted to give television exposure to certain parliamentary candidates and back-bench MPs. The Liberal Democrats' agenda committee is active in making sure that slots are available in debates for presentations by party spokespersons. A similar picture emerges in the planning of the Labour conference timetable. Debates at Labour conferences are 'presented by shadow cabinet member[s] who are not necessarily members of the NEC and wound up by a member of the NEC'.[35] The Shadow Cabinet and members of the NEC are given more time to reply to debates, as Wintour (1995b) notes: 'more shadow cabinet members are given a chance to speak, consuming time that used to belong to delegates . . . even more, presentable prospective parliamentary candidates in targeted seats are called to the rostrum to make a local media splash.'[36] In addition organizers request that 'regional press offices suggest one or two potential star speakers from constituency delegates and parliamentary candidates'.[37] The Liberal Democrats' conference committee also actively seeks to maximize the exposure their parliamentary candidates receive on television. A source noted:

> We obviously want to give maximum media exposure to our parliamentary candidates. I had eight cards in from parliamentary candidates in winnable seats but six of them were in the south-west and although it was a long debate there was simply no way that you can call six parliamentary candidates from the south-west to the debate, conference just won't stand for that. So you have to work that out with the agent. We won't guarantee to call parliamentary candidates in winnable seats, but what we tend to do is to ask them to nominate a couple for each debate, so we don't end up in a situation with them all competing to speak in the same debate.[38]

A Conservative source suggested that the 'star' speakers needed to be spread throughout the week: 'You have your big beasts, your great speakers, your great orators, people who move the conference, they need to be spread out. There is no point having them all speaking on the same day.'[39] This view arose from experience of unforeseen consequences, such as personality clashes. A Conservative source gave an example from their 1994 party conference:

> You will have some personality clashes. One or two Ministers who don't particularly want to speak on the same day as some others because they

think, for example, that if they speak on the same day as Michael Heseltine, however big the announcement, it is bound to be over-shadowed simply by the reaction to him. That was particularly the case in 1994 because Michael Heseltine had not been able to speak in '93 and therefore his return speech in '94 was always going to be a big event. There were a number of senior ministers who said "I don't want to speak on the same day as Michael Heseltine because whatever I say will be drowned out by him". Michael Heseltine's speech was alongside Portillo's. In retro-spect that was probably an unfortunate fact. On the other hand there were so many other people who were not prepared to speak on the same day, and frankly Michael Portillo didn't have any objections, point one. Point two, at the time, although he was spoken of as a future leadership contender, he was still a relatively junior member of the cabinet and there-fore if you had much bigger beasts who were saying "I'm not prepared to speak on the same day as Michael Heseltine", they could not be pushed around, and Michael Portillo to an extent could – although as I say he did not particularly raise any great objections.[40]

The jewel in the publicity crown

The party leader attracts significant media attention and is rarely out of their gaze for the conference week. The leader's speech is the 'highlight' of each conference[41] and regularly gains a large amount of news coverage compared to other events. Consequently a lot of planning goes into the speech in order to maximize its publicity potential. Each leader prepares his or her speech in September. Working with their advisers they prepare a series of drafts; the speech then goes through a con-tinuous process of revision, in which drafts are commented on. The speeches are written to include a number of themes – the health service, foreign affairs, home affairs – and, importantly, to deliver newsworthy policy announcements. In fact such announcements are saved for delivery in the leader's speech to enhance the coverage they receive. The presentational aspects of the leaders' speeches are also planned care-fully. Dan Clifton, a former Labour broadcasting officer, described a meeting prior to Blair's 1996 speech with himself, Peter Mandelson, Jackie Stacy and some media professionals to discuss the presentational elements of the Labour leader's speech.

> Sitting on the sofa we batted around a number of ideas. Could the leader's speech be moved into television prime time? The broadcasters would be compelled to cover it, securing a better audience. We talked about improving the seating arrangements during the speech, radically redesigning the set by extending the stage, and using video inserts to improve the presentation. Most of the suggestions proved impracticable, but some ideas were incorporated by Jackie Stacy.[42]

Similar ideas were discussed and implemented by the Conservatives prior to the 1994 conference. A party source commented:

> He (Major) is a magnetic character when close to people, you get within five feet of John Major and you're hooked, so it was bringing him further forward down towards the front of the platform, so that he was very much closer to the audience, that was something which maximized his natural talents and that was something that was done in conjunction with the conference organizers.[43]

Careful consideration is given to the placing of the speech within the conference timetable and there has been a lot of experimentation with each speech's placement for publicity reasons. The Labour leadership in 1995 removed the 'merit awards' ceremony for party service, traditionally held immediately before the leader's speech, to enable a greater build up to the speech. With the co-operation of the agenda committee, communication specialists in the Liberal Democrats have tinkered with the placement of the leader's speech in the timetable, aimed at improving their coverage. In 1995, in order to benefit Ashdown and enhance publicity, the Liberal Democrats moved the slot allocated for Ashdown's speech from the Thursday, the last day of conference, to the Tuesday afternoon. Several promotional advantages flowed from the move:

> It gives the opportunity to schedule different items pre and post Paddy's speech. Before, everything was before Paddy's speech – anything could have happened. This way he can make comments on so and so's remarks or on such and such. Afterwards, he can concentrate on the message he wants to get across on behalf of the party to the world at large.[44]

Another party source concurred:

> By having the speech at the end of the conference we are actually losing some of his best skills. We put to Paddy the suggestion that he might like to move it, both to make it easier to himself and to make it easier for our people to be more constructive in the use of the [media] – and he jumped at it. Also if things are beginning to go wrong – which will inevitably happen sometimes – it gives him an opportunity to rescue it rather than just letting it build.[45]

The Liberal Democrat leader's speech has since returned to its original slot on the last day of the conference under the new leader Charles Kennedy.

John Major's speech was also brought forward in 1995 from its usual slot on the Friday afternoon to the Friday morning, replacing a second balloted motion and a second speech by the Party Chairman. The idea behind this decision, taken by the party's leadership and the Party Chairman in particular, seems to have been twofold; first, it freed up the Party Chairman to take a more active role in media management; and, second, it provided greater publicity opportunities for the leader's speech. By relieving the Party Chairman of having to make his second speech, this freed him up to act as an important media briefer for the party after delivering his first speech to conference on the Tuesday. The Chairman was 'able to take a more strategic overview of management of the conference and also in part the arrangements for the media because he didn't have this other thing at the back of his mind'.[46] In addition, another source suggested, 'and of course it was difficult to interest the media in the second speech by the same person'.[47]

Bringing the leader's speech forward created greater publicity for it, as a former Chairman suggested:

> The added advantage of bringing the Prime Minister forward to before lunch was that his speech could be on the lunchtime news, which is increasingly important, rather than having his speech in the afternoon on the Friday and missing the lunchtime news and then having crowded evening news programmes. And that seemed to go very well indeed.[48]

This point was reinforced by another source who suggested:

> I think it turned out to be right to move. First, by putting him on in the morning he of all the three party leaders was the only one who was tele-vised on BBC 1 as opposed to BBC 2. And you will know an identical programme at an identical time will get double the ratings just because it is BBC 1 compared to BBC 2. So he spoke to a live audience of between three and four million people when you count that Channel Four was on air at the same time, whereas Blair and Ashdown spoke to less than half that simply because they were BBC 2. We also had a perennial problem in terms of the lunchtime bulletins . . . You have a different audience, although there may be an overlap, it is a different audience and quite an important audience separate from the evening bulletins. Also by bringing it forward into the morning it was felt that the atmosphere in the hall would be even more stoked up than it had been in the past – because they [representatives] wouldn't all have to sit twiddling their thumbs through lunch.[49]

For the 1999 conference the leader's speech was brought forward to Thursday in line with changes in the conference timetable.

All three leaders are additionally used as a key promotional resource in conference week. The communication teams use the appeal of their leader to attract the cameras. Photo-opportunities featuring the leader, from a tour of the exhibition stalls in the conference venue, to visiting a local school, are planned in advance. Careful consideration is given to the interviews with the different broadcasters. In addition the party leaders are also used to inject a bit of excitement into conference proceedings. Special question-and-answer sessions in which the leader fields questions from the audience in the hall are now a standard feature of each conference. The leaders are involved in other choreographed stunts for the cameras such as Major's kiss of Lady Thatcher on the main stage of the 1996 conference as a public sign of the reconciliation between them. At recent Labour conferences Blair's departure has been part of a well choreographed climax to the conference. For instance, at the 1996 conference the Blairs left Blackpool by helicopter to visit nearby marginal constituencies.

Selling party policy

Leading members of communication departments in liaison with the leadership and the relevant heads of departments set about developing the appropriate strategies to 'sell' the planned policy announcements. This involves both logistical planning and the planning of communication strategies.

The success of the communication operation depends heavily on logistical factors being in place. At the Conservative and Labour parties there is one section of the head office especially devoted to the informational needs of the broadcasters. As one source said, 'There were the media people . . . working with the television companies and the press about all the arrangements that had to be made for them at conference . . . '[50] Planning the installation of the press office is crucial. With a large number of journalists present all the equipment necessary to cater for their needs has to be in place.

The press office acts as an information nerve centre for conference week. A Conservative source outlined the function of their press office as,

> processing the press releases, issuing them, organizing the briefings for the regional lobby, being there to answer any inquiries and in organizing the sheer horrendous sort of logistics, like making sure every phone works. That stuff is certainly bigger than would have been the case ten years ago, but about the same level it has been for the last three or four years.[51]

The press office catered for journalists' demands for background information on speeches and debates, but also kept journalists informed of any changes in the timetabling of events in the main hall. Within all three parties, managers in communication departments are responsible for planning the installation of the press office. An effective press office requires not only numerous photocopiers and printers to produce the sheer bulk of speeches and press releases demanded, but also requires an army of staff. All three parties have expanded their press office during recent conferences using volunteers. One Conservative source noted: 'We always expand greatly for party conference week. We bring in a lot of volunteers . . . '[52] A Liberal Democrat source remarked how the operation of the press office was 'more professional operation, unlike the days when it used to be "two men and their dog", and the job of the media office was to hand out press releases. And the journalists would probably go away and follow them up.'[53] The managers also have to provide a suitable space for press conferences in case they are needed, usually consisting of a platform and a series of chairs. They also plan the distribution of internal communication devices such as bleepers and cell phones, a key resource in ensuring that all spin doctors keep in contact with each other.

Communication teams, in planning, try and maximize the publicity afforded to each planned event. They know that unless speeches are newsworthy they attract little attention and journalists look elsewhere for a story. There was a noticeable belief amongst those interviewed that the journalists at conference need a 'big idea', an 'interesting angle', a 'story', or else they will go and find one themselves and that means trouble. One spin doctor noted:

> You have to be able to keep one step ahead of the journalists because if you are not very careful and not supplying them with material and interesting angles they'll go off and do their own stuff. I think I can tell when things go wrong, it's when they [journalists] start interviewing each other about how they think the conference is going. It's a sure sign that it's not going very well, they really [should] be interviewing our people.[54]

In response the communication professionals continually try to ensure that ministers and spokespersons make the most of the opportunities afforded them. In government, the Conservatives sought to ensure that ministers in the different departments produced speeches that were 'forward looking' and importantly contained policy announcements. Indeed ministers' speeches had to be cleared beforehand in order to ensure that they fulfilled these criteria. This emphasis has been continued by the Labour government. In the Liberal Democrats there is similarly a general encouragement to spokespersons to make sure their speeches are well prepared.

With such announcements the communication specialists can develop a story for the journalists. One Conservative spin doctor suggested: 'The alpha and omega of all media relations is that they are interested in a story. If you have got a story, it is much easier to sell than if you haven't.'[55] Another Liberal Democrat spin doctor suggested: 'The strategy as far as the media is concerned is to make it interesting and keep supplying them with stuff which keeps them occupied.'[56] The importance of a story and announcements in speeches was also emphasized by two sources at Conservative Central Office. The first suggested: 'You can't gag them. What we try to do is to make sure that there are stories all ready for the taking, so that they don't make them up themselves.'[57] The second added:

> To my mind content is more important than how it is sold. There were always going to be problems in selling party conference speeches in the past where the only announcement was a new motorway service station, or widdle stops as the *Daily Mail* calls them. And equally it is going to be much easier to sell a speech of the sort we had last week [1995] which had a big idea, 'The Enterprise Centre of Europe', but also a range of significant announcements, such as five thousand extra policemen.[58]

The needs of the broadcasters shape the nature of the strategies being planned. All communication specialists seek to exploit broadcasters' desire for newsworthy information in an attempt to ensure that policy announcements receive the maximum coverage possible. Successful plans are reused, but to some extent the onus is on the communication professionals, with their daily experience of journalists, to find new and more effective ways of promoting the party.

Designing the main stage

The main conference platform is the central showpiece of the conference, the stage upon which the main drama unfolds. The set is increasingly designed to make a strong visual impact; this has become a minimum requirement – a 'bottom line' below which no party would want to fall for fear of looking amateurish. Its importance to the conference now means that it is designed by specialists. For the conference managers the right set design can enhance the presentation of policy to a television audience, just as the wrong one can undermine it. They therefore take a particular interest in the planning process that leads to the final platform, logo and seating arrangements, and make their own input into that process. Any suggested changes are incorporated into the final product by the design team and by those responsible for planning the seating arrangements.

The Liberal Democrats tender design out to a private firm.[59] A Liberal Democrat source suggested: 'We'll put it out to tender and they come forward with designs.'[60] In January 1994 Labour created a specialized internal body for the job, the Events and Exhibitions Unit, consisting of a manager, an events officer and an exhibition organizer, whose tasks include 'designing the floor plan, marketing and promoting the exhibition, liaising with exhibitors . . . '.[61] The proposed design of the main stage is relayed to the leadership. Labour's head of organization, quoted in *The Times*, suggested: 'I don't get involved in policy. I just think about presenting what they come up with in the best way.'[62] The Conservatives' design has been carried out since April 1994 by CCO Conferences Ltd, a wholly-owned subsidiary of World Conference Travel, an international firm of conference management and organizers. A Conservative source said that 'We basically tell them what we want. They then go away and come back with ideas.'[63] As noted, these specialist organizations work in tandem with the communication departments and committees and leaderships.

As the centrepiece of the conference the set has to be functional and aesthetically appealing. The broadcasters place certain practical limits on the size of the platform and its colour, there also needs to be seating room. The sets combine these factors with increasingly more elaborate designs – designs that combine colour, lighting, logos, video screens to create the right ambience for speeches and debates.[64] The design of the main stage has changed a lot since Harvey Thomas provided the 1979 Conservative conference with the first professionally designed set.[65] For both the Tories and Labour, a new platform is required each year. The 1990s saw a rash of new platform designs each seeking to overcome the mistakes of previous years and provide a new aesthetic look to the hall. Resources are the only limiting factor, particularly in the case of the Liberal Democrats, who have a much bigger resource constraint and so have a design which 'serves a number of conferences'.[66] With the advent of the professional set design there have been numerous subtle trends. One in particular is a move away from high-fronted platforms to ones which look less formal and obtrusive on television, as one Conservative source noted:

> The stage has got to be user-friendly and viewer-friendly. We got to the stage a few years ago of a very big stage set which looked more like the Politburo, a lot of people sitting up there, all you could see was their heads . . . So last year [1994] we changed it and used steps up so it made a gradual rise to the level of the platform.[67]

For the 1998 conference the Conservatives removed the traditional rows of seating on the main stage and replaced them with an informal array of comfy brightly coloured 'Tullsta' armchairs from Ikea.

The platform has also begun to change shape during the conference, a trend led by the Conservative party. The main idea here is to augment the presentation of the leader's speech on television. The evening before the leader's speech the platform is extended into the audience – something a former Party Chairman took credit for.[68] While it may have been this informant's idea, John Major also took an active part in changes to the design. 'He was . . . of course, naturally, being so exposed and out at the front there, I won't say he was concerned, but naturally he wanted to take part in going through the planning of that particular staging.'[69] The Liberal Democrats in 1995 also changed the shape of the platform, at the insistence of Paddy Ashdown, for his speech. One Liberal source said: 'The set this year [1995] was slightly redesigned because Paddy wanted to change his style of presentation on the leader's speech, so it was less talking from top table and more talking from nearer the people.'[70]

Just as much planning goes into choosing the colour of the main platform. Colour schemes are worked out between the party organizers. An important consideration is whether the colours are easily picked up by the cameras. One Conservative source suggested that the colour blue 'is a very difficult colour for the cameras'.[71] There has been much experimentation with colours. Labour's 1994 conference backdrop of 'pistachio green' was thought to have looked poor on television and was replaced with a more sober 'television white' in 1995, merging into red and white in 1996. Quoting Joy Johnson, Labour's former Director of Campaigns, Election and Media, Wintour notes: 'TV white, she said, is clean and sharp on TV – even though in real life it is grey. By contrast, pistachio green . . . was "hideous, awful and cold" and "did not combine well with human flesh" . . . '[72] Colour is important in that its function is to complement the general ambience of the platform, without being the focus of news media attention itself. The Liberal Democrats changed the colour of their set to make the most of yellow, the party colour, one with which a television audience could easily identify. A source noted: 'Up to [1993] yellow wasn't being used at all, the only yellow you saw was a tiny little bird. All the rest was black and grey which I thought was wrong... Yellow is a cheerful colour, it's an optimistic colour and makes a bright and futuristic image.'[73] In 1998 the Labour conference platform backdrop changed colour for different speakers: green for Margaret Beckett, purple for Tony Blair, red for John Prescott. The Conservatives' 2000 conference stage set used the same idea, changing colour with each debate. As one commentator noted, 'blue for Toryism, purple for women, and red, white and blue for the constitution.'[74]

A lot of thought also goes into the conference slogan on the platform backdrop. The slogans are designed to capture the theme of the conference and are placed in a position clearly visible to the television cameras. Each year there is a different slogan[75] selected by the parties' leaderships. In the Conservatives' case, the Party Chairman recommended certain slogans to the leader:

> He [the leader] was terribly involved in the choice of slogan. The slogan, after all, is now more and more important. And I can remember for Bournemouth, for instance, I actually put to him a wide range of slogans, which could be narrowed down to two and he very firmly picked one.[76]

Great attention is paid to selecting the right slogan for the conference. Hogg and Hill (1995) note that conference themes encapsulated in the slogan occupied many anxious hours of discussion in party headquarters. 'Some words bob up time and again: "Britain", "winning", "forward", "right", "strength", "future" . . . '[77] The reason for the attention to detail is that the wrong conference slogan, like the wrong colour, can divert news media attention. The backdrop to the main platform for Labour's 1990 conference, contained with the slogan, five eight-foot-high pictures of so-called 'ordinary Labour voters', one of whom was a woman. Attention for the week, particularly amongst the press and then amongst the broadcasters, focused on finding out who the woman was; for the party it was 'irritating, unpleasant and unrelenting as toothache'.[78] Since then, the platform backdrop has never featured photographs.

The latest technological gadgetry, an integral part of the main platform, is used to improve the presentation of speeches for television. Key innovations, such as the 'head-up display unit' and 'electronic adjustable height lectern', introduced for the first time by the Conservatives in 1982, are now standard features of all conference sets. These technologies crucially allow the speaker to look directly into the cameras and provide a clear shot of the speaker. The 'head-up display unit' – the so-called 'sincerity machine' – allows each speaker 'to read his/her text from unobtrusive, transparent perspex screens, thus creating the illusion that the orator is speaking without notes'.[79] The 'electronic adjustable height lectern' allows the cameras a clear view of the speaker whatever their height. While the three current party leaders and senior actors in all parties use such technology for their set-piece speeches, John Major abandoned it in favour of reading his speech from a script. However, such equipment remains part and parcel of the main platform.

Giant video screens are now integrated into the conference set design. Their primary purpose is to entertain the conference audience with the hope that the footage will be captured by the cameras present for the wider television audience. The screens show short films, mainly party promotional. The number of screenings increased over the 1990s, with every speech by major party actors being introduced by a short film. The Labour platform backdrop acts as a screen on which short videos and the results of ballots, particularly the results of the National Executive Committee (NEC) elections, are shown. All three parties now regularly enhance such screenings through dimming the main lights in the hall – a technique first pioneered in US presidential conventions[80] – thus forcing the TV cameras to focus on the images. This practice is now routine in the build-up to the leader's speech, which is trailed by a mixture of biographical videos and videos of the party's achievements. However, while broadcasters sometimes schedule small out-takes or commentary slots for such occasions, to avoid the impression of carrying 'party propaganda', the conference managers still see this as a worthwhile exercise.

The control of seating arrangements at conference is nothing new in itself, Cockerell notes of the early televised party conferences: 'The Tories' publicity men had arranged for the Party's most attractive women to be seated behind Churchill for his conference speech.'[81] With the cameras in mind, conference organizers spend an increasing amount of time planning the seating arrangements on the main platform. Since Harvey Thomas's time in the late 1970s, the belief that the platform should present an uncluttered image for the cameras is taken for granted by all parties.[82] It is now standard practice to isolate the speaker's rostrum from the seating area to make sure the viewer isn't distracted by activity going on behind the speaker.[83] Now very few people actually sit on the main stage through debates and speeches, and those that do are senior party actors or distinguished guests. At each conference, the number of seats on the main platform is carefully planned for each speech and debate in order to avoid any excess seats, which might give the impression to the broadcasters that either had been under-attended. Conference organizers use advance information to regulate the number of people who are able to sit on the platform at any one time. A Conservative source suggested:

> The planning that goes into it has increased over the last two years, simply because one believes in attention to detail. And certainly up until two years ago we always made sure that the front row of the platform was clear, that there weren't rows of seats behind. In the past, people could just pop up if they wanted to, but in most cases we found that there were empty seats at the back and the front row was full. Well I don't think you can do that on television.[84]

At the Labour conference seats on the platform are strictly limited to members of the NEC and the leadership. For the Liberal Democrats' conference, access to the stage is controlled for key speeches and allocated to senior party members. The regulation of seating arrangements reached a high point at the Conservatives' conference, where they changed for each debate, a responsibility that fell at the time to the National Union Secretary, who suggested:

> I now, session by session, debate by debate, three times in the afternoon, three times in the morning have a different seating plan. You're talking about fifty people, so every debate it changes. Different people come on, other people come off, there is an average six and half minutes between one debate finishing and the next one starting because of the turnover and ministers getting ready and all the rest. So now this year what I'm doing is people sitting in the second row are the people who are going to be in the front row in the debate afterwards. So as soon as the debate finishes, the front row leaves, they just come forward and we are ready to go again . . . They [those on the platform] have all got to have a detailed seating plan of every debate so they know when they are going to be on the platform. On the Friday, the last day of conference, you are talking about ninety people on the platform and you cannot afford to have mistakes . . . they can't just meander on. This year [1995] they are going to be regimented backstage into a line.[85]

He also suggested that the party leadership take an active interest in the planning of their own seating arrangements to make sure that there is no adverse publicity.

> The position of each Minister on the platform has to be planned, I have to go to 12 Downing Street and go through it with the Chief Whip so that we are both happy that it is right. There are no two ways about it, you have got the PM in the middle, Michael Heseltine nearest him, but then you've got Ken Clarke that side so you move out that way, so you end up every one next to each other to each end. Again if you get it wrong (a) they'll be unhappy; (b) the media will pick it up. That's why Peter Lilley, demoted, will be one down lower than Virginia Bottomley, when he should have been one above her.[86]

The managers sought to improve on the previous year's planning, making the platform a more effective instrument for the delivery of policy announcements. The platform has become an outward sign of the professionalism of each party, an image which they are keen to convey through the broadcasters to the electorate.

Conclusion

Long-range conference planning is controlled and directed by an increasingly image-conscious party leadership towards the promotion of certain policies and actors and the exclusion of others, in order to generate the right image. Final decisions – on agenda and timetable, media strategies, and platform design – are taken by an inner core of professionals and specialists close to the leader. These decisions are made mainly with the broadcasters in mind although the press, also an influential factor, is taken into account. Communication professionals increasingly occupy a central role in the planning process, devising strategies, advising individuals and encouraging the agenda committees to consider the publicity implications of their decisions. The agenda committees increasingly give precedence in the timetable to policy formulated within the adhocracy over motions from delegates and affiliated organizations – although these are not ignored. The aim is increasingly to use television to promote chosen policies and individuals to the public. A 'promotional psychosis' permeates all areas of the conference planning process. Nearly all aspects of conference planning are now promotionally oriented, focusing on trying to maximize the publicity potential the broadcasters' presence offers and minimizing the risks. Planning is 'reflexive' (Schlesinger and Tumber 1994; Thompson, 1995), with plans being continually improved to enhance the achievement of these goals. The final product of the planning process is a complete promotional package. Pre-prepared official policy – containing deliberately newsworthy announcements – is given in advance to selected news outlets, later it is delivered by a recognizable member of the party leadership, live on camera, on a platform designed to minimize distraction and amplify both the policy and the presenter[87] – all for the benefit of the television audience beyond the conference hall.

2

Negotiating Coverage

Both the broadcasters and the parties are involved in planning the party conferences' TV coverage.[1] It is an increasingly important aspect of the overall planning process because of the large number of news outlets broadcasting from conferences. Conference coverage takes a relatively long time to plan, starting in one interviewee's words 'as soon as the conferences are finished'.[2] This year-long process, however, really begins in earnest in the February before the autumn conferences, 'slowly at first, then come June, July it starts hotting up in to a sort of planning whirl'.[3] The broadcasters and the parties are in effect engaged in a cycle of planning: as soon as one round of conferences finish they start planning for the next. The great majority of coverage planning is carried out simultaneously by a series of professionals within the main body of both the broadcasting organizations and the parties, and forms part of a wider process of logistical planning for the conferences. Throughout the process, both organizations are in continuous contact informally and formally through a series of meetings. These meetings involve a certain level of negotiation to bring about desired aims of both actors.

This chapter focuses on those elements of logistical planning that concern conference coverage. It outlines the organizational structures and the parts of the broadcasters involved in planning. It examines joint planning, negotiation and co-operation between the broadcasters and the parties' professional administrators.

Planning in the conference unit

The broadcasters' planning is conducted simultaneously by political units based mainly at 4 Millbank, and by parts of a departmentalized administrative structure at the BBC and ITN headquarters. The overall responsibility for logistical planning at the BBC lies with its Westminster political unit. The planning of coverage and the prerequisite logistical factors is co-ordinated by the Conference Unit (CU) at 4 Millbank in liaison with Sports and Events (the Outside Broadcast Unit, OBU). There is a certain element of routine in the planning. A senior BBC source remarked, 'these things are so much in the history and culture of the place . . . if there are any problems, we have discussions, but because we have always done it like that it tends not to vary from year to year'.[4] The Conference Unit is involved in making key decisions on matters such as personnel numbers, allocation of resources and timing, as well as meeting with the parties and liaising with the engineers of the OBU. The manager of the Conference Unit acts as the central co-ordinator. In addition the Political Research Unit (PRU) at Millbank also plan for the conferences. The PRU produce 'The Conference Guide' for journalists, which is a comprehensive 270-page book. The Guide provides explanations of conference procedure at the three main parties' conferences, as well as detailed background information on the issues likely to be raised at conference and is a useful aid in news gathering.

The planning of coverage at ITN is carried out by News Resources at its headquarters on the Grey's Inn Road, and at a programme level by ITN's Westminster operation at Millbank. Logistical planning is co-ordinated by a News Resources manager at headquarters:

> My role in terms of the party conferences is [to] look after the budget and the overall strategic part of conference planning. So I liaise with the various customers that ITN has for the service which are: our main news outlets on ITV and Channel Four; the ITV regional companies; and one or two other people who make programmes at the conferences.[5]

His role also involves him co-ordinating with ITN's equivalent of the Outside Broadcast Unit . However, on a general level the role of the ITN planners is less delineated than at the BBC. There is more 'multi-skilling', where individuals charged with planning are responsible for a combination of different tasks. This reflects the growing financial constraints faced by ITN in an increasingly competitive news environment. Their planning is also marked by a certain degree of routine, with the commitments of News Resources not changing in any significant way throughout the period 1993–6. As with the BBC, logistical planning includes accommodation, the allocation of resources and the timing of operations.

The conference commitment

While operational decisions are made at the unit level, the policy direction is decided by News and Current Affairs in the BBC's case and within the main administrative body at ITN. The broadcasters' attitude towards the conferences determines the commitment of resources to their coverage. They both continue to see each conference as an important event deserving of coverage but the commitment to coverage (the amount of live coverage and the number of programmes being produced at conference) has to take into account costs and varies between the BBC and ITN and from conference to conference.

The commitment of the two organizations differs in size, with the BBC as the remaining public service broadcaster providing in addition to television news coverage, live, regional, national and international, radio, television and Internet coverage. As one BBC source said: 'We've got three national radio stations . . . thirty-eight local stations, the World Service, news bulletins, live TV coverage, Breakfast News, [and] On the Record.'[6] This presence is partly replicated in the commercial sector. ITN is committed to providing news coverage on ITV, Channel Four, Channel Five and for its new 24-hour news channel as well as coverage for use by the ITV regions and others who want the service.

The size of the commitment, in terms of the number of programmes, determines the number of crews to be sent.

> We are actually providing the crews this year for news. So if someone says we want seven one-man crews which will cover breakfast news and news for the regions, they have to be provided. Newsnight will provide their own camera men, their own editing equipment and their own staff who they are used to working with, whereas the rest of it we will take from a pool.[7]

At ITN, a source suggested that at the conferences:

> There would be two crews for each of the main customers. So Channel Four would have two crews there, ITV news would have two crews. I would take three crews for general use and they are hired out by the hour and half hour to the regional clients. Then there would be OBU camera men in the hall covering the proceedings.[8]

The size of the crews subsequently determines the amount of accommodation and equipment needed. Where there is a commitment to live coverage as well then this necessitates in addition an outside broadcast unit (OBU). ITN is committed to covering each party leader's speech live for Channel Four, whereas not for ITV and Channel Five and therefore has to incorporate the use of an OBU into its plans. Both the BBC's and ITN's commitment varies between the conferences. Both organizations continue to put fewer resources into the coverage of the Liberal Democrats' conference than into Labour's and the Conservatives'. As one broadcaster suggested:

There is a difference between say the Liberal Democratic conference and the Labour and Tory conference. I refer to the Liberal Democratic conference as a minor conference and to the others as major conferences . . . As far as we are concerned we don't normally front programmes from the Liberal Democrats, whereas we do from Labour and the Tories.[9]

There has been an endeavour by the planners to build in some flexibility into the allocation of crews, allowing them to be dictated more by news priorities. As the same source noted: 'If a big story broke they could easily send more, so they will probably send one to start with and wait to see what comes up on the agenda. If the . . . conference[s] move up the running order of the bulletin they will send extra resources.'[10]

The negotiations

The main broadcasters (ITN, the BBC and Sky News) co-operate with each other in the planning of television coverage and engage in a series of regular negotiations with the political parties in the build-up to each conference. The broadcasters co-operate on a series of coverage matters, sharing information vital for planning between the departments inside each organization. Through co-operating the broadcasters hope first, to gain cost benefits through reducing the duplication of technical resources, and second, to utilize efficiently the existing venue space, partly because of its inherent scarcity, and partly because the parties limit the space broadcasters can have. Managers at the BBC, ITN (and Sky) are regularly in contact with each other in the planning stage, with information being passed on informally by phone and in formal meetings. This regular contact is facilitated by the fact that some are based at 4 Millbank and its vicinity. As one source said, 'I do meet up with them other than at the meetings we go to, because they work in this building'.[11] She added 'the relationship between us, ITN and Sky is very good and it's helpful'.[12]

Negotiations with the parties take place in a series of formal meetings at the conference venues prior to the conferences starting and in a series of smaller informal meetings on specific issues. The main meetings occur in February, March or April each year before the autumn conferences. These meetings act as a forum for discussion between the principal actors and other interested groups – such as the venue's management, the fire brigade and the police. 'There were 50 people there, for big ones, Labour and Conservative, that's the average. You'll find there is more there than at the Liberal Democrats . . . '.[13] For example, prior to the Conservatives' conference in Bournemouth in 1994:

> You've got the Conservative party themselves, Securicor [running con-
> ference security], the Bournemouth Centre people, Sky News, the
> conference hotel, BBC News, Linda Parker [BBC], a producer, a director,
> an engineering manager, BBC Public Affairs, Roy Graham [architect],
> Meridian TV, GMTV, two people from ITN, a representative from the ITN
> press office, Central Broadcasting and the police. It's just a big talking
> shop round a huge square or rectangular table.[14]

Like all regular meetings that develop over time, these events are
routinized. As one party source said: 'We'll sit there and say "The
same as last year, or is there something else?" . . . We've been doing it
long enough, and if there is no objection to how it was done last year
they [the broadcasters] say "Fine", unless they have a particular
request.'[15] There are often 'particular requests' for more venue space,
new and better camera and commentary positions, more leniency on
accreditation (number of media personnel), and lighting,[16] all seen as
key for effective coverage by the broadcasters. Each issue is the subject
of negotiation. As one party source said: 'They constantly make
demands. We go through this thing every time you know . . . They
want the best for them – that is their job. My job is to fight for my party's
interests . . . But we always reach an amicable agreement.'[17] However,
the broadcasters are more limited in what they are allowed in some
areas, such as venue space, compared to others like accreditation.
Some topics on the agenda provide more scope for negotiation, if not at
the main meeting, then in the long run over several conferences.

Accreditation

The broadcasters want to ensure that they have the requested number
of media personnel at the conferences to achieve their coverage goals.
The number of staff the broadcasters need for any one conference varies
according to their commitment. All personnel, however, need to be
accredited by the parties for security reasons. The parties are in part
alarmed by the increasing numbers of media personnel attending
conference; one party source suggested the figure to be as high as two
thousand. 'We issue 2,000 press and media passes. Two thousand of
these guys [sic] running round – not all at the front with cameras, thank
God! But there is 2,000 people of press and media.'[18] However, in terms
of the numbers of broadcasting personnel attending conference, a
source from ITN suggested that the parties are 'very understanding
about the number of people we need . . . We have a very good relationship over accreditation.'[19] But one BBC source referred to the parties
questioning the number of their staff and saw a degree of conflict:

The BBC has a constant battle over credentials. We have far and away the hugest output of any of the organizations covering the conferences. So, say *The Times*, a daily newspaper, maybe it would credit a dozen people. We probably need something like 180. And they'll just say: "Hang on a minute. *The Times* has only got 12 and you've got 180".[20]

When asked about the numbers of BBC staff that were accredited, a Conference Unit manager refused to divulge a number, saying: 'This was a problem. I don't think I should really tell you that . . . enormous.'[21] But he added: 'for the Liberal Democrats obviously less [were] accredited than for Tories and Labour.'[22]

The Independent suggested that for the 1996 conferences, 'the BBC had more than 400 staff at the Labour party conference in Blackpool, and more than 500 converging on Bournemouth for the Conservative conference'.[23] The Labour leader's press secretary Alastair Campbell noted in *The Sunday Times* that the BBC had accredited 410 people to the party conference.[24] The lack of willingness to discuss numbers is in part explained in terms of pressure from ever-questioning parties but also from the press. One source explained: 'It gets into *The Evening Standard*, you know, all the sort of BBC freebies, millions of people there, free parties, John Birt parties. And it makes it sound like a debauched set up rather than something everybody works extremely hard for.'[25] The impact of these pressures was a decision by managers to make an across-the-board cut in the numbers of BBC staff accredited in 1995: 'We are having an accreditation bash at the moment. This has been going on since last October–November to keep numbers down. We are trying to cut it down by some 7 per cent which might not seem a lot.'[26]

Even with the cut, such numbers are far in excess of the other broadcasters present. A source from ITN suggested: 'Fifty to fifty-five people. I take a team of about somewhere between eighteen and twenty. And then there are a few more technical people and then the journalists/presenters, so it is around the fifty mark.'[27] Sky News suggested: 'We probably put in eighty applications and out of that send twenty-five to thirty people.'[28] One reason for the BBC's need to accredit so many staff is their wide-ranging commitment to conference coverage. However, in addition, a problem facing all the broadcasters is that they never know exactly how many people they need and so accredit far more than actually go. One broadcaster explained:

We tend to accredit more people than we need, which is a privilege really. From a security point of view [the parties] would like to accredit the fewest number of people possible. But they understand our difficulties –

that the one person we may have accredited might be on a story somewhere and not be able to get back.[29]

The parties indeed recognized this and made allowances.

Venue space

Space for edit suites, offices and the transmission trucks is vitally
important for the broadcasters. The discussions usually concern,
according to one source, 'where we are going to build and what we all
want, offices and everything else besides'.[30] The broadcasters need
enough space to utilize all the facilities necessary for coverage. Of the
four venues regularly used by the parties since 1993, the Blackpool
Winter Gardens, the Bournemouth Centre and Glasgow's Scottish
Exhibition Centre provide the planners with a large open space in the
form of a car park or hall next to the venue. The broadcasters then fill
this with prefabricated structures which become the news rooms.
However, at the Brighton Conference Centre the space available behind
the scenes is more restricted.[31]

While the amount of space at each venue has remained fixed, the
demand for space by the broadcasters at each venue has increased. A
reason for this, a BBC source suggested, is 'the news room have
increased in size.'[32] because, in his words:

> There was an awful lot more things happening that never used to. For
> instance, [the BBC] have moved radio in, which has four edit suites and
> five studios, and they have things like the language service and
> Newsnight and Breakfast News. These are all separate programmes that
> they do while they are at the conferences which they never used to do.
> They've changed everything over to what they call bi-media. At one time
> the radio and television were separate units, but now they have all moved
> together so they can pool information and everything else. There are
> seven edit rooms in all just for the hand-held cameras, the live cameras
> are controlled from the vehicles.[33]

The greater demand for space is not limited to the BBC, the commercial
television sector has also increased its presence at conference. To
prevent any unnecessary conflict, the broadcasters allocate existing
space more efficiently through centralizing the design of the conference
layout with one designer, which has the bonus of allowing them to
present a united front in negotiations with the parties.

At the formal meetings pressure is put on the conference administrators to concede more space to the broadcasters. The response of the
parties has been twofold. First, to try to charge commercial rates for

the space occupied. The broadcasters either refrain from using such a space or negotiate a reduced fee. Second, to block any encroachment by the broadcasters in the main hall. Requests are weighed up by the party managers against the requirements of the party members present to have a good view of the main platform. This point is reinforced by what seems to be a general belief amongst party actors that conceding too much space to the broadcasters during negotiation can be counter-productive and not beneficial to the conference, a point echoed by one source, who suggested: 'If they had their way, they'd take all the audience out . . . and just turn the whole thing into a big studio.'[34]

Camera positions

The broadcasters are continually looking for new camera angles to supplement material from their large studio cameras situated on the balconies. Outside the main conference hall cameras are free to wander where they want, but in the main hall their movement is controlled. In their negotiations with the parties, broadcasters have pushed for closer and more revealing camera positions particularly on the floor of the main hall. As one Conservative source put it, in a somewhat exagger-ated way: 'They want coverage right up on the platform so they can cover people sitting on the platform and zoom in on their notes. They wanted a camera back stage so they could see all the ministers as they go on.'[35] The number of hand-held cameras allowed on to the conference floor is a source of contention in negotiations. The shots from fixed studio cameras can be worked out in advance by the parties, so as to provide the best pictures of the platform, logo and speaker's rostrum. One Liberal Democrat conference manager explained: 'A visit is made to the venue with an experienced conference organizer during which camera angles are decided.'[36] Another party manager suggested:

> When designing the stage set I consult with the media for the look on tele-vision. You don't want [things] coming out of the left ear or something, so you look at that carefully. We don't actually put up the . . . logo and the words until we are doing a camera position check so we have got some-body at the lectern and we can get the height and the distancing right and just the right camera angles. Prior to that we have drawn up the camera angles on the stage set design and the seating area so [we know] where they are coming from and what are they looking at.[37]

However the footage produced by hand-held cameras is often close-up to the platform and less controllable. The parties feel it is intrusive. A party manager commented: 'They get their cameras at the front of the hall which is very irritating for our own people. They promise they'll stay in one place. Two minutes later they're in another. They are a law unto themselves.'[38] Initial resistance to hand-held cameras has not stopped the broadcasters' pressure: 'We'll push for whatever we can get away with. And if they agree to it, fine! If they don't, we'll push it a bit.'[39]

The outcome of negotiations is an innovative compromise that enables the broadcasters to get some of the close-up shots they want, but be less intrusive and more controllable for the parties. A broadcaster outlined the solution. 'What they have agreed is that we can put little hot heads on, which are small cameras on top of a pole. And someone is sat in a chair below them with a little control box to move the camera so there is no need for standing.'[40] However footage from this new camera position is shared between the broadcasters. Indeed there is a 'me too' process in planning camera positions. If one of the broadcasters manages to negotiate a new camera position then the others insist that they have it too. This has been particularly the case with new 'pin hole' cameras placed in the set behind the speaker's rostrum to 'get a shot over the shoulder of the delegates sitting.'[41] One broadcaster confided:

> The BBC had . . . a rear view camera coming out of the back of the set. Then we wanted one, to which [the parties] said "No" to begin with because we were too late in the day to start drilling holes in the back of the set. But they agreed the following year . . . If the BBC or ITN say we want an extra camera . . . that is going to get a much better shot that nobody has had before, the answer is so do we.[42]

The parties take a fairly pragmatic approach to the competition between the broadcasters for closer and closer coverage. The parties force the broadcasters to share any new camera positions or block them completely.[43] A broadcaster suggested:

> The party says "Unless you can sort it out between you, none of you are going to get it". So they don't actually say to the BBC or us or ITN "Yes, that is yours and nobody else can have it". They have got to keep everybody happy. If it is a really nice shot and we have got a camera there, everybody gets it.[44]

Commentary booths

Commentary booths are a broadcaster-inspired idea, first used on the balcony overlooking the Empress Ball Room in Blackpool. They have now become a standard feature situated in the halls at all venues.

Indeed, Channel Four News and occasionally Newsnight anchor their news coverage out of these observation hides. Each broadcaster wants to have their own balcony studio from which to present commentary on the conference, conduct interviews and generally provide the feeling of a ring-side seat for the audience. A source suggested, that they are also helpful when it comes to the autumn weather:

> What we found last year was that we ended up at the mercy of the weather. We were outside, it was a great shot, everybody was very happy with it. But if it had been foul weather we would have been caught short because we would have had nowhere that would have told you that we weren't standing in front of a board in London and that doesn't look good. So this year we decided that we will build a studio in the hall a bit smaller than we would normally use.[45]

While the commentary booths in Blackpool have the benefit of an already existing balcony, the broadcasters have to make a room on the conference floor to build such booths at the other venues.

While the construction of such studios is the responsibility of the broadcasters, permission to build and their location is decided through negotiation. The parties see these as intrusive structures, particularly where they have to be built on the conference floor. The broadcasters have persuaded the parties to let them build. As one source noted: 'I think also one or two of the reservations of the parties to us building these things in the hall are a bit less strong than they used to be.'[46] The same source was mindful of the imposition the broadcasters caused in constructing the commentary booths:

> It is a question of you are better off asking the parties to know how they feel. We are very mindful that we have got to get their delegates in. It is very easy to say: "Well, can't we just nick a few seats here and a few seats there?" And they go: "That means somebody doesn't get a seat in the conference venue". I think it is a difficult balance for them, they have got to balance how it looks on the TV where they have the audience which they need to address, against the party members who want seating in the auditorium.[47]

This was why he suggested the broadcasters offer a 'carrot' to the parties during negotiations. 'I think that is why we do things like provide a video wall, it is part of helping that balance. It's saying "Well we know we impose a great deal, but you want us there". It is a balance you strike, you have to be sensitive.'[48] In a partly related development, the broadcasters also share in the provision of courtesy monitors for the parties for the transmission of speeches and debates to other areas of the venue. The cost of these sets is met by the three broadcasters.

Lighting and sound

The lighting and sound are an integral part of television coverage of the conferences, but how their cost is distributed is the source of negotiation. In the past the BBC took a leading role in the provision of lighting, as one interviewee noted, but with the advent of new technology the broadcasters do not need to floodlight the whole proceedings[49] and do not think they should bear the cost for it all. After discussion with the parties a scheme was implemented whereby 'the stage lighting [was] done by the parties . . . and the BBC [lit] the audience'.[50] A party source confirmed the point: 'We all came to an arrangement. We will light the stage and they light the audience. As simple as that.'[51] Similarly with sound, as the largest broadcaster present, the BBC take responsibility for providing sound for the other broadcasters who then share the costs.

The cost of these technical prerequisites (space, cameras, booths and lighting) is discussed amongst the technical managers and varies from venue to venue according to its size. The BBC benefits as it shares the cost of provision with ITN and Sky, as a CU manager suggested: 'When we do the scaffolding and lighting then obviously they have got to put in a share of the costs as well, because there is no point them doing it: so we share.'[52] None of the sources were willing to reveal the cost of the operation. As to the manner of how the costs are distributed, one informant suggested that the BBC paid the 'lion's share', around 65 per cent and the others the rest.[53] The costs are also shared according to the amount of space occupied by the broadcasters: 'It is done on square footage basically, on the percentage of area we use.'[54] Overall, the sources interviewed were very cost-conscious and a general theme of many interviews was a conscious desire to reduce the overall cost of the operation.

Conclusion

The vast majority of logistical and long-range planning is carried out by both the parties and the broadcast organizations. Their interaction focuses on making the production of conference news easier and more effective, and trying to provide the best possible coverage of the event. Both sets of organizations are mutually dependent on each other and share many of the same overall planning goals, although these sometimes diverge. The period of planning is essentially routine and characterized by intermittent interaction between party conference organizers and their opposites in the BBC and ITN (and Sky), focused in formal and informal meetings on a specific agenda. At such meetings, amongst many routine issues, active negotiation occurs around certain key issues crucial for coverage. In these areas the broadcasters have to push for change, which is rejected and then sometimes conceded, either because the parties see benefits for themselves in coverage terms, or because the broadcasters compromise.

This is not to deny that there are occasional conflicts on certain areas. But a compromise solution always seems to be reached. The broadcasters in particular are willing to make a trade-off to ensure that they achieve the best coverage possible. Practical limitations and costs mean that co-operation is necessary between the broadcasters, and between them and the parties, if goals are to be achieved. Co-operation is aimed at sharing facilities and coverage, and at the problems involved in allocating limited space at each venue in the face of increased demand created by an expanding broadcaster presence. These meetings highlight the extent of mutual adaptation and co-operation between all the actors involved in logistical planning, and are an important part of TV coverage of the conferences.

3

The Broadcasters by the Seaside

With facilities already in place the broadcast journalists arrive on site the day before each conference starts. While many are seasoned hands, familiar with each seaside location having covered previous party conferences, there is still a certain amount of anticipation about the week ahead. With copies of the weekend newspapers and an outline of the conference agenda supplied by the party, they have an idea of what the most newsworthy events of the week are going to be, whether they are a speech by a leading light or a defeat for the leadership on a particular balloted motion. They are also attuned to other occurrences, such as speeches on the fringe attacking party policy by prominent party actors. Throughout conference the journalists are always looking for the most newsworthy story. During news gathering they are continually in contact with each other. Many of the media actors involved have established relationships with politicians prior to each conference and are immersed in the political culture of Westminster. This chapter examines the process of information gathering: it focuses on the influences on the gathering process, broadcasters' attitudes, interaction between journalists and spin doctors, and the competition and relationships between them.

News teams and news values

Each broadcaster sends its team of Westminster-based political journalists plus additional producers and editors to report on the conferences. The BBC has by far the largest journalistic presence, with on average sixty presenters, editors, producers, assistants and correspondents in regular attendance at Labour and the Conservative conferences.[1] The BBC Millbank team plays a central role in news gathering, providing news items for all the BBC news outlets. The team is the news gathering core on which individual BBC programme editors draw. As a BBC source noted: 'My aim really is to develop conference coverage as our normal Millbank operation . . . to provide political coverage to all the different outlets across the BBC.'[2] In charge of the Millbank team is the editor of political news and an assistant editor. They work alongside the political editor and chief correspondent and other political correspondents. However, certain programmes such as *Newsnight* are editorially independent from this structure: its team includes its own programme editor, along with a producer, a presenter and a maximum of two or three correspondents.

While ITN sends three news teams to the conference their overall presence is much smaller in comparison to the BBC's. Each team is editorially independent of the others, for instance the bulletins for ITV have their programme editors, producers, a political editor and a team of one or two correspondents. Channel Four's editorial set-up is similar, with the addition of the programme's presenter:

> You'll have the editor of the programme, the home desk editor, the political producers and political reporters and myself, plus our two producers and the on-the-day programme producers . . . In conference weeks one of those producers will go to the conference venue and will be specifically in charge of everything that comes out of there and the one other programme producer stays at home and does everything else.[3]

Deciding on the main story

The news teams meet on a daily basis to determine what the 'big' stories or the most newsworthy events are going to be that day. The BBC and Channel Four teams meet at least twice in the morning before the official start of conference proceedings. A BBC source suggested: 'One of the things we are trying to develop there [at the conferences], which reflects what happens here [at Millbank] now, is to have our own editorial meetings in the morning of all the correspondents, producers, the news organizers, the Research Unit and the Live Programme.'[4] A Channel Four source noted: 'We'll tend to sort of meet for breakfast in a hotel, then there will be a fuller meeting at nine o'clock, just before the first conference debate.'[5]

However an ITN source argued: 'We are a much smaller team. We tend to say: "This is the story, let's do it". You go down on the floor, you come back and ring the programme editor, who says: "Right, go and do it". I think that's the way it works best.'[6] Where meetings do take place, judgements are made about what events that day are likely to be the main story. These judgements are guided by a series of professional, organizationally derived attitudes towards events at conference. While everyone attending these meetings has a say, the editorial team's preferences are made clear to the others and the final selection of stories rests with them:

> It'll be carved up. The political editor . . . has really quite a lot of say. But sometimes the programme producer has a very strong idea in their head and they just pull rank and say, "It is my programme. I'm doing it this way". But for the most part the political editors can get their way.[7]

Conference news values

A study of broadcasters' attitudes towards Parliament, by Blumler and Gurevitch (1995), provides a structure that can be transposed to the coverage of the party conferences. They argue that broadcasters have two fundamentally different attitudes to Parliament as a source of news. The first is 'sacerdotal': it considers that parliamentary developments 'deserve a regular and prominent airing as an inherent right and regardless of news value calculations'.[8] The second is 'pragmatic': in this approach, 'the treatment of politicians' activities is based on . . . assessments of their intrinsic newsworthiness . . . [so] that consequently the prominence given to the stories reporting these activities, the amount of time or space allocated to them will be determined by a strict consideration of news values.'[9]

Blumler and Gurevitch (1995) further argue that orientations 'towards a given institution will reflect the interaction between two sets of influences – its more or less abiding sacerdotal standing . . . and its momentary weight on news value scales'.[10] In other words with resources already committed to conference coverage it is likely that there is going to be at least one report in each bulletin on the conferences throughout the day. However the 'news value scales' determine what the main story is. On some days decisions are relatively straightforward – the leader's speech or a big debate will invariably be the main news feature, while on others they may have to choose between a range of competing events. The news teams try and make a decision beforehand between competing events. Is the most newsworthy attraction going to be the planned debates and speeches in the main hall or internal divisions on certain policy issues evident on the fringe or a wider issue affecting the parties – such as the petrol crisis in September 2000? As one source noted: 'You see we try and make so many guesses beforehand . . . [about] what is going to be the big story on the day.'[11] So what are the news value criteria used by the news teams?

Capturing the big beasts of the conference jungle

Different criteria are applied to speeches and debates at conference. In terms of speeches the main factor is who is making the speech. Generally the more senior the party actor the more newsworthy and deserving of coverage the speech is deemed. Seymour-Ure (1996) notes that decisions about which political actors receive coverage, and the amount of coverage, are based on a hierarchy of status or power. The amount of coverage party actors receive at conferences conforms to a similar pattern, with the set piece speeches by the so-called 'big beasts' (senior ministers, their shadows and party spokespersons) receiving the most attention and the individual delegates the least. For Seymour-Ure those at the top of the hierarchy are assured news coverage while those at the bottom have to struggle to gain it.

The news teams see certain events, like the party leader's speech, as deserving of coverage every year without reference to its newsworthiness. One ITN source suggested:

> We are now much more news driven, except for the leader's speech . . . You start from the premise that the leader's speech is important because it is one of the high points of the political year. Then you report what's in it . . . We have got to get the leaders. We can't cut Paddy Ashdown back if it is a busy news day and if it is a quiet news day when Blair's on give him a lot of time. That is just unfair. The easiest thing to do is say: "Give them a big chunk each. Don't ask any questions". It is a must.[12]

Evidence for this attitude can be seen in news coverage of each of the party leader's speeches over a four-year period. Table 3.1 shows that the Conservative and Labour leaders' speeches, in particular, were consistently at the top of each bulletin's running order with no variation over the four years.

Table 3.1 The prominence of reports on the leader's speech by party, 1993–6 (cell contents show reports in each position as a proportion of total conference news items and the actual number in brackets)

	Report Position					
	1st place to 4th place		5th place or more		Total Reports	
Conservative	100%	(24)	0%	(0)	100%	(24)
Labour	100%	(24)	0%	(0)	100%	(24)
Liberal Democrat	62%	(15)	38%	(9)	100%	(24)
Total	84%	(63)	16%	(9)	100%	(72)

However party seniority does not automatically guarantee sub-stantial coverage. There is a second determining criterion – a speech's content and/or the dramatic context in which it is delivered. The further one moves out along the series of concentric circles from the party leadership the more these criteria matter. Senior ministers, their shadows and senior spokespersons' speeches receive attention, but the amount of coverage, unlike the leader, depends upon the announce-ments their speeches contain. The more radical and significant the announcements, the greater the speech's newsworthiness, the greater the chance it will receive prominent coverage. The coverage of a lead-ership actor's speech is also influenced by the dramatic context in which the speech is made. In fact in some instances this acts as a compensating factor for a lack of announcements, raising its newsworthiness. This is particularly the case where the speech is part of an unfolding conference drama.

The operation of these values can be seen by examining coverage given to speeches by the Chancellor, his shadow and the Liberal Democrats' Treasury spokesperson over four conferences from 1993 to 1996. There is little doubt that the broadcasters considered these speeches important, with regular coverage across the time period. However, each speech was not considered equally important and news values largely determined the coverage.

Table 3.2 shows a clear variation in the attention given to the then Chancellor Kenneth Clarke's speeches over the period. In 1993 and 1996 it was seen as an important event, with reports being placed in the top four in 1993 and as the lead story across all bulletins in 1996. The speeches in 1994 and 1995 in comparison received little prominence or coverage. The fluctuation can be explained in part by the drama surrounding it. The 1993 speech was considered important because of its dramatic context. Clarke's speech was a defence of his decision to

Table 3.2   *The prominence of reports on the Chancellor's speeches at the Conservative conference by bulletin, 1993–6 (cell contents show the position of the report in each bulletin's running order)*

| | Report Position | | | |
	1993	1994	1995	1996
ITN 5.40	3rd	0	0	1st
ITN News at Ten	3rd	0	2nd	1st
BBC Six O'clock News	2nd	0	3rd	1st
BBC Nine O'clock News	4th	0	2nd	1st
Channel Four News	1st	7th	5th	1st
Newsnight	2nd	9th	0	1st

Table 3.3 *The prominence of reports on Shadow Chancellor's speeches at the Labour conference, 1993–6 (cell contents show the position of the report in each bulletin's running order)*

| | Report Position | | | |
	1993	1994	1995	1996
ITN 5.40	2nd	5th	1st	1st
ITN News at Ten	1st	3rd	1st	2nd
BBC Six O'clock News	3rd	1st	1st	4th
BBC Nine O'clock News	2nd	2nd	1st	4th
Channel Four News	1st	1st	1st	2nd
Newsnight	1st	1st	0	3rd

impose VAT on domestic fuel in the face of stinging criticism levelled at him by his predecessor Norman Lamont the same day. Animosity between an existing and a former chancellor was clearly newsworthy; only the degree varied between bulletins. Similar dramatic qualities can be seen surrounding Clarke's 1996 speech. The speech was a response to the critics of his pro-European views in the party and the cabinet members who had been demanding his removal. His overt pro-European views and the hostility with which some sections of the party held him, particularly having not delivered much sought-after tax cuts, raised the importance of the speech. In 1994 and 1995 speeches by other party leading lights were seen as more newsworthy.

Table 3.3 shows that there was less fluctuation in the coverage of the then Shadow Chancellor Gordon Brown's speeches. They were seen consistently over the period as newsworthy. In 1993 the speech was placed in the top three, in 1994 in the top five, in 1995 with the exception of Newsnight it was seen as the most important story at conference, although it fell back in 1996. The prominence of Brown's speeches was

Table 3.4 *The prominence of reports on Treasury Spokesperson's speeches at the Liberal Democrat conference, 1993–6 (cell contents show the position of the report in each bulletin's running order)*

| | Report Position | | | |
	1993	1994	1995	1996
ITN 5.40	0	5th	7th	4th
ITN News at Ten	0	5th	5th	5th
BBC Six O'clock News	0	10th	4th	4th
BBC Nine O'clock News	8th	5th	5th	4th
Channel Four News	0	7th	2nd	0
Newsnight	4th	2nd	0	3rd

linked to his status within the party and to a combination of the speeches' content and dramatic factors. Brown's speeches were considered more newsworthy, because of his centrality to New Labour and because he used it as an opportunity to present party economic policy. All speeches were enhanced by the fact that they were part of an active debate on party economic policy where criticisms of Brown's economic policies, particularly the level of a minimum wage, were voiced by some of the largest trade unions. In addition Brown's speeches were on Monday – the official opening of the conference – and as a senior party figure he received little or no competition from his colleagues.

Table 3.4 shows that the Liberal Democrat Treasury spokesperson's speeches when compared to his rivals were seen as less important. Their content was not seen as particularly newsworthy, nor were any of the speeches part of a wider newsworthy drama unfolding at conference.

Fishing for critical minnows

Actors outside the leadership circle receive coverage according to a 'strict consideration of news values'.[13] Speeches by back-benchers, 'old stars' (recognizable former leadership actors) and union actors at the Labour conference, receive attention only if they fulfil a particularly narrow criterion and that almost always is being critical of the party leadership and party policy. One source suggested: 'interest is inevitably nearly always a function of the extent to which there is criticism of the leadership, particularly in the case of a government.'[14] These actors, freed from collective responsibility, can voice their concerns about party policy and attack former leadership colleagues. As another journalist suggested: 'If there is dissent we report it . . . if there is a fringe meeting when the line is criticized then we will probably use it because you are reflecting what is a real tension in the party.'[15] All leaderships have their critics, but the newsworthiness of what they say fades over time. If a former minister, particularly one who has recently been sacked or resigned, makes a critical speech it will receive a lot of attention; the following year a similar speech by the same actor may receive less attention.[16]

In addition news teams are more likely to cover a critical speech if it is delivered by a recognizable party actor. A BBC source suggested: 'Who the speaker is is crucial. You know, if Norman Lamont, say last year [1994] or the year before [1993], is appearing on the fringe, then you have to be there because it is clearly important.'[17] This point was echoed by a senior Channel Four source: 'Television in some measure in political terms is about recognition . . . if you have a room of unrecognizable

Table 3.5 *Prominence of reports on speeches critical of leadership policy by conference (cell contents show the number of reports in each position on all bulletins)*

	\multicolumn{5}{c}{Report Position}					
	1st	2nd	3rd	4th	5th +	Total
Conservatives						
Lord Lamont (1994)	6	0	0	0	0	6
John Redwood (1995)	3	1	0	0	0	4
Labour						
Lord Hattersley (1995)	3	2	1	0	0	6
Lady Castle (1996)	0	0	2	2	2	6
Liberal Democrats						
Lord Rodgers (1996)	0	0	1	3	2	6
Total	12	3	4	5	4	28

faces . . . that sounded bad and the rest of it, it doesn't make terribly persuasive television. It is hard to persuade the audience that some great moment is unfolding.'[18]

The actors highlighted in table 3.5 were all recognizable critics of some aspect of their party's policy. When they did not disappoint journalists and lambasted the leadership in a speech it was given attention. Table 3.5 which provides a sample of critical speeches, shows that former Labour deputy leader Roy Hattersley's five-minute speech criticizing Labour's education policy at the 1995 conference received prominent coverage, as did major speeches delivered outside the main hall on the fringe by SDP founder Lord Rodgers in 1996 and by former Conservative ministers Lamont in 1994 and Redwood in 1995. This example clearly shows that critical speeches by recognizable former members of the party leadership are considered very newsworthy and are given prominence. The bulletins and journalists otherwise see speeches by leadership actors as more deserving of an airing because of their status in the party: their contributions are amplified even more if they are newsworthy. Conference delegates, however, are used primarily as a 'vox pop' element in reports, largely as an illustratory device, a way of registering party opinions. The final determining factor is when a speech occurs. A critical speech is more likely to be covered if it is easy for journalists and camera crews to capture.

Titillated, scintillated and attracted by conflict[19]

If we look at the news value criteria for debates, journalists express a particular preference for conflict on policy issues between clearly divergent sides in a party and are fairly indifferent to debates that are anodyne. The constraint of television as a medium means in practical terms that debates are hard to relay unless there are obvious, overt differences of opinion identifiable with particular actors.

> It is very difficult once you have got to condense it into, let's say, News at Ten's three and a half minute report or even Channel 4's twelve-minute report. It is very hard to say: "Okay, let's devote four minutes of that to Robin Cook commentating on the debate on foreign affairs". It is a ten-ton pencil, it is the most dreadful medium to operate creatively, the worst and yet the best when something physically happens. But for television politics is death unless there is a real fight.[20]

The weight of a debate on the 'news value scales' is further influenced by the actors involved and the issue. Conflict that involves the leadership is more newsworthy than conflict that does not. As for the issue, broadcasters prefer issues to be ones that are significant to the party and their viewers; if the debates end in a ballot so much the better.

The operation of these values can be seen by the attention given to debates with visible levels of conflict involving the leadership compared to those without. At the Liberal Democrat conference in 1994 of a total of some twenty-five debates on various motions only three received coverage. These were debates where the delegates defied the wishes of the leadership. In two debates they voted for the legalization of cannabis and for a set minimum wage and narrowly voted for the leadership line in a third – namely, voting to keep the monarchy. Of a total of eleven reports on these debates four were top four news items and seven in the fifth place or lower. These debates were some of the most prominent between 1993 and 1996. Other debates without these qualities – on asthma and air pollution, the health service, nuclear power, school meals and Northern Ireland – received no coverage at all.

A similar picture emerges in the coverage of the Labour conference. Of a total of fifteen debates in 1993, coverage focused mainly on one – the titanic conflict between the two biggest trade unions and the Labour leadership over the introduction of OMOV (One Member, One Vote) and the downgrading of the block vote. This debate possessed all the criteria mentioned and was subject to a total of eighteen reports over three days – all top three news items. Similarly prominent coverage was afforded the 1994 debate to reaffirm the party's commitment to Clause Four in the face of Blair's announcement to rewrite it. Here the six reports on the debate were all top four news items. In 1993 and 1994 other debates without these characteristics – on the environment, electoral reform, modernizing the National Health Service and education – were ignored.

At the Conservatives' conferences debates in the main hall were usually seen as anodyne affairs by the news teams. Indeed during the 1993 conference, of a total of seventeen debates in the main hall only one was considered newsworthy enough to receive prominent coverage. This was over the introduction of VAT on fuel and public expenditure and was highly visible with all six reports being in the top four positions in the running order. The other debate the news teams covered on the European Union was not formally timetabled and occurred on the fringe. This was the subject of twenty-one reports, eighteen of which were in the top four positions. Formally timetabled debates on defence, agriculture, foreign affairs, education, health, and transport received no coverage at all.

The debates over OMOV (One Member, One Vote), the introduction of VAT on fuel and Europe, and over the legalization of cannabis and abolition of the monarchy, received prominent coverage across all the bulletins. This was because unlike the other debates, they possessed certain qualities that made them newsworthy – namely they were on important issues, and there were openly divergent views held by two sides (one side being the party leadership). If conflict-laden debates do not occur in the main hall, as was the case of the European debate at the Conservatives' conference, then the news teams comb the fringe. A BBC source noted: 'There are particular events where you would have to be, the Tribune rally, the Tory Reform Group or whatever.'[21]

Having made their original choices, news teams weigh up speeches and debates comparatively throughout the day – is the debate X the main story or debate Y? Is it speech A made by a senior minister or speech B by another? Important comparisons are also made as to whether the main story is the debate or a set piece speech by a minister or their shadow. The more the speeches and debates fulfil the different criteria the more they are likely to be subject of a report. However, unexpected newsworthy occurrences during the day such as a gaffe, a resignation or a sacking can move the focus of reports away from the planned agenda.

Expanding the news

Once a decision is taken, further judgements are then made as to whether the news teams are going to expand upon the issues raised in a speech or debate they are covering through an additional news item. The BBC and ITN are committed to expanding the coverage of particularly newsworthy occurrences at conference. There are three forms of

Table 3.6   *The type and number of additional news items used by bulletin,
1993–6*

	News Bulletins					
	NN	Ch 4	BBC9	ITN10	BBC6	ITN5.40	Total
Pegged Items	42	31	24	21	18	1	137
Interviews	69	59	0	1	1	0	130
Two-ways	8	15	9	10	12	26	80
Total	119	105	33	32	31	27	347

(BBC6 = BBC Six O'clock News; BBC9 = BBC Nine O'clock News;
ITN5.40 = ITN News at 5.40 p.m.; ITN10 = ITN News at Ten O'clock;
Ch 4 = Channel Four News; NN = Newsnight)

additional news item. (1) The 'pegged' item or report – additional
reports scrutinizing the impact of policy proposals made in a particular
speech and seeking the reactions and opinion of other elite players, both
in and outside the parties. (2) Two-ways. These are question and answer
sessions between anchor in the studio and the journalist in the field,
which seek 'to assess or make sense of a political event'[22] and also importantly involve speculation[23] and scrutiny of events. (3) Interviews and
discussions with members of the party leadership, with the rank and
file, or with journalists. These also seek to explain, speculate and scru-
tinize and are at times confrontational, particularly with members of the
party leadership. Table 3.6 gives some idea of the preference exhibited
by the evening news broadcasters over a four-year period.

The most frequently used form of additional news item is the pegged
report, closely followed by interviews, with two-ways being used the
least. The table also shows that the different bulletins prefer different
ways of expanding the conference agenda. The BBC and ITN almost
solely used pegged items and two-ways, with the overwhelming
majority of the ITN 5.40's additional news items being two-ways.
Channel Four News and *Newsnight* largely prefer the use of interviews
and to a lesser extent pegged items and two-ways.

The decisions reached at meetings largely determine the subsequent
gathering activity of the news teams and the deployment of additional
mobile Electronic News Gathering (ENG) camera crews. Of course
decisions can be 'blown out of the water' by a newsworthy issue which
suddenly and unexpectedly arises, such as an MP's defection from the
party (which happened at the 1995 Conservative conference) or
the sacking of a shadow minister (which happened at the 1996 Labour
conference).

Trawling for news: gathering and the conference news community

After the meetings the follow-up gathering of information and video footage occurs in linked stages. The first involves gathering from routine events the news teams have decided to cover. The second involves gathering information from briefings and conversations and additional visual material. Gathering is a continuous process throughout the period of the conferences, with deadlines acting as pressure on journalists to get the latest film material available, and prepare scripts, in time for the link-line to London. In the first stage, gathering is largely passive and requires little effort. Footage of speeches and debates comes from cameras already in the main hall, and further information on these events is given to the journalists in the form of press releases.

The passive gathering of information from routine events involves little direct interaction with other actors, whereas the second stage of news gathering often means direct face-to-face contact, whether on or off camera, with a host of different actors. A Channel Four source provides a useful example from his experiences:

> A typical day will begin with a breakfast. [If] it is an event-breakfast, like one that Channel 4 stages, in which case you are likely to be sitting between two cabinet ministers or a cabinet minister and somebody else's wife . . . Then you go on to the 9.30 opening of conference and that morning period, first, in immediate terms, is to find what's swilling about for the day. And second, for a more long-term period, is to get people in the margins who came out of a debate bored perhaps with the immediate subject in hand and more than happy to have coffee and grit through some of the things which are not immediately on the agenda. I team up with the assistant editor of *The Times* and we in fact have a remorseless programme of dining cabinet ministers and front-bench spokespersons throughout the week. I mean my diary for last year, there would certainly be a lunch and a dinner every day with somebody who was worth having dinner with . . . The fringe obviously is a moment, again in immediate terms, to see how passions are running on particular subjects. And in the more long term it's possible to make contact with people who are rather germane to a subject but do not have heads above the parapet. They may be people from think tanks, pressure groups or whatever, who in subsequent times will become useful, should the issue be important. Take Europe for example: obviously there are endless people who materialize to input in a European debate in the fringes who may well subsequently become useful.[24]

This second stage of gathering involves acquiring the reactions of party actors, particularly the leadership, and finding new sources of visual material often from outside the conference hall to supplement existing coverage. This gathering is driven by the need to incorporate new material into reports before the next deadline to freshen them up, which is an almost continuous process throughout the day. Some of this additional gathering observed at several conferences[25] involved 'door stepping' senior party members for comment in numerous different locations, talking to the spin doctors in the press room, and taking notes from impromptu briefings and press conferences. In particular the conference hotel is the haunt of evening news gathering (Baker, 1993; Prior, 1986). One former Tory Party Chairman described a typical scene in the hotel foyer. 'Radio mikes are pushed in front of you; television crews record you entering, being searched, checking in and chatting to friends. If you have to wait for the lift then you are trapped, and comment can only be refused by being churlish.'[26] There is also lots of social interaction in the hotel bars, restaurants, parties and fringe meetings usually in the evenings – gossiping about particular party actors and policy. Indeed, conferences provide a greater access to senior party actors than at Westminster. One source highlighted the advantages of such open access at conference.

> The lobby system at Westminster although it is a system of access it is fairly restrictive access . . . At conferences you have . . . social access . . . [and] it is much easier for stories to slip through the net of the spin doctor. It is much easier to talk to the party mavericks, it is easier to talk to politicians when their guards are down.[27]

In general journalists can usually find a member of the party elite who is prepared to express an opinion that differs from the official line, even if it is given off the record. However, interaction with other party actors and the delegates is more spasmodic and usually on the journalists' terms: As one journalist suggested: 'you're not really getting any sort of insights into the grass roots . . . The theory is we go down there and get in touch with party grass roots, but I think we spend much more time talking to each other and to senior politicians who we know quite well.'[28]

Follow-up gathering also involves the news teams in interaction with rival broadcast journalists and those from the press. As one journalist commented: 'I would say as much time is spent lurking around with the hacks, as is spent with the politicians, spinning between ourselves.'[29] Together these actors form a loose 'news community' (Sigal, 1973), which 'shapes perspectives for its members'.[30] Direct contact between members of the 'news community' occurs off camera around the press room. The broadcast journalists frequently visit the press room during gathering. One noted: 'I would normally go in there [the press room] in the morning, maybe for twenty minutes, to see what everyone is up to, and then go back late afternoon. By then they will know what their stories are.'[31]

After a speech or a debate, journalists were often observed in a huddle talking to spin doctors finding out the leadership line on events. They were also observed in conversation with each other, as one journalist noted: 'We are constantly nattering to each other all the time: "What did you think of that speech? Do you think they were applauding much? Do you think the conference like him? Doesn't he look hung over?" and that sort of thing.'[32] Much of this time is spent discussing the leadership position on a motion, speculating about the likelihood of a defeat in a ballot, trying to decipher what the 'real' significance of a particular announcement is, and reconfirming their views with each other to see if they have the main point. As one source noted: 'The story often emerges after the event when people talk about whether it was what it really was.'[33] Conversations with 'opinion formers' (usually senior journalists) also help journalists provide insights into the reasoning behind the latest policy announcements or generate informed speculation.[34] The 'opinion formers' have specialized knowledge on policy areas which the broadcast correspondents do not. One noted:

> I might talk to them. Peter Riddell [*The Times*] is a very experienced guy and very friendly. And you might say: "What do you think about that?" and he'll say "I was very struck by x,y,z". If they have got time it will be helpful to put something in context, because they have been doing the job a lot longer than you have.[35]

Many of the press journalists are also actively partisan. For instance, Charlie Whelan – Gordon Brown's former media aid – spins for the party from his column in the *Mirror*, a tactic Alastair Campbell as a former journalist with *Today* used in the early 1990s. The senior journalists are also important sources of information for news reports. Over the period of the study, they were used by journalists to provide comment on particular developments at the conferences.

In addition conversations with news community members provide broadcast journalists with an idea of what stories are being followed by which outlets.[36] It enables a confirmation of the journalists' news priorities – a test to see if they are widely held. The same source noted: 'There is a lot of "Hey chaps, what's the line? What are you doing? What are you up to? Well the *Mail* are doing this, are they". They are keen to know what *News at Ten* are leading with and you are always keen to know what the papers are going to say.'[37] Another source indicated that the others acted as a sounding board: 'Initially it informs priorities. You test to see if they agree with you that x is a priority, that it may be at the top of a story rather than the extent of the story or the bones of it. But then equally on some issues it may assist with an analytical structure.'[38] If challenged by the programme editors, the correspondents can always point to the common definition originating within the news community.

> They are quite happy to tell you, because if *News at Ten* runs something that they are not a bit certain about, it gives them a bit of back up that the broadcasters have done the same thing. But it is incestuous, I have to admit that. It is not as if everyone there comes to their own conclusions.[39]

In sum the news community acts as a 'safety blanket' (Mancini, 1993) for its members; the community is a source of reassurance during gathering.

In this vein the BBC brings its own specialists – the Political Research Unit (PRU) – to the conferences. They act as an important source of information for the BBC journalists, providing back-up research and a conference guide. The PRU also acts as a further 'security blanket' for the BBC journalists. A source suggested of the PRU:

> It really does come into its own at conferences, because what it specializes in is policy, background, knowing the history of particular policy areas and so on in a way that the cab rank correspondent [doesn't]. To have people who have that at their finger tips is a fantastic resource for the correspondents. If you were working without that, and other organizations do, you would feel in the dark. If nothing else it is a security blanket.[40]

The presence of the PRU may mean that BBC journalists do not have to rely on the views of the news community on certain issues.

A cosy coterie of friends

Broadcast journalists in the news community tend to be at least familiar, if not on first-name terms, not only with each other but also with the spin doctors and senior party actors. As a correspondent noted:

> You walk in and there is one familiar face after another and it's a journalist's joy . . . It is a road show, you meet them at by-elections, you meet them all day long at Westminster, all year round I should say. Once a year you meet them away from home like a sort of journalist's holiday and there are an awful lot of familiar faces there.[41]

The depth of the relationship built up between these journalists and the party elite – in particular their spin doctors – is an important factor when considering the formation of television news agendas. As the same correspondent suggested: 'I think you'd be right in thinking that you have the most contact with the people you are most familiar with.'[42] A significant proportion of broadcast journalists have pre-existing relationships with party actors as members of the Westminster Lobby. These relationships are based on the exchange of information for publicity. The same source suggested:

> It is a lot like it is in Westminster, it's symbiotic. We look to them for favours and any gossip. We look to them to give us off-the-record a line which they haven't given the BBC, they haven't given a colleague. They look to us presumably to get their point across. I don't think they look for exceptionally favourable coverage: they don't expect us to be totally uncritical.[43]

Another correspondent concurred: 'If you like, it is a trade off.'[44] However within this tight-knit group of actors relationships are hierarchically differentiated (Franklin, 1994). There are formal exchange relationships. These are based on the routine exchange of conventional information (the latest announcements and the related facts and figures) for publicity; bearing in mind the number of broadcast journalists present, the majority have these relationships. However, there are also a series of close relationships. Many of these relationships have developed over lengthy periods of time. Such closeness is also the product of the provision and reporting of accurate information and insight into leadership thinking.

The exchange of more 'personalized information' (details about future direction of the party, personal character assassinations) takes place between principal spin doctors of the senior party actors and the television opinion formers, the political editors and 'star' presenters. This is the inner sanctum of information exchange. The exchange is personal and intense, and often involves the trade of exclusive personalized information for informed representation. The journalists are interested in and anxious to learn the opinions of the party elite actors, who are often unavailable for continuous comment. One elite source highlighted the courting of the journalistic elite by the principal spin doctors:

> Their [the spin doctors'] most valuable and remorseless expenditure is on the electronic media. Oakley and Brunson are powerful. If you go back a decade or more I don't think you would find the political editors of the electronic media anything like as influential as they are now. Influential because they get attention from the parties, and influential because they are sort of mouthpieces, the first brig in the political line. They are courted the whole time by the parties.[45]

Marr (previously Oakley), Sergeant (previously Brunson), Goodman, Snow, Wark and Paxman share a privileged relationship with the senior spin doctors in each party. As their interpretations carry a lot of weight with their junior colleagues, and they have tremendous credibility with other journalists in the news community, they are the conduit through which such personalized information passes. To a certain extent this 'matchmaking' does not exclude brief exchanges developing between 'suitors who would generally consider themselves above such a partner'.[46] However, in the main, the interrelationships between the spin doctors and the correspondents and producers are formal and based on publicizing more conventional information.

The broadcast journalists are less receptive in general towards the information provided by non-leadership actors and delegates unless they have something newsworthy to contribute and this means being critical of the leadership. Journalists have preconceptions about the particular political views of these actors. These shape their preferences in choosing non-leadership sources, particularly delegates. Journalists tend to pick a source to represent a particular view that they think is prevalent in the party. As a Channel Four source confirmed:

> One does find a risk that you go towards the person who you think will reinforce your prejudice. And you ask them whether they think John Major is a weak leader, and funnily enough they say, "well, yes actually". Because we are not immersed with these people, we really are in that greenhouse across the road all year round, and once a year we are supposed to know what the grass roots are like.[47]

Non-leadership sources are indexed as representatives of particular critical views that the journalists think are held by a wider section of the party.

Competition at conference

While acquainted with each other journalists are still in competition to be first or at least not last (Tunstall, 1970) in reporting an event, and to get an exclusive quote or interview with a leadership actor. Competition occurs on a daily basis within the same organization both between journalists and between news teams and simultaneously between the different broadcasters and between journalists in the news community. However, the first stage of news gathering tends not to be particularly competitive. As the big stories often occur in the main hall, the chances of one individual getting a story their rivals do not have is slim. As one source suggested: 'Because of the competition with your colleagues, they might get a story you missed. But on the whole, the story happens in the arena, so you tend to get it.'[48] Competition between journalists is more intense during follow-up gathering. Journalists need to constantly update the reports between deadlines to include the latest developments outside the conference venue, the latest views of the party leadership, and reactions of delegates to events to supplement coverage of the main events. This is compounded by a fear particularly amongst BBC journalists that they may miss a particular development. This point was illustrated by a senior BBC source's expression of worry about missing a story:

> One of our difficulties often is the fact that the newspapers, even more so than at Westminster, are all under the same roof. At a lot of conference venues they are at one end of the building: we are at the other. The newspapers are all together, so a rumour can go round like wildfire, which if we are not careful we can be completely excluded from. As ITN are much smaller, their proximity to the newspapers will be much better than ours. And it is quite possible, even though we have lots of people at the conference, for us to miss a story which suddenly finds itself across the newspapers and ITN. So we are quite vulnerable to stories slipping by us there, and it is something you have always got to be aware of at conferences because it is a rumour mill.[49]

During follow-up gathering the competition that occurs is competition for what is generally termed exclusives. Particularly prized are the newsworthy insights provided by the principal spin doctors. Some broadcast journalists, particularly the political editors, selectively seek to use existing close relationships with principal spin doctors to establish the views of the leadership actors, so as to get an exclusive insight into their opinion on an issue, which their rivals do not have. The BBC and ITN regularly hold receptions, to which party leadership actors are invited, to aid the gathering of exclusive information.

Also important are interviews, particularly with the leading party actors. A BBC source suggested: 'There is considerable competition between the various outlets; for example, which programme got the first full-length Blair interview.'[50] The broadcasters compete for extensive live or pre-recorded interviews. Both bulletins, because of their large time slots, are able to get the interviews with the political actors. *Channel Four News* conducted a total of fifty-eight interviews between 1993 and 1996: six at the Liberal Democrat conference, twenty-five at Labour's and twenty-seven at the Conservatives'. *Newsnight* conducted a total of sixty-seven interviews: eleven at the Liberal Democrat conference, twenty-seven at Labour's and twenty-nine at the Conservatives'. But *News at Ten* and the BBC *Six O'clock News* conducted only one interview each between 1993 and 1996. However, the late-evening bulletins on ITV and BBC did include highlights of interviews in some reports, either conducted by themselves or by *Newsnight* or *Channel Four News*.

In addition, competition can be seen in the drive to gather additional comments to make the reports look fresher. With only a finite number of newsworthy individuals around, the gathering journalists are often forced to engage in 'door stepping' in the hope that they will get a short exclusive answer to a question. The search for exclusive sources of information to provide fresh insights and opinions for reports also takes place at fringe meetings. All journalists jealously guard exclusives they are given: 'If you've had a private chat with someone [in the leadership] you keep it to yourself and run it as an exclusive'.[51]

This competition for exclusives is a source of concern for senior editorial staff, in some organizations. At the BBC, with its large conference presence, there is a worry that competition between BBC correspondents will lead to the various bulletins producing diverging output. In response there has been some movement at an editorial level to co-ordinate competition between bulletins. The BBC has begun to centrally co-ordinate its news gathering operation at conferences, seeking to increase co-operation between the various news programmes. As a BBC source suggested:

> We don't want to pull in all the BBC's coverage and make it the same, but inevitably if you are not going to be competing in a way that is counter-productive you need at least to have that form of trust and communication between the outlets. So I'd like to think if *Newsnight* had some form of exclusive they would at least be able to plan how it came out by talking to me.[52]

While content remains the responsibility of the programme, an overall news co-ordinator brings editors and producers together. The aim is to improve the BBC's internal transfer of information at conference using the existing series of daily meetings. The same source suggested:

> We are trying to pull them all into pooling information. So I will take part in a "conference core" for instance with the television morning editorial meeting and then a little later we will have some form of editorial meeting whereby we try and pull all the strands together.[53]

He admitted, however, that 'they wouldn't be proper journalists if they didn't want their own exclusive and there is an enormous amount of competition',[54] but that there were in place 'editorial structures whereby these things can be sorted out'.[55] These editorial structures, he argued, were 'to make sure the channels of communication between programmes and ourselves exist without trying to standardize everything'.[56] They are also part of an effort to avoid an incoherent interpretation of events within the BBC.

While the news teams decide on the content of each report, each London news room – with one eye on their audience – is responsible for the position of conference reports within the overall bulletin running order and deciding whether the story is worthy of a headline. Competition is not just confined to the conference arena, the main broadcast organizations are locked in competition for audience share. This struggle has become more intense with the presence of three British-based twenty-four hour news channels and the BBC and ITN evening news going head-to-head at ten o'clock for at least three nights a week from early 2001. In the competitive news environment the broadcasters seek to ensure that their bulletins attract a large number of viewers and are not a turn-off. The focus on ratings puts a greater emphasis on the newsworthiness of events at the conferences. While the news teams are concerned with the events at conference, the editors and producers, and the higher executives within the London news rooms, are less involved in news gathering. They are more pragmatically oriented towards conference as a source of news. While events at each conference are guaranteed some coverage, they need to prove themselves in news value terms. The emphasis on news values means that all speeches and debates are not automatically given a high priority. Each London news room compares the newsworthiness of conference with events unfolding elsewhere in Britain and abroad, and adjusts their running order accordingly. The position of the conference changes in each bulletin's running order throughout the day. Even key events at conference are not guaranteed visible coverage by any of the bulletins. In 2000 the Conservative leader's speech was eclipsed on all bulletins by reports on the overthrow of Milosevic in Yugoslavia. On other occasions, such as at the 1995 Labour conference, the leader's speech triumphed over one of the biggest stories of the 1990s – the O. J. Simpson trial verdict.[57] However, *Newsnight* and *Channel Four's News* teams carry greater weight compared to the other news teams in deciding the position of the conferences in their running order. This is primarily because they are anchored out of the conferences. As one Channel Four source suggested, 'It would take a very big story to dislodge the conference coverage from the top of the programme.'[58]

While the political news teams at conference would like their reports to feature prominently in the bulletin, they are in competition with other news teams within their respective organizations. Conference reports have to compete with other stories for prominence. The news teams therefore want to ensure that their reports capture the most newsworthy elements of conference and therefore top the bulletins.

Conclusion

While the main broadcasters are still sacerdotally-oriented to the conferences, news values are a central factor in determining what aspects of conference the news teams cover and the prominence given to the final reports in the bulletins. At each conference the news teams continually make decisions about what the main story of the day will be. Usually this is a timetabled speech or debate in the conference hall, but it may not live up to expectations or something more news-worthy may occur elsewhere. Throughout each day, news teams continually weigh up events against each other to see what is the most important event in news terms – which may or may not be the speech the leadership has spent time planning. Indeed the news teams are particularly attracted to overt intra-party conflict, gaffes and un-expected occurrences involving leadership actors.

Gathering is a continuous process throughout the day, with multiple deadlines to be met. While events in the main hall are easy to cover the news teams also have to make sure that they capture the latest develop-ments outside the main arena. They seek to ensure that their reports contain the latest visual material from the fringe or the conference hotel. The news teams are also alert to missing a late breaking story their rivals might get. Contact with the news community allows them to check what stories are developing and verify their interpretation of events against the one prevailing amongst their colleagues.

Broadcast journalists are a group of actors who enjoy an already strong routinized relationship with senior party actors. Formal pro-fessional relationships exist between editorial staff and party press officers, surrounding the routine matters of conference coverage. However there is also a largely exclusive one between the spin doctors and a broadcast journalist elite of political editors and presenters. Contact with delegates and other party actors is less frequent, and depends on the newsworthiness of those actors, i.e. whether or not they are critical of the party leadership.

While news teams are at the centre of the news-gathering process, overall control of bulletins rests with producers and editors in the London news rooms. The news rooms make the final decisions about the position of conference reports in the bulletin. In the contemporary competitive news environment conferences have to compete for their position in the running order. The following chapter reveals how the party communication professionals aid the gathering process, thereby providing a stable supply of newsworthy information and easing the news teams' work, enabling them to effectively compete with other news teams not at conference.

4

Spinning on the Conference Circuit

During conference each leadership and their management teams want the events they have planned, particularly the set piece speeches, to dominate each day's news bulletins. To ensure this happens the conference managers try and make sure that the information is packaged and delivered in a manner that is attractive to and convenient for journalists, and that any distractions from the main events are kept to a minimum. This is a continuous process throughout the duration of each conference, which sees the managers engaging with party actors and gathering journalists to ensure the news bulletins reflect the preferred leadership agenda. This chapter examines the on-going management process during conference, focusing on the party actors involved, the strategies used, and through the use of a case study how news management works.

The hidden persuaders

In each party there are front region and back region actors.[1] The front region actors are those officials who visibly disseminate information – the party leader, the ministers and their shadows and a loose heterogeneous collective of recognizable personalities composed of prominent back-benchers, external power brokers such as the unions in the Labour party and 'old stars' like former ministers (Heffernan and Stanyer, 1997). The back region actors are the spin doctors and party managers who are active in the planning process but remain largely invisible to the viewer even though they are crucial in conference communication.

It is this army of back region actors who play a crucial role in ensuring that party problems are ironed out behind the scenes, and that communication strategies are implemented and publicity goals achieved. In all three parties these back region actors operate as an organized team. Each team is co-ordinated by the same coterie of senior actors who directed the planning effort. The team – now a permanent fixture at every conference – is a leadership resource working for them alone. This cadre of co-ordinators is comprised of communication specialists and party managers, including experienced and senior party professionals, elected officials and politicians. For the duration of each conference these senior actors meet on a daily basis to fix communication strategy and second guess any problems that are likely to arise and react accordingly.

For example, during the 1995 Liberal Democrat conference their Director of Strategy and Planning worked closely with the others including the Director of Communications, the leader's press officer and key party actors such as Chair of the General Election Campaign (then Lord Holme), General Secretary (then Graham Elson), Director of Campaigns and Elections (then Chris Rennard). This group of actors was responsible for the co-ordination of the management operation. A team member noted: 'They meet every morning. We try to get them together so they can work as a team for the whole week. In the morning we can review what's coming up and advise members how we ought to argue it.'[2] In 1995 Labour's management operation was co-ordinated by an inner circle of actors around the leader. These included Alastair Campbell, the leader's press secretary, Peter Mandelson,[3] the Head of Press and Broadcasting (then David Hill), the General Secretary and other senior party members. The team met every day and 'drew up a "conference planning grid" to plot hour-by-hour the debates, speeches, fringe meetings and media appearances by front-bench spokesmen. It listed the main theme for each day, Labour's preferred media story and the potential problems which might dominate the headlines instead.'[4] The Conservative conference in the same year also saw 'a ruthless centralization and co-ordination of announcements'.[5] Their management operation was co-ordinated via a daily meeting by an inner circle of actors. As one noted:

> This last conference (1995) we had a meeting at 7.30 in the morning chaired by the Party Chairman and present there were, Michael Heseltine, Tony Newton, Alistair Goodlad the Chief Whip, Howel Jones the Prime Minister's Political Secretary, Norman Blackwell head of the Policy Unit, Hugh Colver and myself. Michael Trend was also present as Deputy Chairman.[6]

Each cadre co-ordinate a team of spin doctors whose overall task is primarily to ensure the news media reflect the desired message or adopt a particular interpretation of events.[7] The team consists of professional employees and part-timers and volunteers, the latter actors being activists who have experience of the broadcasters, or MPs with specialist knowledge of a particular policy area. In 1995 the Liberal Democrat co-ordinators oversaw a team including a Head of Press and Broadcasting and sixteen professional press officers.[8] The operation also drew heavily on a series of actors with specialized knowledge. The Labour inner circle co-ordinated a team which included a Chief Press and Broadcasting Officer, a Parliamentary Officer and Broadcasting Officer and six other press officers. In addition there were also press officers from regional headquarters and Scotland and Wales present. There were also notable part-timers used by the Labour leadership. These were MPs or Prospective Parliamentary Candidates, not part of the Shadow Cabinet but ideologically in tune with the New Labour core. Labour's operation involved the press officers of the then members of the Shadow Cabinet. Many of these actors stayed with their masters after the 1997 general election. The Conservative elite oversaw a team of twenty-two staff, including a media consultant, the Head of News, the Head of Scottish Media, four broadcasting officers, three press officers, two photo-opportunities officers, two information officers, a press office manager, three secretaries and two messengers and also MPs.

Each team of spin doctors run the press office and implement communication strategies. The junior employees and volunteers man the press office, aiding journalists with their inquiries and producing the press releases[9] to accompany events at conference. A large volume of releases are disseminated to journalists both before and after events. These take several forms: an outline of the main announcements contained in speeches, on the record quotes by senior party actors, and details of the leadership's responses to various motions under debate.[10] In addition the press office produces copies of all the speeches in full, keeps camera crews up to date with the location of party leadership photo-opportunities,[11] keeps journalists informed of any changes in the timetable, and updates the conference website.

The main task of party managers and those with specialist knowledge is to 'sell' conventional information (the official party line or perspective[12]) to broadcast journalists and the wider news community. In addition there are spin doctors working for individual ministers and shadow ministers who also disseminate personalized information on behalf of their bosses. They are at liberty to trail something different to opinion formers – exclusive information on new directions in party policy providing a new angle for journalists during briefings. This information generally concerns their opinions on an issue or existing policy that is much sought after by journalists, particularly when in government.

Conference management

In order to ensure that the planned agenda is the news broadcasters' main story and reduce the risk of distractions arising, the teams engage in a dual process of party management and news management. Party management is largely a preventative measure aimed at stopping negative or unwanted publicity dominating the news broadcasters' agenda. It makes sure that there are few if any surprises that will deflect journalists away from reporting the chosen agenda. News management seeks to ensure that the broadcasters and the wider news community give the planned agenda the maximum coverage possible. News management involves the implementation of different communication strategies throughout the duration of the conferences. These strategies are designed to ensure that the broadcasters reflect the main conference agenda and give precedence to the leadership line. The strategies adapt the release of information to fit the needs of gathering journalists but in a way that is beneficial to the leadership.

Managing the party

Conferences, despite the planning, remain an unpredictable environment. Not all disagreements can be prevented from an airing in spite of the tight regulation of the timetable and agenda, nor can results favourable for the leadership be guaranteed in a ballot. A particular concern for the Liberal Democrat and Labour leadership is the publicity that accompanies a leadership defeat. Much hangs on whether the leadership position is endorsed or rejected. Any rejection is seen as newsworthy and is often framed by journalists as a snub for the leadership (see chapter 7). The publicity that follows is of some embarrassment to the leadership and detracts from the planned message the communication teams are trying to get across, showing the party instead as undisciplined. Each management team in response engages in a behind-the-scenes attempt at persuasion, aimed at finding a compromise and preventing conflict between the party and the leadership or ill feeling spilling on to the conference floor and becoming news.

At Labour conferences party management is increasingly driven by publicity concerns, as ballots are not necessarily binding on the party leadership. Conflicts between the unions and the leadership are seen as particularly newsworthy – as chapter 3 has shown. These conflicts are often viewed by journalists as a return to the conferences of old, an image which the leadership is desperate to avoid. There is a concerted effort at Labour conferences by party managers to resolve potential problems and prevent embarrassing defeats for the leadership. Such management tactics are not new and have been well documented (Minkin, 1978). During the 1993 conference pressure was brought to bear on the Manufacturing, Science and Finance (MSF) union to abstain in the One Member, One Vote ballot. More recently at the 2000 party conference much effort by senior government actors was put into trying to persuade the then leader of UNISON, Rodney Bickerstaffe, to remit his motion calling for the government to re-establish the link between increases in the level of state pensions and increases in earnings. Management activity also focuses on the delegates. A former agenda committee source admitted that one of their tasks was to calm down disgruntled delegates. The process of management extends to the conduct of key debates. The general consensus amongst observers is that when calling delegates for a debate the platform has knowledge about their views and is able to call or ignore them accordingly.[13]

The Conservatives faced similar problems, although much of the opposition to the leadership was not articulated on the conference floor but on the fringe. Although, as one source remarked, 'there isn't a way of preventing it',[14] the Conservatives' management team engaged in an attempt through the 1990s to persuade former ministers and factions to desist from their attacks on the leadership and party policy on European integration. At the 1995 conference words were had with certain opponents of the leadership. A source noted: 'Mawhinney [then Party Chairman], had conversations with all the people who were likely to cause trouble . . . '[15] In a similar vein Hague's team had words with Margaret Thatcher ahead of their 2000 conference. At the previous year's conference Lady Thatcher had drawn media attention away from the main hall with a high profile speech on the fringe supporting the release of the detained former dictator Augusto Pinochet. Fears of a similar performance drove the conference managers to ask her to take a lower profile at Bournemouth. A conference manager noted 'they recognize that we have to put on television those people that will be ministers and not those from the past. A great deal of effort has been expended to ensure that.'[16]

Exploiting the news machine

Party communication teams employ tried-and-tested proactive communication strategies (Heffernan and Stanyer, 1997; McNair, 1995) to help sell the collectively agreed agenda to journalists. Proactive strategies work through exploiting the competitive nature of news gathering, the accompanying pressure of multiple deadlines, and the journalists' need to check the accuracy of interpretations. They further take advantage of the television news teams' need to be as up to date as possible – capturing the latest twists and turns of a story – their demand for fresh visual material and access to leadership sources for interviews. The strategies provide the broadcasters with what they need but they 'exert some influence over how that something is mediated and presented to the audience'.[17] This can be clearly seen in the two most widely used forms of proactive strategy – trailing and follow-up briefing.

Information is trailed on a daily basis. Trailing involves communication teams in providing an extract of the announcements to be made in forthcoming speeches; trailing has been successfully practised by all three parties for some time. Experience has shown that 'the media are much more interested in something that is about to happen than they are in something that has just happened'.[18] A Conservative source suggested that virtually every speech was trailed at the 1995 party conference.

> We tried every day to have something on the *Today* programme that looked forward to what was going to be happening later that day and what announcements were going to happen. So for example on the Wednesday morning they were trailing the fact that Gillian Shephard was going to be making announcements about new qualifications for Headmasters. On Thursday morning the fact that Michael Howard was making new announcements on sentencing policy. On the Friday morning we gave them the story about the assisted places scheme in the Prime Minister's speech. Now in most of those cases they weren't necessarily the biggest thing in that speech but they were enough for a programme.[19]

The same source suggested that problems had arisen if they did not trail announcements from a speech. 'We had learnt from bitter experience in the past that if you don't give them things, it doesn't mean that they don't trail them: they just make it up. So it is far better if you can trail things.'[20] Trailed information is also embargoed, allowing greater control when it is used. The same source gave a routine example:

> I talked to all the broadcasters who would be putting out programmes in the morning and gave them the story . . . And that was given on a strict embargo basis – they couldn't run it till six o'clock the following morning but they were told that no newspaper would have it, and that it was just being given to the breakfast broadcasters, and it wasn't to be used that evening.[21]

The journalists, having received their advance information, nearly always respect any embargo. The same source noted: 'If they had chosen to break the embargo (which they very rarely do) they could have had it running on the six o'clock and the nine o'clock news bulletins. But they all understood the terms.'[22]

At the Labour and Liberal Democrat conferences, where motions and composites debated are balloted and the leadership's position endorsed or rejected, the outcome of such affairs is of considerable interest to the journalists. The spin doctors seek to shape the expectations developing in the news community about the likely outcome of a ballot. The expectations game played by the spin doctors is based on the construction of a deceptive set of expectations about the likely outcome of future events. The aim of the game is to lower expectations of the outcome in advance of the event. The trailing of these low expectations performs two functions: if the results are known to be close, it gives follow-up spinning more credibility and enables a planned favourable interpretation to be put on the loss. It also enables the spin doctors to claim a victory for the leadership's policy proposal if defeat is avoided, however narrow the margin. The expectations game deliberately reduces expectation in order to maximize the publicity from a victory and minimize the bad publicity from a loss.

Follow-up spin

The period after speeches and debates is a particularly important time for journalists. It is a period where journalists check their interpretations of events with others and search for the latest reactions. Follow-up briefing is designed at one level to prevent misinterpretations arising. Liberal Democrat spin doctors talked about their role as helpers, and as in the other parties, they are available for queries explaining the mechanics of the conferences. Such help and advice is important for the less experienced journalists who regularly descend on conferences. In this sense it is a basic form of risk minimization, preventing mistakes over interpretation developing which could be harder to correct in the future.

However, briefings are about more than aiding journalists, they are also a way of ensuring that key announcements in a speech or leadership's views in the case of debates are taken on board by journalists. Gathering journalists are particularly eager to find out the leadership line (Jones, 1995) and the latest reactions. Follow-up spin plays on this in order to shape the framing of events, minimizing any divergences of interpretation between leadership and the news community in the hope that all outlets amplify the same announcements and views.

The most visible form of briefing is the press conference with senior party actors. Press conferences are an opportunity for journalists to capture on the record comments by leadership actors and a chance for ministers or their shadows to further embellish what they see as the key themes of their speeches (usually on the record), in the knowledge that the footage will be used in news bulletins.[23] However, formal access to particular senior party actors is not always possible. Much of the briefing that also takes place is informal and involves the spin doctors behind the scenes. Speaking on behalf of the leadership gives spin doctors in follow-up mode a considerable weight in the interpretation of events or in emphasizing key announcements. Hours are spent in social functions and the press room briefing journalists about the detail behind a policy proposal indicated in a speech or in reinforcing the leadership line. The author observed press room briefings by spin doctors and senior party actors at all three party conferences. For example at the Labour conference, Alastair Campbell (the leader's press secretary) frequently visited the press room and spent time talking informally to particular journalists. The Shadow Scottish Secretary (then George Robertson) and his press secretary held regular briefings for Scottish journalists, and there were several other briefings by the press secretaries of the other members of the shadow cabinet on their specialist areas, a pattern followed at the other two parties.

The effectiveness of follow-up briefings is often increased through taking advantage of the journalists' daily deadlines. Spin doctors have knowledge of each journalist's deadline or often multiple deadlines, and the impending presence of a deadline offers them an opportunity to exert greater leverage over the interpretation of events. The nearer a news event occurs to a deadline, the less time the journalist has to seek out alternative views to those provided by the spin doctor. This tactic is compounded by the pressure to meet satellite feed times and also to update the report to include the latest developments at conference or just to rework it. In such an environment journalists are more receptive to spin. One journalist gave a not untypical account of how this process worked in 1994:

> Peter Mandelson, acting as Tony Blair's unofficial spin doctor, was bleeping us all day long. He'd rung the news desks to say what Tony was saying in his speech. Tony was speaking quite late, about an hour before the feed-in by satellite down to London. Basically the rule of thumb is that it takes an hour to edit a minute and I was editing something like four minutes in one hour. I knew ahead what was the interesting part of Tony's speech [because] I'd been told what the interesting part was. At least I could write the script line in to it saying "Tony Blair's going to call for this, this and this". It just speeds the whole process up so you're very grateful for it. He [Mandelson] got his lines in my script and a few other people's scripts. That's how they do it. They know when to give you help. They know when your deadline is pressing. The best of them know exactly when to offer you their helping hand.[24]

A senior *Channel Four News* source also confirmed the vulnerability of journalists to spin as deadlines neared:

> They have structured their moments to pounce. There is no doubt that seven o'clock is a very good time. There is only twenty-five minutes to the first edition. Or the timing of their strikes are just before lunchtime where there isn't really time. You know Robin Oakley or Michael Brunson have got to get it on the air and the last conversation they have is with Peter Mandelson or is with Brian Mawhinney, or whoever it happens to be that is the dominant spin doctor. So their availability at moments of panic and crisis for journalists is a critical factor, and they certainly make themselves available or choose their times to call when it is least easy to resist.[25]

Targeting

The party spin doctors seek to make the most of the competition that exists between different news teams by giving certain journalists access to information ahead of their rivals. This technique, known as targeting, is routinely practised. Targeting exploits the journalists' desire for exclusive stories and has the added bonus of allowing the spin doctors' time and effort to be more effectively utilized. A source noted, 'News broadcasters will give extensive coverage if they think it's an exclusive.'[26] The targeting of particular news outlets with exclusive information is worked out in advance. Trailing and follow-up briefing can be aimed at different journalists or broadcasters. Senior spin doctors, many former journalists,[27] are well aware of the strengths and weaknesses of the broadcast journalists present at the conferences and which ones will be the most appropriate receivers of a particular piece of information. The leadership actors and senior spin doctors have established relationships with many of the news community opinion formers, as chapter 3 has shown. They know which of their senior actors present might be most compliant in framing an exclusive in a way they like and subsequently shape the interpretations of their junior colleagues. This knowledge is indispensable in helping decide on where to release certain information.

The spin doctors can also target the different media present at the conferences. As one source suggested: 'You can organize it by medium, so you give some to the newspapers and not to the broadcasters or vice versa.'[28] This allows the spin doctors access to different audiences. For example, regional news broadcasters are targeted with information that is relevant to that particular region. Each party holds regular briefings for Scottish and Welsh journalists, providing information that is solely of relevance to them. As one source suggested, 'We have got a set of what are called regional media co-ordinators who work for all the party in that region and they spend a lot of that week liaising . . . [with] regional broadcasters.'[29] All the parties for the 1996 conferences – the last before the 1997 general election – actively targeted the regional broadcasters in those areas where their Prospective Parliamentary Candidates stood the greatest chance of winning.

Photo-Opportunities

Each party seeks to take advantage of television's 'consuming need for pictures.'[30] To a large extent the choice of pictures is governed by the event on which the report is focused and by the already committed technical resources. However, conference sessions are not a source of dramatic visuals. They provide what can be described as a series of 'talking heads' – a 'second-best' source of visual material (Schlesinger, 1987). There is, therefore, a continual demand from programme editors for additional interesting visual material to illustrate events and to show the same personalities in different settings, such as on the conference fringe and walking between the venue and the conference hotel. As one Liberal Democrat source noted, 'There is a big demand for photo calls.'[31] All communication teams seek to exploit this demand for opportunities to film the party elite in other distinctive locations, and continually try to provide new images to reinforce the party message. With the 'gaze' of the cameras focusing outside the main conference auditoriums, photo-opportunities constitute a direct attempt to adapt to the visual demands of the broadcasters.[32] In providing additional visual material each communication team has three aims. First, to regulate the conference environment so that key individuals – be they ministers, shadows or the party leaders – are less likely to be caught offguard by haphazard 'door stepping'. Second, to make it easier and quicker for the broadcasters to gather footage of key party actors to supplement their core coverage. The same source noted: 'For instance, you know they are all on tight deadlines: they need to know who will be where and when.'[33] Third, to provide visually relevant clips for reports on policy announcements. It is standard practice at all three conferences for ministers, shadow ministers and spokespersons to undertake a visit to a school or hospital in the conference locality, to emphasize policy proposals or the success of existing policies. Such occasions are just for the cameras, with the key protagonists refusing to answer questions that particular journalists lying in wait might ask.

Realizing that the broadcasters are tiring of the trips to schools or factories there has also been an attempt to inject newsworthiness into such opportunities by using party actors who are in demand,

Table 4.1 *The nature of Liberal Democrat photo-opportunities used in reports, 1993–6 (cell contents show the number of opportunities used)*

	NN	BBC9	ITN5.40	ITN10	BBC6	Ch 4	Total
Party leader	3	3	3	5	6	6	26
Education spokesperson	1	1	1	1	0	1	5
Other leadership actors	0	0	0	1	1	1	3
Celebrities	0	0	1	0	0	1	2
Home Affairs spokesperson	0	0	0	0	1	0	1
Treasury spokesperson	0	0	0	0	1	0	1
Total	4	4	5	7	9	9	38

(BBC6 = BBC Six O'clock News; BBC9 = BBC Nine O'clock News;
ITN5.40 = ITN News at 5.40 p.m.; ITN10 = ITN News at Ten O'clock;
Ch 4 = Channel Four News; NN = Newsnight.)

accompanied by other newsworthy actors such as party defectors, showbusiness and sporting celebrities. This is now seen as one way of ensuring widespread media attention. Tables 4.1 to 4.3 show the photo-opportunities used in reports between 1993 and 1996.

Tables 4.1 to 4.3 show that the most widely used photo-opportunities at Labour and Liberal Democrat conferences involved party leaders. Photo-opportunities featuring the Liberal Democrat leader accounted for twenty-six of the thirty-eight photo-opportunities used. The Labour leader accounted for thirty-one of all forty-five photo-opportunities used. Interestingly, photo-opportunities featuring the Conservative leader were less frequent than those featuring the Party Chairman. This was due in large part to the fact that most of these were on the Monday before the start of the conference, when the Chairman was virtually the only leadership member present.

The tables also show the frequent use of photo-opportunities featuring the party leader and other actors, particularly celebrities. Labour held two successful photo-opportunities featuring Tony Blair with football managers Kevin Keegan in 1995 and Alex Ferguson in 1996 (see table 4.2). These featured in all bulletins except *Newsnight*. *News at Ten* devoted its 'And finally' slot to the 1995 Blair–Keegan photo-opportunity. One of their journalists suggested:

If you are a news editor and you are told Blair is doing this, Blair is doing that, you have got to cover it because if you miss it and something

Table 4.2   *The nature of Labour photo-opportunities used in reports,*
1993–1996 (cell contents show the number of opportunities used)

	NN	ITN5.40	BBC9	BBC6	ITN10	Ch 4	Total
Party leader	1	3	4	6	4	4	22
Leader & celebrities	0	1	1	1	2	1	6
Leader & wife	0	0	1	1	1	0	3
Shadow Education Secretary	1	0	1	0	0	1	3
Other leadership actors	1	0	0	0	0	1	2
Shadow Home Secretary	1	1	1	1	1	2	7
Union	0	0	0	0	1	0	1
Shadow Chancellor	1	0	0	0	0	0	1
Total	5	5	8	9	9	9	45

(BBC6 = BBC Six O'clock News; BBC9 = BBC Nine O'clock News;
ITN5.40 = ITN News at 5.40 p.m.; ITN10 = ITN News at Ten O'clock;
Ch 4 = Channel Four News; NN = Newsnight.)

Table 4.3   *The nature of Conservative photo-opportunities used in reports,*
1993–6 (cell contents show the number of opportunities used)

	ITN10	NN	ITN5.40	BBC6	BBC9	Ch 4	Total
Party leader	1	0	1	4	2	2	10
Leader & Lady Thatcher	0	0	1	0	0	0	1
Party Chairman	1	1	1	2	5	4	14
Party Chairman & Event	0	1	1	0	0	2	4
Labour Party Stunt	0	1	1	1	1	1	5
Total	2	3	5	7	8	9	34

(BBC6 = BBC Six O'clock News; BBC9 = BBC Nine O'clock News;
ITN5.40 = ITN News at 5.40 p.m.; ITN10 = ITN News at Ten O'clock;
Ch4 = Channel Four News; NN = Newsnight. Labour Party Stunt = the parading of a
Conservative defector to Labour outside the 1996 Conservative party conference.
Party Chairman and Event = a football practice with the Party Chairman and
Bournemouth FC youth side.)

happens or he says something you look a complete idiot. But inevitably if you are told nice pictures of Blair in front of a tank, nice pictures of Blair playing football, we are television – good pictures is the name of the game. We are going to use them and they know that.[34]

These visuals are more popular with the broadcasters than those that are designed to provide a peg for particular ministerial or shadow ministerial announcements. Generally, those broadcasters interviewed did see themselves as partly compromised by overt attempts to manipulate the use of visuals, but they were also limited in their responses:

> I think any journalists in our profession would all strongly dispute going down the line they wanted but maybe paradoxically we do. We do what we think is a professional way of covering it and they achieve something they want to achieve because they get nice pictures of Tony Blair. We can't say: "We won't use these pictures of Tony Blair, we will use shots of the stage" just because we don't want anything to do with it. It doesn't work like that. So if you like it is a trade off.[35]

The press office also faces competition from other sources in the photo-opportunity stakes. The parties have taken to organizing stunts at each other's conferences, particularly the Labour party, whose 1996 parade of a Conservative defector outside the Conservative party conference received wide coverage (see table 4.3). At the Labour conference some of the big unions regularly hold photo-opportunities to emphasize one of their campaigns. While generally the leadership's opponents do not have the resources to provide large-scale planned photo-opportunities, they are aware of the 'pictorial imperatives' of television news and are willing to pose impromptu for the cameras.

Leadership actors schooled in media techniques (Franklin, 1994) also respond individually to the pictorial demands of the broadcasters. With the proliferation of lightweight Electronic News Gathering (ENG) cameras searching for additional visual material on a virtually twenty-four-hour basis at conference the leadership are aware of being caught offguard, of being 'door stepped' at any moment. The spin doctors seek to control door stepping to some extent, especially around the party leaders. In particular their arrival and departure at the conference hotel and main hall and their tours of the conference exhibition stands are increasingly stage-managed. Such situations also provide potential publicity, and the elite actively seek to co-operate with camera crews in the production of important set-up shots for news reports. During observation in the press room at the 1996 Labour conference, frequent co-operation was observed in the setting up of short interviews for reports. On two separate occasions Gordon Brown's and Alistair Darling's spin doctors helped organize the camera angles, insisting that the party logo featured in the background of their interviews – demands with which the journalists and camera crew complied.

Managing the interview process

The communication teams in each party are fully aware that there is a strong demand amongst broadcasters for interviews with key leadership actors. The spin doctors use this to secure the best possible outcome for the leadership. At each conference they regulate access to the party elite for interviews. This point was emphasized clearly in the responses of various journalists. One said: 'Increasingly, I'd say through the Thatcher years, the parties have taken a much tougher grip on that whole process and they decide who they are fielding.'[36] The point was reinforced by a senior BBC source who argued: 'there is a trend towards greater control of their leading players and where they appear and how they appear.'[37]

All the broadcasters have to bid for interviews in advance through the press office. A political correspondent remarked: 'There are two types of bids. There is a bid for a pre-recorded interview for a package, which we might put in ourselves or might ask the producer to do. And there is a bid for a live interview on the programme.'[38] The communication teams then pick and choose in advance which news programmes leadership members will be interviewed by. These decisions, if need be, can be made on an 'hour-by-hour basis'[39] determined by events at conference. Interviews are regularly monitored, with the aim of improving the way senior party spokespersons communicate particular party policies. A not untypical example occurred at the Liberal Democrats' 1996 conference. Here the Director of Communications used a team of volunteers to monitor all interviews and provide feedback on the strengths and weaknesses of each spokesperson's performance.

Being in demand means the leadership can gain further advantages. The communication teams are able to decide who to put up for interviews. The spin doctors want to ensure whichever leadership actors are making the big speech that day follow it up with a series of interviews to reinforce the main points raised in the speech. To ensure this is the case, all communication teams put forward their preferred candidates and reject bids for interviews with other senior party members. A political correspondent commented: 'At the conferences they'll decide who they want to put forward.'[40] A similar gambit is to insist on being interviewed by a certain journalist in preference to another. However, there is a certain amount of negotiation between the two sides, with both sides aware of how far they can push their demands. A senior BBC source suggested:

> They will constantly have battles about who is available and on what day, people pulling out at the last minute and substitutes put up. You have to be prepared to indulge in some brinkmanship. If we are going to complain against the conditions they are putting up, we have to be prepared to sometimes say: "Well, if you are only offering over these conditions, fine, we won't bother". And we have to judge how important they think it is to go on the air. There is an awful lot of that.[41]

Sometimes negotiations ended amicably, in other cases party insistence backfired. On the day before his keynote speech to the 2000 conference, Conservative leader William Hague insisted that his pre-recorded interview with the BBC should be with the corporation's new political editor Andrew Marr – who had interviewed the Prime Minister the previous week. The BBC refused to give a guarantee that any future interview would be conducted by Marr and instead put forward Paxman. An angry Hague, in response, refused to do any interviews with the BBC, including a pre-planned slot on Radio Four's *Today* programme – but he still gave interviews to their rivals ITN, Channel Four and Sky News. An aid to Hague noted that, 'William doesn't mind tough interviews, but he doesn't want to do an interview with Paxman because he doesn't think Paxman does a fair job as an interviewer.'[42]

Tough on crime: the Home Secretary's speech

This example shows the simultaneous use of two proactive media strategies by Conservative spin doctors at their 1995 conference and the response of the news broadcasters. This not untypical example focuses on the trailing and targeting of *News at Ten* with information from the then Home Secretary Michael Howard's speech. *News at Ten*'s political editor was provided with an exclusive trail of the content of the Home Secretary's speech. *News at Ten* was targeted because the source suggested it was 'by far the most important news programme'.[43] The Tories' aim was to maximize publicity for the Home Secretary's announcements, as the other bulletins would pick up on the information and carry it too, and the announcements would be further reported the following day after the speech.

The report lasted four minutes and twenty-one seconds on Wednesday, 11 October 1995. It was the lead story on *News at Ten* and dealt mainly, although not exclusively, with the trailed information. The information was framed in the following way:

Anchor: Good evening. The Home Secretary Michael Howard is planning much longer jail sentences for serious crime, including a "Two strikes and you are out" policy for some sex offenders. He'll tell the Conservative party conference in Blackpool tomorrow that anyone found guilty twice for the most serious sex attacks will be locked up for life, most other prison sentences will be served in full . . .

Political editor: Tonight the Home Secretary was on the social circuit, but after hard argument with his cabinet colleagues, he'll not only suggest tomorrow that the courts should send far more burglars to prison but will seek to end two situations within the criminal justice system which he believes ordinary people find offensive: criminals apparently getting out of jail early and criminals who repeat very serious crime. Mr Howard will say here in this hall tomorrow that in the future the sentence the court hands down will usually be the time actually served; 15 years will mean 15 years. And judges must take that into account in future, suggesting that present arrangements for remission for good behaviour are about to be ended. And when those who have served time for very serious crimes like sex attacks and then commit the same offence again once they are out of jail, Mr Howard will announce that in many cases, they will face the certainty of life imprisonment . . .

The same Conservative source suggested that this 'didn't actually stop them devoting another five or six minutes the next day to what he'd just said even though they had reported it, but they were able to give themselves a nice pat on the back. Mike Brunson [the political editor] was saying "As *News at Ten* reported yesterday . . . " and all this sort of stuff.'[44] There was some truth in this. Wednesday's report was followed by a three-minute, thirty-two second report on Thursday where the political editor did state 'as we reported last night'. However, the second report also focused on the reactions to the announcements. *News at Ten* obtained a reaction from the Lord Chief Justice. In fact, the report's introduction suggested that the speech 'Almost immediately ran into trouble with the Lord Chief Justice. Lord Taylor . . . issued a statement saying he didn't believe the threat of longer periods of imprisonment would deter habitual criminals, he suggested more police might.' The response of the Lord Chief Justice was also included in the report, reinforcing the commentary. The report also further carried Howard's reaction to Lord Taylor's comments.

Interviews conducted with ITN journalists gave some idea of the attitude of ITN's Political Editor to the use of trailed exclusive information and more generally of ITN journalists' attitudes. An ITN source explained their orientation through a story of a trailed exclusive but on a different issue:

> Once I was scooped by my opposite number at the BBC because he got a leak of the inflation figures and I was very pissed off. So I took this high moral tone and said that he was deliberately leaked them as part of the Department of Employment's news management operation. I remember discussing it with Mike Brunson and I said "Would you have chosen to rise above it and not get abused like that?" And he said, "To be quite honest, if you get the inflation figures it's a good story. It doesn't matter what the motive is. You've got the inflation figures the night before, you use them. It doesn't matter if someone is trying to manipulate you". Well he didn't quite say that, but he was right.[45]

It seems that the newsworthiness of the trailed information was the priority for the Political Editor. The fact that *News at Ten* had been used for the advance release of information was secondary. The same journalist suggested:

> I don't think we have the right to withhold something from the public just because we think we are being used with bits and pieces of information. I think if you start taking that line you're in grave danger because you'll end up reporting nothing – you'll end up filtering material just on some abstract principle.[46]

Through co-operating, both the Conservative leadership and ITN benefited. ITN received their 'exclusive' before their rivals and the Conservative leadership gained maximum publicity for the announcements. This example further shows that proactive strategies worked through adapting to the competitive desires of the broadcasters to be first, ahead of their rivals, and have exclusive material. Successfully executed proactive strategies provide benefits for both the leadership and the journalists.

Conclusion

The increasingly news hungry broadcasters want the conferences to generate newsworthy information, the leadership want coverage of the events they have planned. In order to achieve their goals the spin doctors have to fulfil the news broadcasters' demands. They have to ensure that planned events live up to journalists' expectations in news terms. If the spin doctors do not provide newsworthy information and the visual trimmings, the news teams will be more likely to focus on newsworthy events elsewhere. The implementation of communication strategies can be seen as a structured way of reducing the chance of this happening by ensuring that both groups of actors get what they want out of the conferences. The parties provide a complete package for the broadcasters; newsworthy announcements, with interesting visuals and access to leadership actors for follow-up interviews. The official message of the day is made easy to gather through the use of 'information subsidies' (Gandy, 1982). Party managers further try to make sure that the journalists' attention is not distracted by ministers or shadow ministers talking at cross purposes, or dissenting unions or factions. The strategies ensure that the policy announcements are reported over the welter of other information.

The broadcasters in turn adapt to the information environment constructed by the conference managers. They are aware of management strategies but co-operate. While several interviewees grumbled about the stage-managed nature of the conferences, they also admitted there are certain advantages to the set-up. They receive a regular supply of newsworthy information, the access they need to senior party actors, a supply of diverse visuals and a share of exclusives – indeed, the regulated flow of information makes gathering predictable and enables a more efficient allocation of resources and aids the Westminster news teams in their competition with other teams in their organizations. The mutual benefit will be seen clearly in the following chapter, which examines the reporting of the leader's speech.

5

Packaging the Leader's Speech

Coverage of the leader's speech provides each party with an unrivalled opportunity to promote policy and internal party messages to an audience of millions outside the immediate conference environment. As part of this promotional drive, the spin doctors routinely add gravitas to the event through the use of promotional videos, lighting and changing the shape of the main stage. For the news broadcasters the speech is the centrepiece of each conference. The speech provides newsworthy developments or pronouncements about the direction of the party and policy announcements that help ensure the political correspondents' reports gain prominence in the news bulletins. The broadcast journalists not only relay extracts from each speech but also process them for audience consumption. They act as 'packagers' (Blumler and Gurevitch, 1995), compiling various extracts from which to form a report.

The packaging process consists of a series of activities. First, selection. The correspondents and political editors can only capture certain parts of each speech due to the limited size of the time slot within which they have to fit the report. Journalists therefore have to decide which are the most significant passages of the speech. Second, there is then an attempt to explain for the television audience the meaning and significance behind each particular passage. All passages are accompanied by 'contextualizing remarks'[1] (Semetko *et al.*, 1991). In addition the journalists in their commentary also try and contextualize the whole speech in terms of the bigger political picture. The significance of the leader's speech is often explained to the viewer in terms of the pressures of party competition; contemporary political events; the positioning of the parties in the political spectrum; and attempts to rally conference delegates. Reports also make frequent references to the leader's performance and to the immediate reception of the speech by the party. Occasionally comparisons are also drawn between the current speech and those of a previous leader. These narrative features are mainly visible in the reports' introductory and concluding remarks. The correspondents also exhibit discretion in being able to solicit reactions from those in the conference hall or other media professionals. Reports often carry favourable and unfavourable reactions of these actors to the speech. Finally, the bulletins expand their coverage of certain news-worthy issues raised in the leaders' speeches through a combination of additional news reports, two-ways[2] and interviews.

This chapter examines the packaging of the three party leaders' speeches by six evening news bulletins in 1995. The analysis focuses on key elements of packaging the selling of the speeches by the parties, the selection of passages by journalists, the contextualization of the passages and the whole speech, and the expansion of the news agenda through the production of additional news items.

Selling the speech

A great effort is made by party spin doctors to maximize the publicity fallout from the speech. Announcements from the leader's speech are particularly heavily trailed. The broadcasters use the information to 'freshen-up' their evening conference reports. Between 1993 and 1996 at all three conferences, table 5.1 shows that the news broadcasters trailed information on each leader's speech a total of thirty-one times.

Table 5.1 also shows that the late evening bulletins (the BBC *Nine O'clock News* and *News at Ten* in particular) carried the greatest number of trails and the early evening bulletins, the BBC *Six O'clock News* and the *ITN 5.40*, the least. Since early evening bulletins had covered the day's events prior to the speech, the later programmes were looking for (and were provided with) newsworthy information about the content of the leaders' speeches next day. Trailing continues on the day of the leader's speech itself, with spin doctors feeding information to both the

Table 5.1 *The number of news items containing trailed information on the leaders' speeches by conference, 1993–6*

	ITN5.40	BBC6	Ch 4	NN	BBC9	ITN10	Total
Liberal Democrat	2	1	3	3	2	3	14
Conservative	0	0	0	2	3	5	10
Labour	0	1	1	0	1	4	7
Total	2	2	4	5	6	12	31

(BBC6 = BBC Six O'clock News; BBC9 = BBC Nine O'clock News; ITN5.40 = ITN News at 5.40 p.m.; ITN10 = ITN News at Ten; Ch 4 = Channel Four News; NN = Newsnight.)

live and news programmes airing before the speech. In addition advance information on the content of the leaders' speeches is also fed to the broadcasters to aid the production of additional news reports.

At the 1995 conference all three parties issued press releases and briefing documents ahead of their leader's speech. The Liberal Democrats issued a two-page press release outlining key passages from the speech. At the Labour conference, all the journalists before Blair's speech were given a twenty-four page briefing pack. This document outlined some thirteen new policy initiatives to be delivered in the speech together with supporting background facts and figures and the phone numbers of specialists. Conservative spin doctors circulated two documents prior to Major's speech. The first, five pages long, high-lighted the fourteen key announcements in the speech and key quotes from the speech on each announcement. The second was a briefing document that provided background facts and figures – in a similar manner to Labour's.

A quart into a pint pot

There is a tremendous amount of compression in the editing process, squeezing what is often an hour-long speech into a report from around three to four minutes long on the shorter bulletins to six minutes on the longer ones. The journalists, usually the senior correspondent or polit-ical editor, sift through the footage of the leader's speech selecting what they see as the most significant passages. These are the most news-worthy passages, and are usually the ones that contain policy announcements or initiatives. These handful of newsworthy passages

Table 5.2   *The mean number of passages used from each party leader's speech, 1993–6*

	ITN5.40	ITN10	BBC6	BBC9	NN	Ch 4
Lib Dems						
Mean 1993–6	4	4	5	5	5	7
St.D.	0.9	1.5	1.0	1.2	0.8	1.3
Labour						
Mean 1993–6	6	6	7	8	9	7
St.D.	0.6	1.5	1.8	1.0	1.3	2.5
Conservative						
Mean 1993–6	7	7	9	9	8	11
St.D.	1.5	1.5	1.8	2.2	1.3	1.3

(St.D. = Standard deviation. BBC6 = BBC Six O'clock News; BBC9 = BBC Nine O'clock News; ITN10 = News at Ten; Ch 4 = Channel Four News; NN = Newsnight)

Table 5.3   *The mean length of soundbites (in seconds) in reports on each party leader's speech, 1993–6*

	BBC6	BBC9	ITN5.40	ITN10	Ch 4	NN	Av
Lib Dems							
Mean 1993–96	15	15	19	22	22	26	20
St.D.	7.1	7.3	7.0	6.8	8.7	9.3	7.7
Labour							
Mean 1993–96	15	18	21	20	21	27	20
St.D.	6.9	8.0	9.8	7.5	8.2	12.8	8.9
Conservative							
Mean 1993–96	14	16	21	23	19	25	20
St.D.	6.1	6.9	9.7	9.6	8.6	8.5	8.2

(St.D. = Standard deviation. BBC6 = BBC Six O'clock News; BBC9 = BBC Nine O'clock News; ITN5.40 = ITN News at 5.40 p.m.; ITN10 = ITN News at Ten; Ch 4 = Channel Four News; NN = Newsnight)

tend to dominate any single report. Table 5.2 shows the average number of passages used by the different news bulletins over four conferences between 1993 and 1996. The table shows journalists used a comparatively small number of extracts from Ashdown's speeches when compared to the other two leaders. The journalists also have to decide on the length of each passage used.

Table 5.3 gives an indication of the mean length of selected passages in reports, and shows that soundbites from each leader's speech were on average twenty seconds long. Tables 5.2 and 5.3 show that the BBC *Six O'clock* and *Nine O'clock News* consistently provided more soundbites from each leader's speech than both ITN bulletins, but they were of a shorter length. There seemed to be a trade-off in reporting the leaders' speeches within the limited time slot available on these bulletins – namely, more breadth at the expense of length. Such a trade-off did not affect *Channel Four News* or *Newsnight*, whose lengthier bulletins could contain a greater number of longer extracts from the leaders' speeches. The leaders therefore had more opportunity to get their message across using the longer (but less watched) bulletins.

Paddy's overture to New Labour

All bulletins saw the most important aspect of Ashdown's 1995 speech as the outlining of the conditions for co-operation with Labour after a general election, especially in the light of the leadership's abandonment of the strategy of equidistance[3] earlier in the year and in respect to Blair's

Table 5.4 *Which passages from the 1995 Liberal Democrat leader's speech were used in reports by bulletin*

	Identification number of the passage						
	1	2	3	4	5	6	7
ITN5.40	x	x	x	x	x		
BBC6	x	x	x			x	
Ch 4	x	x	x	x		x	
BBC9	x	x	x	x	x	x	
ITN10	x	x	x	x	x		x
Newsnight	x	x	x				x

(1 = an extract from a joke postcard. 2 = call to renationalize Railtrack. 3 = opposition to tax cuts. 4 = a call to get rid of the existing government. 5 = a challenge to the other parties to confront the issues. 6 = a call to reform the existing voting system and implement proportional representation. 7 = the Liberal Democrats' role in a new government. BBC6 = BBC Six O'clock News; BBC9 = BBC Nine O'clock News; ITN5.40 = ITN News at 5.40 p.m.; ITN10 = ITN News at Ten; Ch 4 = Channel Four News)

offer of closer co-operation the previous day. The speech's aim, according to reports, was to highlight areas where co-operation with Labour could be considered. All the reports focused on what they termed the challenges Blair would have to meet for co-operation. The BBC *Six O'clock News* called these a 'checklist of challenges', the BBC *Nine O'clock News* 'challenges for Labour', *Channel Four News'* report called them the 'terms of readiness to work with Labour', and *Newsnight* the 'decisions Labour should not duck'.

A total of eleven passages were used from the 1995 Liberal Democrat leader's speech. Table 5.4 shows which passages were selected by each bulletin. There was considerable overlap between all the bulletins in the passages they selected as the most important from the speech, with most of the reports using the same passages. Indeed seven of a total of eleven passages from the speech were used in more than one report. All reports sought to put each passage used[4] in its context for the audience.

The first passage, used by all reports, showed Ashdown reading out a joke postcard in response to the Labour leader's call for greater co-operation.

PASSAGE 1

Dear Tony, Having a wonderful time in Glasgow. We've always believed in working with others where we agree. But first you must be clear where you stand. We are. Let us know when you are. Yours, Paddy.

All reports saw this as Ashdown's response to Blair's offer of co-operation. *ITN 5.40* and *News at Ten* contextualized the response in terms of its confidence, suggesting that Ashdown was 'confident enough to send Tony Blair, after his approaches, what amounted to a saucy postcard'. The *Six O'clock News* suggested that the passage's significance lay in the fact that his party wanted to hear 'his reply to Tony Blair's petition to talks and possible co-operation.' *Channel Four's* report suggested it was 'designed to open up a dialogue without giving the impression he was rolling over at the first approach'. The *Nine O'clock News* referred to Blair's offer of co-operation as 'destabilizing' but suggested that Ashdown had turned it into 'an advantage by lambasting his potential allies for retreating on key policies'. *Newsnight's* correspondent noted that it 'struck just the right mocking tone'.

The second passage was contextualized as a challenge to Labour to co-operate with the Liberal Democrats in opposing rail privatization, and was emphasized as being popular with the delegates.

PASSAGE 2

> We must retain public control of Railtrack. And once again my message to Labour is very, very simple. Join us, join us in that pledge and if you do, no one would buy the shares and together we could stop this crazy rail privatization dead in its tracks.

The *ITN 5.40* and *News at Ten* emphasized both the popularity of its reception and the challenge to Labour: 'The biggest applause came when Mr Ashdown spoke about rail privatization and said Labour should join them in keeping Railtrack under public control.' The *Six O'clock News* referred to this as an example of co-operation: 'Labour should join them too in pledging continuing public control of Railtrack.' *Channel Four News* suggested: 'so to the loudest applause for his speech, he challenged Labour to block rail privatization.' The *Nine O'clock News* focused on the reception and noted 'his insistence that they could between them stop the privatization of Railtrack won him his loudest applause.' *Newsnight* suggested: 'the biggest applause came when Mr Ashdown spoke about rail privatization and said that Labour should join them in keeping Railtrack under public control.' The popularity of the reception of this passage made it more salient in the eyes of the journalists than other elements in Ashdown's list.

The third and fourth most frequently used passages concerned re-affirmation of existing party policy on tax and education, and a critique of the other two parties. The third passage, used by all reports, was seen as both evidence of his continuing commitment to the policy of increasing tax to fund education and as a challenge to the other parties to be honest on taxation.

PASSAGE 3

> If you promise never to put up taxes, then the rest of your pledges are no more than pipe dreams. What's so depressing is that Labour now seem as keen to play this party trick on the electorate as the Conservatives. Well, let me make it clear now, deceiving the electorate on taxes is not a game this party intends to play.

The *ITN 5.40* and *News at Ten* highlighted the passage as a spending pledge and as an attack on the other parties: 'Mr Ashdown once again promised more spending on education and the environment which might indeed mean higher taxes about which other parties never spoke the truth.' The *Six O'clock News* did not mention the spending pledge but saw it as a criticism of Labour: 'It was also depressing that Labour now seemed as ready as the Tories to hide the truth about taxes.' *Channel Four News* contextualized it differently, in terms of tough choices: 'Throughout he positioned the Liberal Democrats as the party that was prepared to take tough choices in contrast to Labour's timidity.' The *Nine O'clock News* made no mention of the criticism of Labour but suggested: 'Riskily, Mr Ashdown promised that his party would tell the truth on tax.' For *Newsnight* the significance lay in terms of the tax-cutting agenda of the other parties. The report suggested the passage was a taunt: 'On tax he taunted Labour's timidity.'

The fourth most-used extract (ignored only by *Newsnight* and the *Six O'clock News*) was contextualized as a call for the government 'to go'.

PASSAGE 4

> I want to use this moment as the start of a great campaign, up to and through the next election, in which we say simply and plainly how Britain must change and how the Liberal Democrats will guarantee that change. And the first change that Britain needs is a change of government. This government must go, and every vote and every seat that we win at the next election will see that they go.

The *ITN 5.40* and *News at Ten* suggested this was Ashdown's 'clear alternative message for Britain once the Tories were slung out'. *Channel Four* said that it showed Ashdown 'was unambiguous in his deter-mination to get rid of the government.' The *Nine O'clock News* described it rather oddly, saying 'he didn't spend too long discussing the Tories'.

The fifth passage used by both ITN reports and the *Nine O'clock News* was contextualized as a critique of the other two parties for failing to confront the 'issues'.

PASSAGE 5

> Labour won't confront the issues because they are frightened of the electorate. The Tories won't confront the issues because they're frightened they'll divide their party.

The *ITN 5.40* and *News at Ten* suggested the passage was an attack on 'the constant fudging of the issues by the two old parties'. The *Nine O'clock News* noted that Ashdown 'assailed' the other two parties 'for timidity and a failure to tell it like it is'.

The sixth, used by both BBC One reports and *Channel Four News*, was contextualized as a critique of Labour's policy on proportional representation (PR).

PASSAGE 6

> Well let me make it absolutely clear, electoral reform is not an optional extra. It is not leadership to ask others to decide when you won't decide yourself. Holding a referendum is not an alternative to holding an opinion.

The *Six O'clock News* suggested it was Ashdown's critique of Blair's stance on proportional representation: 'In areas such as electoral reform he should stop being half-hearted and timid. He must say whether he supports proportional representation.' *Channel Four*'s report similarly focused on the critical nature of the passage: 'Tony Blair's promise of a referendum yesterday was welcome, but not enough.' The *Nine O'clock News* suggested: 'he wants the Labour leader to come out in favour of PR, not just to stage a referendum on it.'

The seventh passage, from the speech's close, was only used by *News at Ten* and *Newsnight*. It was contextualized as a restatement of the 'Liberal Democrat Guarantee' document[5] to be the guarantors of change in the next parliament.

PASSAGE 7

> Within the next eighteen months, perhaps before we meet again, we will be called upon to show that we have the courage and the firm answers and the strong vision to be the lever of change, the guarantee of change, in our country once again. Let them then say of us, that was their challenge and they rose to it.

News at Ten's report suggested: 'Come the general election the party would need to show it has firm answers and a strong vision to be a lever of change.' *Newsnight* attempted to draw some historical comparisons. It suggested 'tellingly Mr Ashdown ended on a conciliatory note, something of the spirit of Labour's landslide victory in 1945, noting the vital contributions the Liberals Beveridge and Keynes made to post-war Britain, he said it was time to play that role again'.

In addition there were four passages from the speech used by only one of the reports each. The *Six O'clock News* used another quote to illustrate Ashdown's call for co-operation with Labour. *Channel Four's* report used another extract to illustrate Ashdown's attack on the Conservatives' education policy, suggesting this was an example of another policy area over which Labour and the Liberal Democrats should co-operate. *Newsnight* used a further two extracts to highlight the role of the Liberal Democrats in a future parliament after the next election. The statements trailed in the press release on education, taxation and the Liberal Democrats as guarantors of change were used by nearly all reports.

Performance, reception and reactions

In 1995 there were no remarks on Ashdown's performance when making the speech. Table 5.5 shows the frequency of comments on Ashdown's performance made in other years. Overall there were nine comments, mainly concentrated in reports on the 1996 conference speech and on the ITN and BBC main news bulletins, with one on *Channel Four* and none at all on *Newsnight*.

In addition the reports were keen to convey the speeches' reception by delegates in the main hall. These comments usually came at the end of a report but were also linked to a specific announcements. Table 5.6 shows that there were seventeen references to the speeches' reception

Table 5.5 *The number of references in all reports to the performance of the Liberal Democrat leader in making his speech by bulletin and year, 1993–6.*

	BBC9	ITN5.40	BBC6	ITN10	Ch 4	NN	Total
1993	0	0	0	1	0	0	1
1994	1	0	1	0	1	0	3
1995	0	0	0	0	0	0	0
1996	2	2	1	0	0	0	5
Total	3	2	2	1	1	0	9

(BBC6 = BBC Six O'clock News; BBC9 = BBC Nine O'clock News; ITN5.40 = ITN News at 5.40 p.m.; ITN10 = ITN News at Ten; Ch 4 = Channel Four News; NN = Newsnight.)

Table 5.6   *The number of references in all reports to the reception of the Liberal Democrat leader's speeches by bulletin and year, 1993–6*

	ITN10	ITN5.40	Ch 4	NN	BBC6	BBC9	Total
1993	1	1	1	0	0	0	3
1994	1	1	0	0	0	0	2
1995	2	2	2	1	1	1	9
1996	1	0	1	1	0	0	3
Total	5	4	4	2	1	1	17

(BBC6 = BBC Six O'clock News; BBC9 = BBC Nine O'clock News;
ITN5.40 = ITN News at 5.40 p.m.; ITN10 = ITN News at Ten;
Ch 4 = Channel Four News; NN = Newsnight)

over four conferences. Both ITN bulletins consistently referred in their reports to the speeches' reception by delegates, whereas the BBC bulletins made only one mention of the speeches' reception. In 1995, in addition to the reception already noted for the passage on rail privatization, five reports also specifically referred to the speech's final reception. The report on the *ITN 5.40* suggested that the speech 'earned Paddy Ashdown a noticeably warm ovation' and *News at Ten* that the conference 'rose to give Paddy Ashdown a noticeably warm ovation'. The BBC *Six O'clock News* report said that it 'won him more than a standing ovation'. The *Channel Four News* report said that after the speech 'delegates insisted on Mr Ashdown taking a second bow today', and *Newsnight* noted that 'Mr Ashdown's speech went down so well he was even called back for a sort of encore'.

In addition to referencing the speeches' reception the journalists also included the reactions of other actors to the speeches. *Newsnight* and *Channel Four News* provided considerably more reactions to Ashdown's speech than the other bulletins over four conferences. Table 5.7 shows the reactions to the leader's speech initiated by journalists.[6]

The overwhelming number of reactions initiated by journalists after

Table 5.7   *The number of positive, negative and neutral reactions to the Liberal Democrat leader's speeches by year, 1993–6*

	Positive	Negative	Neutral
1993	0	0	3
1994	2	0	6
1995	0	0	9
1996	1	0	2
Total	3	0	20

Ashdown's speech were neutral over the four years, with no negative reactions. On the 1995 speech only three reports carried reactions, all neutral. The BBC *Six O'clock News* recorded the reaction of MPs Liz Lynne and Simon Hughes; *Channel Four*'s report included Liz Lynne, Charles Kennedy and a delegate; and *Newsnight* covered Lord Holme and three delegates.

Concluding remarks

The concluding remarks of the reports despite emphasizing the upbeat finale to the speech clearly alluded to the potential problems for Ashdown from certain sections of the party over his overture to New Labour. Indeed the negative consequence of any future deal for the party was spelt out in no uncertain terms in some reports. The *ITN 5.40* report suggested: 'Thumbs up, another sign of his confidence that being up-front on tax and other issues will mean more votes and seats and influence in the next parliament.' *News at Ten* similarly suggested: 'Thumbs up, an indication that Mr Ashdown believes he is carrying his supporters with him over his "Yes, we'll put taxes up if we have to" strategy.' The report also noted there could be problems from 'a sort of hair shirt tendency inherited perhaps from the old Liberals . . . and evident today as it voted to ban National Lottery instant scratch cards . . . but most of the representatives here seem to be backing Paddy Ashdown's view.' The *Six O'clock News* report said that he had succeeded in keeping 'the door open to increased co-operation but his language was sufficiently uncompromising to make it sound more like a challenge'. *Channel Four* similarly noted the possible response of the party: 'He deliberately didn't respond too warmly to Mr Blair's talks, knowing that might produce a backlash, as a result he kept the party with him . . . Despite the applause Liberal Democrats won't be rushed into talks with a party that its vocal minority still regards as the enemy.' The *Nine O'clock News* raised the same dilemma as the other reports: 'The Lib Dems have been pleased to be wooed by Tony Blair but they are by no means convinced they want to start walking out. But he's kept the doors open whilst boosting his party's confidence.' *Newsnight* was more forthright in focusing on a deal with Labour. Tension between delegates and MPs was raised as one potential outcome: 'This week has revealed a tension between MPs and officials, who would dearly love to pull that lever for change inside a government, and activists who would split the party rather than contemplate coalition.'

Tony's vision of New Britain

All the bulletins saw the most important aspects of Blair's 1995 speech as both his vision for Britain and his policy initiatives. The BBC *Six O'clock News* suggested that he set out 'his vision for a new young Britain' and said the speech was designed to 'answer those critics who complain that he's full of fine words but his promises lack substance'. The BBC *Nine O'clock News* noted it was 'prescription . . . to change Britain.' *Channel Four News* said it was 'his vision for Britain under Labour' and observed that 'Mr Blair's advisers wanted this speech to be seen as full of policy'. *News at Ten* came out with 'a vision of a new young united Britain . . .', and both ITN bulletins remarked that 'perhaps sensing in advance that the Tories might try and attack the speech today for being without substance it came with a twenty-four page briefing paper'. *Newsnight* noted that the aim was to 'reposition Labour as the party of the future' and in addition, 'this is a party that has been increasingly restive, wondering "Where is the beef?" Mr Blair offered up some red meat'.

A total of seventeen passages were used from Blair's 1995 speech. Table 5.8 shows which passages from the speech were selected in reports. Many of the reports used the same passages from the speech. Table 5.8 shows that nine passages were used by more than one of the reports. The first two most widely used passages specifically concerned policy pledges. The first quote, used by all and summarized by *Newsnight*, concerned the connection of every school to the Internet via British Telecom (BT).

Table 5.8 *Which passages from the 1995 Labour leader's speech were used in reports by bulletin*

	Identification number of the passage								
	1	2	3	4	5	6	7	8	9
ITN5.40	x	x	x	x				x	x
BBC6	x	x	x		x				
Ch 4	x	x	x	x		x	x		
BBC9	x	x	x	x	x		x		
ITN10	x	x	x	x				x	x
Newsnight		x	x	x	x	x			

(1 = A deal with British Telecom to connect schools to the Internet. 2 = A pledge to renationalize the railways. 3 = Labour as the patriotic party. 4 = A joke referring to Blair's nickname. 5 = The leader's love for his party and country. 6 = The leader's vision of a new Britain. 7 = The importance of education and technology. 8 = The uses to which revenue from a new windfall tax would be put. 9 = A critique of the Conservatives. BBC6 = BBC Six O'clock News; BBC9 = BBC Nine O'clock News; ITN5.40 = ITN News at 5.40 p.m.; ITN10 = ITN News at Ten; Ch 4 = Channel Four News)

PASSAGE 1

> I can tell you that we have been these past weeks in discussion with British
> Telecom. In return for access to the market I can announce that they have
> agreed as they build their network to connect every school, every college,
> every hospital, every library in Britain for free.

The *ITN 5.40* and *News at Ten* restated the aim of the passage but added
a caveat: 'The cable television market currently closed to British
Telecom would be opened up, but at a price.' The *Six O'clock News*
emphasized the advantages for both schoolchildren and BT: 'each child
to have access to a computer and British Telecom to have greater
freedom to compete.' *Channel Four*'s report suggested the passage was
symbolic. It symbolized 'both Labour's commitment to education and
technology and to a partnership between the private and public sectors.'
The *Nine O'clock News* suggested the passage was both visionary and
practical. Its vision was 'of a country with every schoolchild having
access to a laptop computer, medical centres of excellence linked to the
electronic super highway. To underline its practical purpose Labour has
done a deal with the privatized BT'. *Newsnight* summarized the
announcement: 'Labour would allow British Telecom to use cable technology to the full in return for promising to connect up every school . . .
in Britain for free. And he [Blair] also said that there would be discussion
about how to ensure that every child has access to a laptop computer.'

The second passage was a pledge of tight public spending controls
but with a caveat that there would be a publicly owned railway under
Labour. The popularity of this announcement was emphasized by reference to the applause it received on the *Nine O'clock News*, *News at Ten*
and *Newsnight*.

PASSAGE 2

> I don't give blank cheques in any area of policy, including this, no matter
> what the pressures. But to anyone thinking of grabbing our railways, built
> up over the years so they can make a quick profit, as our network is broken
> up and sold off, I say this: There will be a publicly owned, publicly
> accountable railway system under a Labour government.

The *ITN 5.40* and *News at Ten* emphasized the careful wording of the
passage: 'After welfare into work for single parents, transport. But there
will be no blank cheques in any policy area' and noted the reaction: 'The
applause for that, led by Jimmy Knapp the rail union leader.' The *Six
O'clock News* described the passage as a 'pledge' on 'taking a privatized
British Rail back into the public sector'. *Channel Four* emphasized its
reception and made reference to its careful wording: 'Most popular of

all, public ownership of the railways. But the commitments were very carefully phrased.' The *Nine O'clock News* focused on the passage's reception: 'But if New Labour are warming to the markets, Mr Blair still got his loudest applause of the day for a pledge to reverse a controversial privatization.' *Newsnight* referred to the passage as 'a promise of a more traditional kind', its aim 'to delight the audience in the hall'.

All the reports referenced the passage of the speech that sought to label Labour as the patriotic party and attack Conservative patriotism.

PASSAGE 3

> So let us say with pride, we are patriots, this is the patriotic party, because it is the party of the people. And as the Tories wave their Union Jacks next week, I know what so many people will be thinking, I know what people want to say to those Tories. It is no good waving the fabric of our flag when you have spent sixteen years tearing apart the fabric of the nation.

The *Six O'clock News* suggested simply: 'today he also took hold of the Union Jack.' *Channel Four* noted the passage as an attempt to occupy the moral high ground: 'Mr Blair returned to his theme of trying to occupy the moral high ground with an appeal for patriotism.' The *Nine O'clock News* located the significance of the passage in terms of Conservative attacks on Labour's European policy: 'Mr Blair knows the Tories will attack him at the next election as soft on Europe and so he has sought to stress that his party is a party of patriots.' The *ITN 5.40* and *News at Ten* saw the passage as a critique of the Conservatives' patriotism: 'The Labour leader knew what ordinary people would be saying to the flag-waving Tories at their conference next week.' *Newsnight* framed the passage as part of Blair's strategy: 'Labour the party of patriotism! an audacious move in itself', but added: 'the hall cleared, there was not a single Union Jack among the debris.'

In addition to repositioning and policy pledges there was also an interest in humorous passages from the speech. All reports except the *Six O'clock News* contextualized the fourth passage, as a joke in which Tony Blair sought to respond to critics of his style of leadership.

PASSAGE 4

> Last year I was Bambi, this year I'm Stalin. From Disneyland to dictator-ship in twelve short months. I'm not sure which one I prefer. OK, I prefer Bambi honestly.

Channel Four News framed this as 'dealing with criticism of his leader-ship with a joke against himself'. In the *Nine O'clock News*: 'The struggles for party reform were dismissed with a joke.' On the *ITN 5.40* and *News at Ten* there was no mention of a joke. The passage was seen as showing that 'Labour could change Britain for the better since the party itself had changed'. *Newsnight* suggested that the passage showed that Blair 'laughed off the criticism that he's centralized power in his hands'.

The fifth, sixth, seventh and eighth most frequently used passages concerned a mixture of the reiteration of existing beliefs, a vision of the future and an attack on the Conservatives. The fifth passage, used by both BBC One reports and *Newsnight*, was seen as a straight attack on the Conservatives.

PASSAGE 5

> I love my party, I just hate being in opposition. And I love my country and hate what the Tories have done to it.

The *Six O'clock News* saw this as 'one of his overall themes' and the report suggested it was 'underlined by the appearance of the widow of one of his most successful predecessors'. The *Nine O'clock News* in a similarly descriptive manner suggested 'time for a change was the theme'. *Newsnight* suggested the passage was a gesture to old Labour: 'It was time to display a little tenderness to old Labour members who often feel unloved by Mr Blair.'

The sixth passage, used by *Channel Four News* and *Newsnight*, was contextualized as a vision of a new Britain.

PASSAGE 6

> Where people succeed on the basis of what they did for their country rather than what they take from their country. Not saying "This was a great country", but Britain can and will be a great country again. A country that will build the new economy of the future. No more bosses versus workers, partnerships at the work place. No more public versus private, co-operation to rebuild our nation's roads and rail and inner city and regions. No more boom and bust economics . . .

Channel Four contextualized the passage in terms of President Kennedy: 'His language as he described his vision of Britain as a young country could have been borrowed straight from President Kennedy.' *Newsnight* treated the passage somewhat sceptically: 'In a curious phrase he promised a young country. Indeed this man who has steered clear of firm promises made some rather extravagant ones about new Britain.'

The seventh passage, used by *Channel Four* and the *Nine O'clock News*, was contextualized as Blair reaffirming the importance of education and technology.

PASSAGE 7

> Education is the best economic policy there is for a modern country. It is
> in the marriage of education and technology that the future lies. The arms
> race may be over, the knowledge race has begun.

Channel Four interpreted this passage in a descriptive way: 'The key to
the future he claimed was education and technology.' Similarly the *Nine
O'clock News* suggested 'he made education and technology the key'.
The eighth passage, used by both ITN reports, concerned uses of the
windfall tax for a welfare-to-work programme.

PASSAGE 8

> And we will use that money too and end up saving money by giving
> single parents the chance not to live on benefits but to plan their future,
> organize child care and training so that they can support themselves and
> their children.

This was highlighted as the 'biggest programme of work and education
ever put forward in Britain'. The ninth passage, used by both ITN
reports, was the closing passage of the speech.

PASSAGE 9

> I will do all that I can to get these Tories out and I will devote every breath
> that I breathe, every sinew of my body, to ensuring that your grandchil-
> dren do get to live in that new Britain, in a new and better world. New
> Labour, New Britain. The party renewed, the country reborn.
> New Labour, New Britain.

This was highlighted by both bulletins as a promise 'to those ordinary
people among the flag-waving crowd on VJ day'.
    In addition there were a further eight passages used by the different
reports – four by *Newsnight*, two by *Channel Four News* and one each by
the BBC bulletins. *Newsnight* contextualized Blair's introduction of Lord
Wilson's widow (Mary) in terms of reaching out to his own party,
'which perhaps he has deliberately failed to do over the past year', and
as a tribute to Lord Wilson, 'the last man who won power for Labour'.
It used a passage to show Blair's definition of socialism, another passage
to illustrate the theme of education and technology, suggesting 'Mr Blair
dreamed of surfing the net', and another passage on the family stating
that 'family values were Labour values'. *Channel Four*'s report used two
further quotes to illustrate Blair inspiring the next generation and
retaining traditional values as the party of the family. These were
decoded as the Labour leader 'trying to position Labour as the party of
the future' and trying to 'reclaim some traditional values from the

Table 5.9   *Which further passages from the 1995 Labour leader's speech were used in reports by bulletin*

	Identification number of the passage							
	1	2	3	4	5	6	7	8
Newsnight	x	x	x	x				
Ch 4					x	x		
BBC6							x	
BBC9								x

(1 = The introduction of Lord Wilson's widow. 2 = The leader's definition of socialism. 3 = The importance of education. 4 = Family values. 5 = Labour as the party of the future. 6 = Traditional values. 7, = National Health Service. 8 = The party's position on Europe. BBC6 = BBC Six O'clock News; BBC9 = BBC Nine O'clock News; Ch 4 = Channel Four News)

Tories'. The *Six O'clock News* referenced the passage on his support for the NHS suggesting 'the NHS would become a service again', and the *Nine O'clock News* referenced a passage on the party's position on Europe, which it saw as Blair 'nailing his colours firmly to the European mast'. Of the thirteen new policy initiatives trailed in the briefing document only five found their way into news reports. Initiatives on a people's lottery, getting single parents into work and a fair deal for consumers, for instance, did not feature at all.

Comparisons

In 1994 there were a few comparisons made on *Channel Four News* and *Newsnight* to Gaitskell and his attempt to rewrite Clause 4, but they were not as widespread as the comparisons to Wilson and Kennedy made in 1995. The commentary drew comparisons between Blair's speech and that made by former Labour leader Harold Wilson in 1963, known generically as the 'white heat of technology' speech, and between Blair's language and that of President Kennedy. The *Six O'clock News* report compared one section of the speech dealing with new technology to Wilson's: 'Like Harold Wilson he put great emphasis on education and technological change.' The *Channel Four* report made a similar link: 'There were echoes of Harold Wilson's "white heat of technology" in his speech.' The report also made comparisons with Kennedy: 'Together with an almost Kennedyesque appeal to the next generation and patriotism.' The link with Kennedy was further emphasized: 'His language as he described his vision of Britain as a young country could have been borrowed straight from President Kennedy.'

The BBC *Nine O'clock News* report, like the previous two reports, drew a comparison with Wilson. After highlighting the introduction of Wilson's widow (Mary) to the conference, it suggested that the last Labour leader to end a long period of Conservative rule 'did so preaching the white heat of technological change. Mr Blair too suggested the Tories had let Britain become a tired old country'. The report further reinforced the comparison: 'like Lord Wilson he made education and technology the key.' *Newsnight's* introduction, like *Channel Four News'*, drew the comparison between both Wilson and Kennedy: 'His speech tried to cast himself and his party in the mould of Wilson against Douglas Home, Kennedy against Nixon.' The historical comparison was further developed in the report – 'just as Wilson won power from the white heat of technology to drag Britain into the 1960s Mr Blair dreamed of Britain surfing the Internet'; and then, 'there was also more than a hint of the vision thing, a touch of Kennedy's Camelot'.

Performance, reception and reactions

Table 5.10 shows that the leader's performance was commented on some eleven times in reports over the period. Most of these remarks were focused on the Labour leader's 1996 speech. Overall there were marginally more references to the leader's performance on ITN than on the main BBC bulletins. However, there were no references to Blair's performance in reports in 1995.

The reports were also keen to convey the reception the speech received from the audience in the conference hall. Table 5.11 shows that there was frequent reference to audience reception. The late evening bulletins made more references than the early evening bulletins, with the exception of *Newsnight*. In 1995, four of six reports referenced the speech's overall reception. The *Six O'clock News* suggested: 'there was

Table 5.10   *The number of references in all reports to the performance of the Labour leader in making his speech by bulletin and year, 1993–6*

	Ch 4	ITN5.40	ITN10	BBC6	BBC9	NN	Total
1993	1	1	1	0	0	0	3
1994	0	0	0	1	0	0	1
1995	0	0	0	0	0	0	0
1996	2	1	1	1	1	1	7
Total	3	2	2	2	1	1	11

(BBC6 = BBC Six O'clock News; BBC9 = BBC Nine O'clock News;
ITN5.40 = ITN News at 5.40 p.m.; ITN10 = ITN News at Ten;
Ch 4 = Channel Four News; NN = Newsnight)

Table 5.11   *The number of references in all reports to the reception of the Labour leader's speeches by bulletin and year, 1993–6*

	BBC9	Ch 4	ITN10	ITN5.40	BBC6	NN	Total
1993	1	1	1	1	1	1	6
1994	2	3	1	0	0	0	6
1995	2	0	2	1	1	1	7
1996	1	1	1	1	1	0	5
Total	6	5	5	3	3	2	24

(BBC6 = BBC Six O'clock News; BBC9 = BBC Nine O'clock News;
ITN5.40 = ITN News at 5.40 p.m.; ITN10 = ITN News at Ten;
Ch 4 = Channel Four News; NN = Newsnight)

of course a long standing ovation.' The BBC *Nine O'clock News* said that 'the hour-long marathon won Labour's leader rave reviews from most of his audience'. *News at Ten* noted that 'its reception inside the hall confirmed the extent to which Mr Blair is carrying his party with him'. *Newsnight* somewhat disdainfully pointed to an 'inevitable standing ovation', and argued that 'rhetoric that would have offended and shocked this conference a few years ago now genuinely pleased most here'.

The reports also included reactions to the speech by other actors. Table 5.12 shows that the majority of reactions initiated after the Labour leader's speeches were positive. There was a high proportion of negative reaction used by journalists, particularly after the 1994 conference, which contained Blair's announcement that he had decided to rewrite Clause Four of the party's constitution. In 1995 *Channel Four*'s report used the reactions of two delegates and Diane Abbott MP, all positive; The *Nine O'clock News* used three delegates, two positive, one negative. *Newsnight*'s report suggested that 'critical voices were hard to find' and carried positive reactions to the speech from Harriet Harman (then Shadow Social Security Secretary), Clare Short MP and a delegate, and

Table 5.12   *The number of positive, negative and neutral reactions to the Labour leader's speeches by year, 1993–6*

	Positive	Negative	Neutral
1993	1	2	2
1994	14	13	1
1995	8	2	0
1996	5	1	0
Total	28	18	3

a negative reaction from another delegate. In addition the *Six and Nine O'clock News'* reports referred to the critical reactions of both Brian Mawhinney, the Conservative Party Chairman, and Alan Beith for the Liberal Democrats. *Channel Four News* referred to the 'Tories dismissing it as little more than retitled version of Labour in '45 and '64.' *News at Ten* noted that the 'Tories dismissed it as nothing new, the same old plan for dismantling Tory success'.

Concluding remarks

Overall the reports' concluding remarks focused on a mix of policy substance and party positioning, and evaluated the success of the speech. The *Six O'clock News'* concluding remarks suggested that the speech had strengthened Mr Blair's position as leader, noting 'Mr Blair has managed to consolidate his position as a strong party leader'. The consolidation of his position was further underlined by referring to the defeat of the left: 'Earlier the left of the party were easily defeated over the dropping of the left-winger Liz Davies . . . '. In terms of policy substance the report was slightly sceptical, suggesting that 'In some areas, in particular over the overall balance between tax and spending, Mr Blair has not been specific. But at least for the party faithful here, he's provided plenty of fresh ammunition to use against the Tories.'

Channel Four's concluding remarks contextualized policy initiatives in terms of reassuring the party: 'The party has been looking for re-assurance and they got it in the form of a policy commitment.' In addition it suggested that Blair had 'succeeded in going some way to answer what Labour will do with power, without making costly commitments . . . '. But the speech was also seen in terms of positioning the party for the forthcoming election campaign: 'What is important in the long term is how he positions Labour as the party of the future. For now, there is no question of the Tories changing leader, so that could be a difficult strategy for the government to counter'.

The BBC *Nine O'clock News'* concluding remarks ignored the question of policy substance, summing up the speech as a personal triumph: 'Tonight Mr Blair and his colleagues can afford to grin . . . A compliant party occasionally swallowing hard has its sights on the next election.' It further characterized the speech as 'stamped through with Christian Socialism, even prayer book language', suggesting that it had 'pressed nearly all the right buttons, while reassuring middle England with firm words on crime and the family'.

The *ITN 5.40* and *News at Ten's* report contextualized the speech in terms of electoral competition: 'Every word was meant to reflect Tony Blair's belief that Labour can replace the Tories because Labour's moral purpose is higher, their vision for Britain clearer.' In addition the concluding remarks focused on an imagined Blair response to Conservative attacks: 'First he would say that in his view it's a patriotic thing to do, to try and change the country, not a destructive one. And secondly, he was playing for all it's worth the feeling that he has that up and down the country people are saying "It's time for a change".' *Newsnight*'s concluding remarks suggested that 'he had soothed a party that was beginning to get a little restless, and set out a strong vision'. Yet it also suggested that there were potential problems ahead: 'But trying to prove that Mr Blair can afford to build what he calls a young country may still prove to be more awkward.'

John's fight back

All the reports' introductions summarized the main announcements in the speech and sought to contextualize the speech as laying the ground on which Major would fight the next election. The introduction on the *Six O'clock News* suggested that the speech contained Major's 'plan for winning the next election'. *Channel Four News*' introduction suggested it represented 'John Major's manifesto'. The introduction on the *Nine O'clock News* noted the speech as one in which he had 'spelled out the issues on which he'll fight Tony Blair at the next election'. The *ITN 5.40* and *News at Ten*'s introduction suggested the speech as one in which Major had 'stamped his personality and priorities on the . . . party today . . .'. *Newsnight*'s introduction was slightly sceptical in tone. It suggested that Mr Major had promised 'tough choices' on public spending and taxation 'but the week has ended without any clear hint of how he's going to do that'. The introduction suggested the announcements were aimed at persuading voters that the party could still come up with 'election-winning ideas' but posed a question: 'But was there really a big new idea to captivate the electorate?'

Table 5.13 shows which passages from the Conservative leader's speech were selected in reports on the 1995 conference. A total of seventeen passages were used, nine of which were used by more than one news report. The most important passages were deemed to be those that involved the announcement of new policy, the position of the party on Europe and Major's personal history.

The first passage extracted by all reports except *Newsnight* concerned the announcement of extra police on the beat; this was contextualized in terms of its popularity with the Tory representatives although some reports suggested it was part of a drift to the right.

PASSAGE 1

Table 5.13 *Which passages from the 1995 Conservative leader's speech were used in reports by bulletin*

	Identification number of the passage								
	1	2	3	4	5	6	7	8	9
ITN5.40	x	x	x	x			x		
BBC6	x	x	x	x	x				x
Ch 4	x	x	x	x	x	x	x	x	
BBC9	x	x	x	x	x	x			
ITN10	x	x	x	x			x	x	
Newsnight				x	x		x	x	x	x

(1 = 5,000 extra police on the beat. 2 = Party policy on Europe. 3 = Remembering his father. 4 = More state assisted places for private schools. 5 = A pledge to keep on winning general elections. 6 = Caring Conservatism. 7 = Serving the nation. 8 = A pledge to reduce taxes. 9 = An attack on Labour's plans for devolution. BBC6 = BBC Six O'clock News; BBC9 = BBC Nine O'clock News; ITN5.40 = ITN News at 5.40 p.m.; ITN10 = ITN News at Ten; Ch 4 = Channel Four News)

> We have found the resources over the next three years to put not 500 but an extra 5000 police officers on the beat.

The *Six O'clock News* suggested this was 'another popular announcement'. *Channel Four* suggested that the passage was part of a wider series of measures: 'He announced new measures to allow the security services to join the fight against drug trafficking, a new national police squad and more policemen.' The *Nine O'clock News* saw the announcement as an ideological 'rightward drift' in the party and highlighted its reception: 'Policy reflected the rightward drift this week of Tory rhetoric. A promise to get the security services involved in fighting crime brought cheers. So did this announcement.' The *ITN 5.40* and *News at Ten* highlighted the fact that the announcement was more substantial than a promise made by Blair and popular with the audience: 'For those who have been asking all week "Where's the big one?" they now had the answer . . . Well, that announcement topping Tony Blair's promise of three thousand more constables over five years was for many representatives not just the best thing in the speech but the best announcement of the week.' *Newsnight* merely described the passage's content: 'then a series of announcements on law and order, five thousand more bobbies on the beat, MI5 to fight organized crime, possibly a national police force.'

The second passage, used by all except *Newsnight*, was on the Conservative party's position on Europe.

Passage 2

> If we want to persuade our partners that their policies for Europe are
> wrong, and I passionately believe that many of their policies for Europe
> are wrong, then we must use our imagination to understand their feelings
> and their motives. But underneath the rational argument we should not
> be misunderstood. If others go federalist, Conservative Britain will not.

The *Six O'clock News* saw the passage in terms of the representatives'
response: 'On Europe some would have preferred a more strident tone,
even though he gave a firm "No" to federalism.' *Channel Four News*
noted the passage as dealing with the 'potentially most difficult issue',
and in terms of Michael Portillo the Defence Secretary's speech earlier
in the week: 'In a polite rebuke to Mr Portillo he said Britain must
advocate its arguments courteously.' The *Nine O'clock News* comments
were descriptive, suggesting that the passage was a 'firm warning on
Europe that a Tory Britain would have no truck with ending border
controls or signing the Social Chapter, we must understand the
motivations of our European partners and argue courteously'. The *ITN
5.40* and *News at Ten* alluded to the positive response of the representatives: 'The message on Europe pleased this audience too.'

The third passage, about Major's father, was used by all the reports,
the journalists saw it as an insight into Major 'the man' and his background.

Passage 3

> He made garden ornaments forty years ago. Some people have
> always found that rather humorous. I don't. I see the proud, stubborn,
> independent old man I love, who ran that firm and taught me to love
> my country, fight for my beliefs and spit in the eye of malign fate. And
> I know the knockers and the sneerers who may never have taken a risk
> in their comfortable lives aren't fit to wipe the boots of the risk takers
> of Britain.

The *Six O'clock News* suggested the passage was a part of a deliberate
attempt by Major to compare himself with Blair: 'Mr Major as a candidate was contrasted with Mr Blair. He the public school educated
socialist. Mr Major the son of a small businessman.' *Channel Four*
suggested the passage showed Major making 'much of his own inheritance or lack of it . . . and recalling his own father's struggles as a
small businessman making garden gnomes'. The *Nine O'clock News* saw
the passage as an attempt to revive the 'core Tory vote', using 'his
personal experience to demonstrate sympathy with key sectors like
small business . . . '. The *ITN 5.40* and *News at Ten* emphasized the

emotion of the passage, suggesting that there were 'tears almost as he spoke of the struggle his father had in running a small business . . . Well, both Mrs Major and the Prime Minister, first biting his lip, and then as the applause continued clearly seen dabbing at his eyes, they seemed to have quite a struggle with their emotions at this stage.' *Newsnight* saw the passage in marketing terms, drawing comparisons with Blair: 'The next step selling Major the man. Unspoken the comparison of John Major, the ordinary bloke, with Tony Blair, the public school socialist. Mr Major reminded his audience his father made garden gnomes.'

The fourth passage used was about education policy and the pledge to extend the assisted places scheme.

PASSAGE 4

> It helps children from lower income homes to go to our best private schools and it has been a magnificent success. But Labour hate it, hate it. And that's true to form. They always claim to want to help people, but in return they demand that people know their place if they happen to have been helped. In Labour's view there is no place for children of low-income families in private schools, no place. So they want to abolish the scheme outright. Labour's message to them is "no choice for the poor".

The *Six O'clock News* framed this passage as an attack on Labour's policy on assisted places: 'On education Mr Major promised to double the number of assisted places at private schools – Labour want to abolish the scheme altogether.' *Channel Four News* similarly drew a comparison with Labour's policy, suggesting it was an attempt to 'undermine Labour's claims to be the party of standards and choice. While Labour last week said that it would scrap the assisted places scheme, he said he would double it.' The *Nine O'clock News* personalized the comparison: 'Mr Major announced the doubling of the assisted places scheme for sending children from poor homes to private schools, the scheme Mr Blair last week vowed to scrap.' The *ITN 5.40* and *News at Ten* high-lighted the popularity of the announcement and the reaction of ministers, suggesting that the popularity of the announcement of more bobbies on the beat was almost matched by 'news about the assisted places scheme . . . a delighted Education Secretary signalled to William Waldegrave, the holder of the Treasury purse strings, that he'd have to find the money now'. *Newsnight* suggested the passage was designed 'to catch Labour out' and contrasted it with Labour policy: 'Singling out Mr Blair's old public school, Mr Major said he would double the number of pupils that the state sends to private schools – Labour would abolish the scheme.'

The fifth passage, used by both BBC reports and *Channel Four News*, involved elements of humour, with Major's pledge to keep on winning elections in the future.

PASSAGE 5

> We've won four and we're going for five, then six, and then seven. And then we'll think again.

The *Six O'clock News* saw the passage as an 'unashamedly traditional' appeal: 'they would wave the flag as they always had, and they would win elections as they always had.' For *Channel Four* it was part of Major's strategy to 'convince them that he had a strategy for winning the next election'. The *Nine O'clock News* noted that the passage was evidence of his new-found confidence, 'boosted by the leadership election gamble in the summer that has given him a new authority'.

The sixth passage, used by *Channel Four News*, the *Nine O'clock News* and *Newsnight*, was contextualized in terms of the theme of caring Conservatism.

PASSAGE 6

> If there's one thing in our Tory tradition that inspires me, that helped bring me into this party, I'll tell you what it was. It was our historic recognition that not everyone is thrusting and confident and fit. Many are not and they deserve our protection. With a Conservative government they can always be certain of getting that protection now and in the future.

For *Channel Four News* the passage was explained as a rebuke of criticisms made by a defecting MP earlier the same week: 'He didn't mention the defection this week of a Tory MP to Labour, but the subtext of his speech was a rejection of Alan Howarth's claim that he had abandoned traditional caring Conservatism.' The *Nine O'clock News* saw the passage in terms of ideological positioning: 'But Mr Major insists that his position is still on the One Nation centre ground of politics.' *Newsnight* was somewhat sceptical, noting: 'If Mr Major did express a vision it was a curious amalgam, of Britain as the low tax Hong Kong of Europe, combined with caring, comforting One Nation Conservatism.'

The seventh passage, used by all except the BBC One reports, was the final section of the speech.

PASSAGE 7

> We carry the scars of battle, that is true. But they are honourable scars. We know that no other party can win the battles for Britain that lie ahead. Our

nation's future is at stake and we Conservatives have served our country in office for longer and better than any other democratic political party in the world. We Conservatives are here, and in the future we Conservatives stand ready to serve on behalf of the nation we love.

Channel Four News saw this as another attack on Labour: 'Mr Major predicted that Labour would make a lightweight alternative.' The *ITN 5.40* and *News at Ten* highlighted Major's emotions: 'at the end of the speech it was all quite different as Mr Major talked of the Tory record.' For a sceptical *Newsnight* it was part of the marketing for the next election: 'all part of a package the Tories hope will woo voters.'

The eighth passage, used by *Channel Four*, *News at Ten* and *Newsnight*, concerned the pledge to reduce taxes at an unspecified future date.

PASSAGE 8

In recession we had to put up taxes to protect the vulnerable. Now the recession is over and, as Ken Clarke said, as soon as is prudent, but not before, we must get those taxes down again. But be in no doubt, I don't only mean income tax. I mean taxes that damage investment and stultify wealth creation. I mean inheritance tax and I mean capital gains tax as well.

Channel Four News decoded this passage in terms of Major's big idea an 'enterprise centre of Europe', based on lower public spending 'and, to the pleasure of representatives, lower taxation'. *News at Ten* noted: 'with the Chancellor listening, Mr Major said taxes must come down.' *Newsnight* noted only: 'he said taxes would be cut and not just income tax.'

The ninth passage, used by *Six O'clock News* and *Newsnight*, was an attack on Labour's plans for devolution.

PASSAGE 9

These are not distant problems to be tossed aside while we worry about day-to-day matters of politics. These are Labour's plans for the first year of the Labour government if they won the election. So take the message of danger to every doorstep in every part of our once united Kingdom.

The *Six O'clock News* saw the passage as a further attack on Labour: 'It was over the constitution that Mr Major reserved his strongest fire power . . . Labour were threatening the United Kingdom itself.' *Newsnight* also saw it as an assault on Labour: 'On the constitution he admitted there was a clamour for change in Scotland but denounced Labour's plans.'

Table 5.14 shows that there were eight further passages used by the

Table 5.14 *Which further passages from the 1995 Conservative leader's speech were used in reports by bulletin*

	Identification number of the passage							
	1	2	3	4	5	6	7	8
BBC6	x							
Ch 4		x						
BBC9			x					
ITN10				x	x			
Newsnight						x	x	x

(1 = Increased annual payments to Victoria Cross holders. 2 = A critique of Labour policy. 3 = Passion for politics. 4 = An attack on drug dealers. 5 = Formation of the National Crime Squad. 6 = The party's economic record. 7 = Government spending cuts. 8 = The importance of welfare. BBC6 = BBC Six O'clock News; BBC9 = BBC Nine O'clock News; ITN10 = News at Ten; Ch 4 = Channel Four News)

different reports, mostly *Newsnight*. The *Six O'clock News* used the announcement of an increase in the annual payment to holders of the Victoria and George Cross, suggesting: 'Patriotism of various forms was highlighted, with the warmest applause going to the increase in annual payment for holders of the Victoria Cross.' *Channel Four News* highlighted Major's attack on Labour for 'double think'. The *Nine O'clock News* used another passage to illustrate Major's passion. *News at Ten* cited Major's attack on drug dealers and his announcement of the formation of a national crime squad, suggesting the passage was heartfelt, giving a greater insight into Major 'the man'. *Newsnight* used passages on the Conservatives' economic record, Major's vision of lower government spending and his belief in the importance of welfare. These were contextualized in terms of the forthcoming election campaign. Out of fourteen key announcements trailed in the briefing documents only eight found their way into reports on the speech. No reports mentioned more freedoms to be granted to specialist or religious schools, aims to make more schools grant maintained or contract work for the unemployed.

Performance, reception and reactions

In all the reports on the Conservative leader's speech, over four years, there were fourteen comments on the performance of the leader. These remarks were mainly concentrated on the BBC, with the *Nine O'clock News* commenting on Major's performance after each of the four speeches. In 1995 four out of six programmes commented on Major's performance. The *Six O'clock News* report said: 'Mr Major was becoming

Table 5.15   *The number of references in all reports to the performance of the Conservative leader in making his speech by bulletin and year, 1993–6*

	BBC9	BBC6	NN	Ch 4	ITN10	ITN5.40	Total
1993	1	1	0	1	0	0	3
1994	1	0	1	1	0	1	4
1995	1	1	1	0	1	0	4
1996	1	1	1	0	0	0	3
Total	4	3	3	2	1	1	14

(BBC6 = BBC Six O'clock News; BBC9 = BBC Nine O'clock News;
ITN5.40 = ITN News at 5.40 p.m.; ITN10 = ITN News at Ten;
Ch 4 = Channel Four News; NN = Newsnight)

an old hand at making conference speeches, and this was his best so far.' It also suggested that his performance had been strengthened by his leadership victory in the summer. *News at Ten* focused on certain performance-enhancing factors in Major's speech, noting that 'the Prime Minister had been practising quite hard at varying the tone and pace and the content of this year's speech'. It further emphasized the 'emotional staging' of the speech: 'Mr Major decided to step out into the centre of the hall to deliver his speech. He wanted to take the audience with him, and those outside the hall too, as he made what came across as a more heartfelt speech, giving us a greater insight into the way his mind works.' *Newsnight* indirectly questioned the spin doctors' line that this was his best speech ever: 'The spin doctors' big line that this was Mr Major's best ever speech was swallowed by many. There was something here for every vaguely Conservative taste.'

There were some thirty-seven references to the representatives' reception of the leader's speech – as table 5.16 shows. While the 'clapometer' was used during the week by the broadcasters, it was never used to register the reception given to the leader's speech. In addition to comments on audience reception for certain passages of the speech already noted, three broadcasters summarized the overall reception of the 1995 speech. *Channel Four*'s report focused on the audience response at the beginning: 'Mr Major's arrival on stage was delayed until he'd heard whether he'd won the Nobel peace prize. He hadn't, but that didn't take the enthusiasm out of his reception from the representatives, who wanted to demonstrate to the watching world that the divisions of the leadership struggle were over.' It also noted the conference's final response: 'The representatives waved their flags in defiance of Tony Blair's claim last week that their treatment of the nation denies them the right to do so.' The *Nine O'clock News* suggested 'the audience loved his sharper new style.' Similarly, *News at Ten* said that the audience 'loved

Table 5.16 *The number of references in all reports to the reception of the Conservative leader's speeches by bulletin and year, 1993–6*

	Ch 4	ITN5.40	ITN10	BBC6	BBC9	NN	Total
1993	2	1	0	1	2	1	7
1994	2	1	2	1	0	1	7
1995	4	3	3	3	1	0	14
1996	1	3	3	1	0	1	9
Total	9	8	8	6	3	3	37

(BBC6 = BBC Six O'clock News; BBC9 = BBC Nine O'clock News;
ITN5.40 = ITN News at 5.40 p.m.; ITN10 = ITN News at Ten O'clock;
Ch 4 = Channel Four News; NN = Newsnight)

the speech', but added: 'they always do, of course.'

Most of the reactions used were favourable and there were no negative reactions used. This pattern was especially marked in 1993 and 1994. In 1995 only *Channel Four* and *Newsnight* included any reactions to the speech from within the party. *Channel Four* carried three positive reactions from representatives. *Newsnight's* report sought positive reactions from two representatives, and neutral reactions from Andrew Lansley, former head of the Conservative Central Office research department, and Trevor Kavanagh, political editor of the *Sun*. In addition the *Six O'clock News* referred to the critical reactions of John Prescott, Paddy Ashdown and Alex Salmond, and the *Nine O'clock News* to the reactions of Prescott and Ashdown. *News at Ten* referenced John Prescott's attack and *Channel Four* a general Labour critique.

Concluding remarks

Overall, the concluding remarks focused on several themes. The speech was seen largely in terms of repositioning the Conservatives on the centre ground, opening up 'clear blue water' between themselves and

Table 5.17 *The number of positive, negative and neutral reactions to the Conservative leader's speeches by year, 1993–6*

	Positive	Negative	Neutral
1993	11	0	3
1994	10	0	0
1995	5	0	2
1996	2	0	0
Total	28	0	5

Labour and raising the morale of the representatives in the face of the looming general election. The concluding remarks on the BBC *Six O'clock News* focused on the speech's target audience: 'Mr Major's whole speech was directed at the election campaign to come. And unlike many of the speeches this week, it was aimed at the electorate outside the hall as well as the party faithful.' Its aim was contextualized as an attempt to reposition the Conservatives: 'The Prime Minister with his brand of 'one nation' Toryism wants to reclaim the centre ground from Mr Blair.' It was also seen as an attempt to move the political 'goal posts', 'so that if Mr Blair is tempted onto the Tories' new territory he would have to move further to the right'. *Channel Four*'s report similarly contextualized the speech as a formula for 'reclaiming the centre ground from Mr Blair', but also alluded to the attempt to open up a difference with Labour on certain policy areas: 'Education is obviously one area in which the Tories believe they can open up "clear blue water" with Labour', and 'the Conservatives intend opening up divisions with Labour over law and order'. Finally the report hinted at the enormity of the task: 'The Tory party want to rally behind John Major. The road to victory will be very long indeed.' The concluding remarks on the *Nine O'clock News* suggested that 'Mr Major is now fully in charge' and that Major had 'focused forward to the millennium, not back to the past.' It saw the speech as giving the representatives 'back some self-belief, and the hope that (with two budgets to come) they can yet get back into election-winning form'. As with the previous year, the BBC's political editor generally summed up all three conferences as 'successes'.

Both ITN's ITV news programmes' concluding remarks emphasized the upbeat ending of the conference week: 'This year the representatives here, and the party at large, had wanted something to bite on. And with the law and order package, a week which had started slowly, tensely, ended with satisfaction and a bit of fun.' *News at Ten* went further, suggesting that the representatives 'agreed with the Prime Minister, that the party had been united, renewed and healed'. *Newsnight*'s concluding remarks contextualized the speech in terms of the forth-coming election. It insinuated that Major had only just started to respond effectively to Labour: 'The conference season at an end, the Tories seem to be getting rid of the debris of three years of infighting. They are only just starting to respond more effectively to Labour.' But it in a further derisory manner suggested that 'they've lost the trust of the nation, and it may be difficult persuading the voters to return to the fold'.

Expanding coverage

The news broadcasters contributed to the news agenda by extending their coverage of what they saw as key issues raised in all three speeches. This was done either through a two-way, via a pegged additional report or by an interview. The bulletins produced twenty-two two-ways after the leaders' speeches between 1993 and 1996. The function of a two-way is to provide the senior correspondents and the political editors with an additional outlet to elaborate further upon different elements of each speech. Prompted by the anchor's questions they focus either on an explanation of a particular part of the speech or on speculation about its impact.

Over a period of four Labour leader's speeches there was a total of eleven two-ways. In 1995 the only two-way was on *Newsnight* between the anchor Jeremy Paxman and the political pundit Peter Kellner. Over a period of four Conservative leader's speeches there was a total of ten two-ways. Two-ways were the main way of extending coverage of the Tory leader's speech particularly on the early evening bulletins. Table 5.19 shows that there were a total of twenty-one pegged news items on information from the Conservative and Labour leaders' speeches (but none from the Liberal Democrat leader's speeches). Table 5.19 reveals that the longer bulletins produced the greatest number of pegged items. It also shows certain differences in editorial approach between the main news bulletins on BBC One and ITV, with the BBC producing the greatest number of pegged items and ITN the fewest. The news broadcasters produced seven pegged items on the contents of the Labour leader's four speeches. The majority of the pegged reports – five – were produced in 1994 after Blair's announcement of the intention to rewrite Clause Four of the party's constitution, which was given no prior

Table 5.18   *The number of two-ways broadcast after the leaders' speeches by conference, 1993–6*

	ITN5.40	BBC6	BBC9	NN	ITN10	Ch 4	Total
Liberal Democrat	1	0	0	0	0	0	1
Labour	3	1	2	3	1	1	11
Conservative	3	4	1	0	1	1	10
Total	7	5	3	3	2	2	22

(BBC6 = BBC Six O'clock News; BBC9 = BBC Nine O'clock News;
ITN10 = News at Ten; Ch 4 = Channel Four News; NN = Newsnight)

Table 5.19 *The number of pegged news items on leaders' speeches by conference, 1993–6*

	ITN5.40	ITN10	BBC6	Ch 4	BBC9	NN	Total
Liberal Democrat	0	0	0	0	0	0	0
Labour	0	1	0	1	2	3	7
Conservative	0	1	2	3	3	5	14
Total	0	2	2	4	5	8	21

(BBC6 = BBC Six O'clock News; BBC9 = BBC Nine O'clock News; ITN10 = News at Ten; Ch 4 = Channel Four News; NN = Newsnight)

publicity at all. There was only one pegged item for each of the other speeches. In 1995 the only pegged item was produced by the *Nine O'clock News*: it examined the background to Blair's pledge to connect schools and hospitals to the Internet courtesy of British Telecom.

The broadcasters' appetite for pegged items was in some respects greater when a party enjoyed the advantages of being in government, so that any announcements made within a speech were likely to become law and therefore to affect the broadcasters' audience in a significant way. There were fourteen pegged items on the Conservative policy announcements raised in the leader's speeches over the four years. The largest number of pegged reports – five – were produced by *Newsnight*, and the main BBC bulletins produced more pegged reports than ITN. There were two pegged reports on the contents of the 1993 speech, four on the 1994 speech, five on 1995 and three on 1996. Both BBC One bulletins, *Channel Four News* and *Newsnight* produced an additional report on the 1995 speech's main policy announcement, the formation of a national crime squad; and *Channel Four News* produced a further report on the planned expansion of the assisted places scheme.

Table 5.20 shows that all full-length post-speech interviews were conducted on *Channel Four News* and *Newsnight*, the two longest bulletins. The party elites' communications teams regulated interview access to certain of their members. In return for access, both *Newsnight* and *Channel Four News* provided the parties with an additional forum in which to develop further the issues initiated in the leaders' speeches.

A wide range of individuals were interviewed by the two bulletins after the Labour leaders speech, not just members of the leadership who had been put forward. There was a total of nine interviews between 1993 and 1996 after the leader's speech, all on *Channel Four News* and *Newsnight*. On *Channel Four News* in 1993 there was one joint interview with Bill Morris and Robin Cook, and in 1994 there was another with Peter Mandelson, Dennis Skinner and John Edmonds. Further inter-

Table 5.20   *The number of interviews broadcast after the leaders' speeches by conference, 1993–6*

	ITN5.40	ITN10	BBC6	BBC9	Ch 4	NN	Total
Liberal Democrat	0	0	0	0	1	3	4
Labour	0	0	0	0	4	5	9
Conservative	0	0	0	0	6	3	9
Total	0	0	0	0	11	11	22

(BBC6 = BBC Six O'clock News; BBC9 = BBC Nine O'clock News; ITN10 = News at Ten; Ch 4 = Channel Four News; NN = Newsnight)

views in 1995 were with John Prescott and another with Robin Cook in 1996. John Prescott was interviewed every year by *Newsnight*, who also produced one interview with three members of the general public in 1994 to solicit their comments on Tony Blair's speech and whether they would be tempted to vote for him.

There were nine interviews around Major's speeches, all on *Channel Four News* and *Newsnight*. *Channel Four News* in 1993 interviewed Douglas Hurd (then Foreign Secretary) and Peter Lilley (then Social Security Secretary). They interviewed Lilley again in 1994 and Steven Dorrell (then Heritage Secretary). In 1995 they produced a joint interview with Charles Moore (editor of the *Daily Telegraph*) and Geoff Mulgan of the think-tank Demos, and in 1996 interviewed Major himself. *Newsnight* in 1993 interviewed David Hunt (then Employment Secretary), and Michael Heseltine (then Deputy Prime Minister) in 1995 and 1996.

Conclusion

The reports of the leader's speech, based on a detailed analysis of 1995, were exclusively 'reactive' (Blumler *et al.*, 1986) namely the journalists acted as 'translators' (Blumler *et al.*, 1986) interpreting the key passages in each speech for the audience. They sought to give an airing to the announcements contained within the speech. There was conformity on what the key passages were. In 1995 the same seven passages were used from Ashdown's speech, the same nine from Blair's, and the same ten from Major's. The main passages selected, while appearing at different lengths, were on policy announcements from the Labour and Conservative leaders' speeches, and about party relationship with Labour for the Liberal Democrat leader. These were seen as the most newsworthy and were often the passages that were trailed by the spin doctors. Other passages were included that dealt with non-policy issues such as the leader's vision or his background.

However, similar to the findings of Blumler *et al.*'s study of the BBC during the 1992 election, reports included a large amount of 'value added'. Journalists were involved in a process of prioritizing, selecting and contextualizing the information they received, and news teams also sought to expand upon the issues raised in each leader's speech through pegged items and interviews (Blumler *et al.*, 1995). The reports also sought to put the speeches in a wider context for the viewer. The selected passages were explained and their significance underlined. This commentary was mainly descriptive rather than directional, although *Newsnight* provided a more sceptical contextualization of the passages than the other reports. There was also an attempt to show the delegates' responses, revealing the speeches' popularity or un-popularity amongst the audience in the hall. The performance of the leader in delivering his speech was also noted. In certain situations there was an attempt to contextualize the leader's speech historically. This was done in the case of the Labour leader's speech – although not the others – through drawing a comparison with speeches made by previous party leaders. The concluding remarks sought to explain the significance of the Liberal Democrat, Labour and Conservative leaders' speeches to the viewer in terms of competition and co-operation between the political parties and in 1995, in particular, in terms of the manoeuvering and positioning of the parties ahead of the general election.

The leaders' speeches underline the shared interests of each leader-ship and the news broadcasters. For the broadcasters, the leaders' speeches represent easily reportable, newsworthy information about an event whose significance is already manifest and does not have to be explained too much to the audience. All they need to do is reflect it. The party elites derive a series of benefits from the news coverage of speeches. Speeches, particularly those made by the easily recognizable party leaders, gain more attention and benefit from the news broad-casters' 'reactive' approach, with the main announcements more or less guaranteed prominent coverage. The leaders' speeches also represent a controllable information channel, one which other dissenting actors cannot affect. However as the following chapter shows, the leaders' speeches are an exception. The conference managers cannot ensure that other stage-managed events gain similar amounts of coverage or ensure that other external events will not drive the news agenda, or prevent, through party management, dissent becoming public.

6

Off Message: the Limits of Agenda Management

Despite the months of planning, there is no guarantee that things will turn out according to plan. The conference managers cannot prevent conflict occurring between different sections of the party, silence all opposition to the leadership or prevent a defeat of a leadership endorsed motion in a ballot. In addition unexpected events occur: these may be surprise findings from opinion polls[1] commissioned by the news media; photo-opportunities may backfire; leadership actors make gaffes; and newsworthy issues originate outside conference such as an MP defecting. Journalists find all these events especially newsworthy, as chapter 3 has shown, and if left unchecked by conference managers they can dominate the conference news agenda. The management teams in response have developed reactive communication strategies, designed to minimize the publicity given to these situations and to limit any damage they may cause the party in the short term and in the long-term to remove the causes. However, the effectiveness of the strategies depends on the extent to which management efforts are plagued by personal animosity between leadership actors and poor co-ordination. This chapter examines the publicity problems that arise for the leadership during conference and how they respond.

Leadership opponents

Each leadership faces strong opposition on certain policy areas. Its opponents range from delegates, mandated to oppose particular policy motions, members of formal groups or affiliated organizations (in Labour ranks the unions), disaffected former ministers, or members of a more tightly-bound faction, who share an ideological outlook. These 'claim-makers' (Spector and Kitsuse, 1987) tend to be interested not only in providing journalists with an alternative point of view to that being disseminated by the leadership but also in promoting their own agenda. In comparison to the leadership they are not always well organized, do not necessarily have the resources to employ a back region team of communication specialists and are unable to provide the same level of information subsidy. However, they are nevertheless determined that their views on policy and other matters are widely reported.

One particularly vocal source of criticism are party 'old stars'. Their backgrounds as former members of the leadership provide these actors with legitimacy in the eyes of the journalists and a quasi-elite status. In the Liberal Democrats the 'old stars' are variously: the founders of the former SDP, Lord Jenkins, Lord Rodgers and Baroness Williams; as well as Sir David Steel, the former party leader; and now Paddy Ashdown and other actors such as Lord Russell and Ludovic Kennedy. In the Labour party the grouping is larger, consisting again of 'old stars': Tony Benn MP, Lord Hattersley, Neil Kinnock (former leader), Gerald Kaufman, Lord Shore, and Baroness Castle. Within the Conservative party the prominent 'old stars' are: Lady Thatcher, Edward Heath and now John Major in their capacity as former party leaders; and Lord Howe, Lord Lawson, Michael Heseltine, John Redwood and Norman Lamont, all former recent members of the party's leadership.

Opposition also comes from recognizable malcontent MPs who are leadership opponents. At the Labour conferences in the 1990s there were numerous recognizable back-benchers on the left who were particularly critical of Blair, such as, Dennis Skinner, Peter Hain, Ken Livingstone, and Diane Abbott. Some of these MPs were part of a wider faction usually on the left of the party such as the Campaign Group. In the Conservative party during the same period there were also a vocal group of Eurosceptic MPs vociferous in their opposition to the Maastricht treaty and to the party's policy on the European single currency. Some of these MPs were part of a wider faction including delegates and organized activists. In the Conservative party of the 1990s there were numerous groups linked to the issue of European integration such as 'No Turning Back Group', or the European Foundation (see Sowemimo, 1996).

Such groupings and actors make use of whatever resources they do have and exploit the opportunities that arise to attract journalists' attention. At each conference there are a plethora of additional forums for dissenting voices – beyond the control of conference managers. These include television and radio studios and particularly the fringe. The fringe – a series of meetings organized by an array of different groups on numerous issues – takes place throughout the week while the main conference is not in session. The fringe has grown (Harris and

Lock, 1995; Norton, 1996) and 'is now a prominent feature of every conference'.[2] Recent research has shown that there has been a dramatic increase in the number of fringe meetings. There were 290 meetings held at Labour's conference in 1995 compared to 166 held in 1986. Similarly the Conservatives' conference had 173 fringe meetings in 1995 compared to 100 in 1986.[3]

The broadcasters' coverage of the fringe provides a platform for dissenting claim-makers to gain wider exposure for their views. The fringe in this sense has become an integral part of these actors' public relations strategies, allowing them access to a wider audience than those immediately in the meeting. Although factions do not necessarily command the same resources or have the same contacts as the leaderships, they realize that broadcast journalists often require reactions broadly for and against the issues under debate and trail planned meetings to journalists, in the hope that they will attend and use the footage as an expression of differences of opinion within the party. In certain situations these actors also time their meetings for the same day as a motion they are opposing is being debated in the main hall. By doing this they increase the chances that their meeting may be covered. As a journalist noted: 'If your line of attack is the economy or it's Europe you make sure you speak on the day the Tory party is debating the economy or Europe, because otherwise the news editor is not going to construct a whole news package just around your speech unless it is extraordinary.'[4]

One of the most successful users of the fringe for publicity purposes have been disgruntled 'old stars'. These actors use their public recognizability and status and contacts amongst journalists to gain attention for their views. The fringe became a key platform for disaffected former Conservative ministers during the 1990s.[5] Certain actors such as Norman Lamont, John Redwood and Norman Tebbit used the fringe to gain publicity. A correspondent noted of one: 'Redwood in particular is very keen to be on the media . . . He is very media friendly, he is always available for a quote. He knows how it works, he sends faxes round of his speeches.'[6] In both 1993 and 1994 Norman Lamont was able to mount a highly successful public relations operation, getting his views and criticisms across on the news bulletins. His success was due in part to the 'capital' he possessed as a former Chancellor, in particular his public recognizability and the fact that his views were seen as representative of a party-wide divergence of opinion on Europe. But he built upon this advantage by internalizing the needs of the news broadcasters. His proactive strategy had two identifiable parts. The first concerned the content of the speech. Both speeches were overtly critical of the party leadership and its policies: the first speech of government policy on the economy, and second of the then Prime Minister and government policy on Europe. One correspondent remarked that he was 'thrilled to have a politician saying something and not couching it in ministerial terms . . . [and added] we are just glad for the story'.[7] In addition to being critical, Lamont delivered his speeches on the same day as leadership actors made their speeches on the same issues, further increasing the likelihood of his speech being included in any news report. Lamont further trailed the content of his evening speech on 11 October 1994 at a press conference, ensuring those bulletins with earlier deadlines widening its exposure. While these factors do not necessarily determine whether claim-makers receive coverage, adopting the logic of news values and timing as a strategy enhances the chance of an actor's views being carried in a report.

In the Labour party the leadership also faces more powerful opponents in the shape of some of the large unions. Union leaders have the resources to be able to employ spin doctors of their own. The large unions did not suffer from the same resource problem as other opponents of Labour's elite and maintained a position of power at conference. While the block vote had been reduced between 1993 and 1996, they still commanded 50 per cent of the votes at conference. The unions are particularly eager to get their interpretation of events across to journalists, aware that the Labour leadership has improved its media operation. Over recent conferences the unions have become more sensitized to the need to run a similar operation. Each of the union leaders present at conference has their own press officers and Jones suggests: 'like the party, they too had developed close links with many journalists. If the unions considered their interests were at stake then obviously they would do all they could to take advantage of the access and opportunities which the news media afforded them.'[8] Some of the unions (particularly the Transport and General Workers, the General and Municipal Boilermakers and UNISON) regularly took advantage of the 'access and opportunities which the news media afforded them' when opposing the party's leadership on a series of issues.

Killing off dissent

What ensues therefore for the duration of each conference is competition to set the news agenda on a series of issues, between the leadership and an assortment of opponents. This intra-party competition varies in intensity according to the issue. Some of the most intense competition occurred between the Labour leadership and the largest unions. There was an intense struggle between these actors to set the news agenda on the One Member, One Vote reforms proposed by the leadership at the 1993 conference, over the level of the minimum wage in 1996 and over party policy on earnings linked state pensions at the 2000 conference. At the Conservative conference there was an on-going visible struggle to set the news media agenda on Europe. Each communication team in response to the competition employs a series of reactive communication strategies combined with party management tactics to try and prevent the conference news agenda being hijacked by their opponents. These strategies have been developed as an essential part of party campaigning activity throughout the year (Jones, 1995, 1999) and are enacted during the follow-up gathering.

Rebuttal is the most common reactive strategy used. It entails a systematic countering of opinions initiated outside the party elite with the aim of 'killing them off' before they develop into a full news story. As a journalist noted: 'Spinning is not just about placing stories, it is about killing them too, either by straight denial or sly innuendo.'[9] This involves targeting opinion formers and the news community with the counter-points to prove that there is no truth in that particular interpretation of events. It is frequently combined with complaining to, and the bullying of, particular journalists. Each of the parties has established a rebuttal unit, with one or more spin doctors responsible for rebutting.[10]

While interacting with journalists the spin doctors are constantly checking to see what interpretation of events is emerging within the news community and whether there is a divergence from the party elite's perspective. When there is a divergence between the leadership's line and the perspective emerging in the news community, then appropriate action can be taken. The message has to be kept on course; the higher the stakes, and the more the message that has been delivered looks like going off course, the stronger the measures needed. Measures principally include complaining and bullying. Complaints are delivered directly to a particular journalist in the form of a rebuke but can also be intimidatory and personal.[11] Journalist Paul Routledge (1995) calls one method of intimidation used the 'shame game'. It involves the spin doctor playing on the insecurities of a journalist, shaming the journalist whose interpretation of events is considered 'out on a limb' into taking the perspective that has been adopted by his colleagues in the news community. If complaining or intimidation is unsuccessful, then 'an approach might be made direct to the relevant programme editor'.[12] If this in turn is unsuccessful, then the spin doctors may appeal to a more senior member of broadcast management. Appealing over the heads of the journalists requires the necessary seniority and authority.[13]

Sometimes, in addition, the spin doctors need to 'up the ante' through mobilizing authoritative leadership sources to attack or condemn their opponents. The effective mobilization of comment is done in off-the-record briefings and through interviews. The off-the-record mobilization generally tends to be pernicious in character, involving a repudiation of the source of the stories. The aim of such a technique is to undermine the credibility of an opponent and condemn his views as unrepresentative of general feeling within the party. Such off-the-record comments may be made by members of the leadership themselves, but are usually made by senior spin doctors on their behalf. However, such strategies by themselves are sometimes not enough – a public attack by leadership actors may also be called for to reinforce the off the record comments.

A public mobilization of comment may also on occasions be necessary in support or denial of a news story. A potentially negative event involving a senior party member often calls for the support of the rest of the leadership or a disagreeable activity might require their collective condemnation, but either way the comments are an important part of reducing the salience of a potentially negative interpretation of events developing amongst the news community.

Tales of the unexpected

Reactive strategies are also used to try and kill off negative publicity generated by certain unexpected occurrences and prevent them 'snowballing' into something that can seriously undermine the planned promotion of policy. Throughout each conference the spin doctors engage in a certain amount of second-guessing. One source suggested that 'you have to have in the back of your mind constantly, what is the potential problem? How can we pull it round [and] get the right people in the right positions to control the story?'[14] All the communication operations constantly monitor news reports each day of the conference to spot potential problems. Rather like 'watching a radar screen for dangerous blips',[15] monitoring enables them to react to the interpretations given to events by various news reports and errant comments. As one senior Liberal Democrat source suggested: 'Somebody can be saying something that can dominate the whole day's coverage and becomes the story, so we have to make sure that's monitored all the time.'[16] The spin doctors need to be in a position to react immediately to potentially negative coverage. In the long term the conference managers seek both to remove the sources of negative publicity and improve their response times.

Mishaps and gaffes

While the activity of leading party actors on the main stage is increasingly choreographed, it does not always go according to plan. When mishaps occur their visual attractiveness is particularly appealing to broadcasters. Paradoxically the more potential mishaps are ironed out in the planning stages, the more newsworthy they become when they do occur. The Conservative Party Chairman's accidental walk off the main platform prior to his formal introduction to the conference in 1994 was one such occasion. A senior Conservative party source remarked:

> I don't know if you saw that little snip last year where the Chairman says I welcome to the platform the Party Chairman, "Oh where has he gone". He's gone because the PM said to him "Jeremy I want to see you now". Jeremy Hanley had been told to stay put, but the tension was building and the adrenaline was pumping and the PM says "Get up Jeremy". Bill, who's the Conference Chairman, can't see this . . . The media have run that story of the missing Chairman time after time after time. They ran it the whole of the Tuesday morning of conference. That was the only thing they referred to: it was very upsetting for the agriculture debate . . . It happened to Norman Fowler [former Party Chairman] the year before [1993] as well.[17]

Reflecting on the mistake, the same source said that he hoped to introduce measures to avoid such occurrences in the future:

> I have got to break the courtesy [and] get the Conference Chairman to welcome the Party Chairman as well. So then if the Prime Minister or anybody else comes on stage we can welcome them too. You only learn these things, it's not something you think of until it actually happens. But I believe that sort of detail is quite important . . . So you have to try to cover yourself. It probably sounds worse than it is, but you always need to get it right.[18]

However attempts by conference managers to prevent mishaps and gaffes being caught on camera may lead in certain situations to unforeseen problems. For instance, at the 1994 Conservative conference, the same Party Chairman implemented a plan to control the movement of ENG camera crews and photographers in front of the main stage in an effort to try and prevent the roving eye of the cameras capturing leadership actors off guard or in an unflattering light. While the crews were willing to co-operate with some restrictions on their movement they resented the Party Chairman's new stricter controls. The outcome was a boycott of subsequent arranged photo-opportunities and the eventual climb-down of the Party Chairman.

The photographers insisted their job was being made impossible, and downed cameras. A tense stand-off developed during the day, with prolonged negotiation between the press and Conservative Central Office yielding little result . . . The first photo-call to suffer was that of Jeremy Hanley the Tory Chairman, who toured the new platform pursued by a gaggle of reporters and a couple of television crews. A football match kicked off by Dame Angela Rumbold, the party's Vice Chairman, was the next casualty – her outdoor event falling victim to the negotiations. Last night it was unclear who would crack first – the Conservative politicians, who want coverage, or the media who need the pictures.[19]

At the 2000 Labour conference Tony Blair made his speech in a blue shirt rather than the usual white shirt, as the image managers thought the lighting had made the white look grey on television. However, while the usual white shirt would have hidden his sweat, in the heat of the auditorium Blair in the blue shirt looked as if someone had thrown water over him. The Prime Minister's sweat soaked shirt received a mention in the conference reports. Party spin doctors were nervous that he would be portrayed as sweating under the pressure of the previous week's petrol blockade. Their immediate response was to put out the line that 'it proves he's a real man'.[20]

While mishaps undermine conference choreography, more serious are gaffes that threaten to damage the promotion of party policy. These often require an immediate reaction. For example, the Labour leadership was forced to act quickly when shadow cabinet member Baroness Turner of Camden openly supported Ian Greer Associates, the lobby firm at the centre of the 'cash for questions' scandal in an interview with *Channel Four News* at the 1996 conference. The later evening bulletins all led with the story. To prevent the story snowballing and overshadowing the last day of conference, comment was publicly mobilized and Blair himself denounced what she had said and she was sacked. The next day the story rolled on but was overshadowed by the deputy leader's speech to conference.

At the 2000 Conservative conference the Shadow Home Secretary Ann Widdecombe in her speech put forward a new policy initiative for a minimum fixed penalty fine for the possession of illegal drugs and an automatic criminal record: 'If someone possesses drugs, the minimum for a first offence will be a fixed penalty of £100.' The announcement was heavily trailed the evening before and was mentioned on all late evening bulletins. However, the idea of replacing cautions with fines was attacked by the Police Federation, the Police Superintendents' Association and various anti-drugs groups as inherently bureaucratic and unworkable. It was also criticized by members of the shadow cabinet, by the Conservative supporting press and by Lord Cranborne who appeared in all reports suggesting cannabis should be decriminalized. All the bulletins led with the story. The leadership attempted to play down the criticism. Hague did an interview on *Channel Four News* where he suggested that the party would talk to police before any change in the law. The Party Chairman and Shadow Home Secretary also engaged in a series of interviews to play down the criticisms. The story rolled on overshadowing the rest of the conference and led eventually to the abandonment of the policy.

A more detailed example from the Liberal Democrat conference serves to illustrate both the party response and the response of the news broadcasters to a gaffe by a party spokesperson. The incident arose at the 1996 conference and concerned an announcement by the health spokesperson, Simon Hughes. In a speech he suggested that certain existing tax loopholes would be closed to provide extra revenue for the NHS. The extract from the speech was as follows.

> Some of the cats – of all sizes – in the City and elsewhere currently receive huge sums from tax-dodging employers who should know better – millions of pounds have been paid in gold bars, life policies and other valuables to avoid paying tax to the Exchequer. Responsible firms shouldn't spend their time thinking up tax wheezes and we wouldn't let them – we'd close this illogical loophole for good.

However, one journalist rang the Inland Revenue that same afternoon to enquire about such exemptions. A source noted:

> John Sergeant [then BBC Chief Political Correspondent] rang the Inland Revenue and said "Is this the case?" And they said "Oh no we have been taxing them for a while". So it looked as if Hughes had dropped a huge clanger by trying to tax something already taxed.[21]

News of the fact that these items were already taxed spread through the news community at the conference. The same source noted: 'So this is where the bush telegraph works . . . somebody said "Oh down in the press room they have all been talking about this gold bars thing" . . . '[22] The Liberal Democrat spin doctors engaged in an immediate rebuttal operation led by their Head of Communications and the Treasury spokesperson's spin doctor. From observation in the press room at the time, they held an impromptu press briefing for all the journalists, fully explaining the party's policy and arguing that this was an example, not a proposal. This stance was backed up with press releases from a tax expert indicating that there were other loopholes that could be closed. The same source, who also attended the briefing, noted:

> I went down to see what was going on and I found Jane Bonham-Carter

[then head of communications] with Malcolm Bruce's spin doctor, who used to work in the City himself. And they had already produced an opinion from a tax expert saying you could raise three hundred million pounds. And they said: "No, what Simon meant was this is what used to happen, but there are lots of other examples" . . . [23]

The rebuttal exercise was combined with a further mobilization of comment. Simon Hughes did a series of interviews for the evening news bulletins where he reiterated the same line. All reports quoted the same extract from the speech juxtaposed with information challenging it. The BBC *Six O'clock News* commented:

But tax experts were puzzled. A leading local accountant explained that a good part of this loophole had already been closed: "Not fine wine and gold bullion bars because those have already been closed down, but there are still ways that national insurance isn't being paid on bonus payments in kind. Those ways are being challenged by the authorities but without a more fundamental change in the rules the task is going to be much more difficult" . . .

The BBC *Nine O'clock News*, before quoting the same source, noted:

The party estimate that 350 million pounds would be saved, but tax experts were puzzled. A leading local tax consultant pointed out that employers couldn't avoid tax by offering gold or vintage wine. The problem had already been tackled by the government.

Channel Four News, News at Ten and *Newsnight* juxtaposed the passage with a reference to government sources claiming that the loopholes had already been closed. The *Six O'clock* and *Nine O'clock News* and *News at Ten* further quoted Hughes explaining the passage.

The rebuttal and mobilization of comment prevented the incident from turning into a full-blown gaffe. None of the reports contextualized the passage as a gaffe. One journalist suggested a reason for this:

Because the speech was ambiguous you had to give them the benefit of the doubt. But they only just got away with it. I still don't know whether it was just sloppily written or they really had just cocked it up and then had to retreat, but they handled it quite well actually. It was quite well spun by them, because they put the fire out quickly once they realized what was going on. They marshalled their forces, got some bits of paper, came down, and that was a partial success from their point of view.[24]

Further, the concluding remarks of the reports left the issue open and did not draw any strong conclusions; this is best summarized in the source's report for *News at Ten*: 'But the Liberal Democrats have had to work hard today to defend their claim to have policies which are clear, costed and coherent.' This example shows that rebuttal prevented the full development of an alternative perspective on the issue through effectively muddying the interpretative waters and mobilizing comment from a tax expert and Hughes himself.

External events

The spin doctors are aware that certain newsworthy events that occur outside the conference environment, over which they have no control, may effectively set the day's news agenda. These situations lead to a temporary divergence between the aims of the broadcasters and the spin doctors, with the journalists eagerly pursuing the agenda and the spin doctors trying to kill it off. It is impossible for the spin doctors to predict what external events will occur or their 'size' and impact upon the planned conference agenda. There were numerous periods during the study when the broadcasters' agenda shifted away from planned events at conference to ones that had occurred externally.

At the Conservative conference it occurred every year. As one Conservative source suggested:

> You always have your meltdown on the Sunday and this has happened so often that I think it's a sort of fixture of the party conference as regular as the Mayor's address at the start on the Tuesday morning. What tends to happen is that one of the Sunday papers or more will have a story which completely comes out of left field as the Americans would say, which you have no warning of, which is absolutely devastating in its impact and which is in serious danger of knocking you for six.[25]

The news agenda on the opening of each of these conferences was dominated by a series of events: in 1993 the publishing of leaked extracts from Lady Thatcher's memoirs in the *Daily Mirror*; in 1994 Mark Thatcher's involvement in the Saudi Al Yamamah arms deal; in 1995 the defection of MP Alan Howarth to the Labour party; and in 1996 the defection of Lord McAlpine, former Conservative party treasurer, to the Referendum party. A Conservative spin doctor outlined the reactive strategy followed in 1995 after the defection of Conservative MP Alan Howarth:

> The first any of us heard about it was when one Sunday journalist rang me up on Sunday evening and said "Have you heard about Alan Howarth MP for Stratford upon Avon" and I have to say I went through in my mind, dead, in bed with a woman, in bed with a man, in bed with a camel

and the last thing that occurred to me was that he had defected to the Labour party – no warning at all. That was clearly a big story, that wasn't a case where you could sort of try a damage limitation exercise. We got the local association's chairman to say basically that this man is a git, we had an exercise of statements from various people, we did try what turned out to be quite a successful fire-break operation in that our concern had been that the story could run for two days rather than just the one and that when the Prime Minister arrived at Blackpool on the Monday afternoon the only questions he would be asked would be about Alan Howarth and that would run the story on into the Tuesday. So a decision was taken by the Party Chairman that we would get the Prime Minister to respond on the Sunday evening, so he came back from Huntingdon deliberately. Instead of going straight into Downing Street he lingered and answered some questions predictably enough about Alan Howarth so all the reaction was done on the Sunday. We knew the Monday papers were lost because they were going to follow up on that, but it did mean that by the Tuesday morning we were beginning to slightly regain the full control of the agenda. But that sort of reactivity really at the beginning of the week is often all that you can do.[26]

The spin doctors also try to 'calculate in advance what may be the worst-case scenario'[27] if the broadcasters' coverage is dominated by an external event. They will then launch a pre-emptive strike to prevent the event overshadowing conference news. A significant example of this kind of activity occurred at the 1995 Labour conference. The leader's speech coincided with the verdict of the O. J. Simpson trial, seen by most journalists as a momentous news event. The leader's principal spin doctor Alastair Campbell, fearing that pragmatic values would take precedence, launched a pre-emptive strike to try and persuade the broadcasters to lead with the Blair speech rather than the verdict of the O. J. Simpson trial. Campbell sought assurances from both the heads of BBC and ITN that Blair's speech would not be displaced from its lead position on their bulletins. One political editor noted that Campbell was 'imploring the broadcasters not to lead their news programmes with the O. J. Simpson verdict'.[28] Another journalist suggested that Campbell had 'urged television news organizations not to swamp the Labour leader's speech . . . with coverage of the trial verdict'.[29] As part of his attempt to persuade the broadcasters Campbell appealed to the then Director General of the BBC, John Birt, and the head of ITN Channel three news, Nigel Dacre. He sent the following fax around midday on the day of the leader's speech.

I write concerning your coverage of Tony Blair's speech on your evening bulletin today. Some of the journalists have suggested to us that we are unlikely to get as much coverage for the leader's speech as in previous years because of the O. J. Simpson trial verdict at 6 P.M. It has even been suggested that there is little chance of Mr Blair's speech leading your bulletins. Whilst of course news judgements must be made in the light of other stories on any particular day, and whilst I fully understand there is much interest in the verdict, I would implore you not to lose sight of the news value and of the importance to the country of Mr Blair's speech. I hope you will communicate our concerns.[30]

While ITN ignored the fax, Tony Hall, then Managing Director of BBC News and Current Affairs, replied immediately, saying that 'the corporation was capable of making its own decisions'.[31] The response of the BBC and ITN was different. Although claiming to be 'capable of making its own decisions', both the BBC's bulletins led with Blair's speech, whereas both of ITN's bulletins led with the O. J. verdict.

Peter Bell, head of the BBC TV news programmes, was quoted as saying in the BBC's defence: 'The order of the Nine O'clock News was determined by the editor Malcolm Balen. His decision was supported by the editorial management, including me. At the time the decision was made the programme editor did not even know Mr Blair's press officer had contacted the BBC.'[32] As to charges that the BBC had 'bowed to Labour pressure' or 'caved in to Labour party complaints' a further BBC spokesman was quoted as saying 'The Nine O'clock News would always have led on Blair. We are quite happy we got it right'.[33] This example shows that such attempts at editorial interference have mixed results. This case also highlights the broadcasters' discretionary power to decide the running order of their bulletins. If the BBC is to be believed, the decision was made on sacerdotal grounds, not because of pressure. Although in terms of the conferences such attempts at editorial inter-ference were far from frequent, the example shows the response of the party elites where news values threatened the taken-for-granted assumptions on the prominence of the leader's speech.

Long-term responses to news management problems

While gaffes and external events require immediate remedies, certain problems are ironed out by party managers as part of the on-going plan-ning process. This can be seen in the way in which the Conservative managers responded to the ineffectiveness of the press conference traditionally held on the day before the conference started. The press conference is designed to promote forthcoming issues and to fill a news vacuum ahead of conference. A party source noted: 'The media's attention has switched to the Conservative party with effect from about midday on Saturday. The Saturday papers try to do a preview of the Tory conference but we don't actually start until the Tuesday morning, and we don't have an exciting speech until noon on Tuesday so you have this terrible vacuum.'[34] However, it failed in that task: the journalists were more interested in pursuing the issues raised by external events such as the Al Yamamah arms deal and the defection of an MP or the former party treasurer. The comments made by those holding the press conference in response to journalists' questions tended to dominate subsequent news reports and keep the stories going. The frustration of the party leadership is palpable in the responses of these three sources.

> The big press conference is a game. It is when the press will try to de-stabilize the conference and blow the Chairman off course. They hunt in packs! And it was Mark Thatcher who was the theme for that Monday, which was a story that died a death within two days, but that was their attempt to try and destabilize it, this year [1995] it was Alan Howarth. You know that is part of the game.[35]

Another source reinforced the same point about the 1994 press conference:

> It was just the four of us. The Party Chairman, the Chairman of the National Union, the President and myself and they're throwing questions at us. Basically they are usually about the agenda and the way things are going to pan out over the next four days etc., perhaps questions about how many people are coming, whether we are down or up, and we are ready for that. Of course the day before on the Sunday something blew about Mark Thatcher and every single question at that press conference was about Mark Thatcher. The Party Chairman said: "Right we've had it, we've had six questions on Mark Thatcher, we are not taking any more, something different" . . . "Adam Boulton Sky, Mark Thatcher etc., etc. Yeah but we want to know". A total waste of time as far as we were concerned and you cannot break them out of it.[36]

Another source suggested:

> Last year [1994] was the last year that we had the Monday afternoon press conference . . . Basically what happens is that an awful lot of fairly obnox-ious journalists come along and scream insults at the Party Chairman until he says something slightly awkward. Last year with Jeremy Hanley they came along and they screamed at him for three-quarters of an hour about Mark Thatcher and he said something slightly unfortunate and then bingo the Mark Thatcher story was running into Tuesday's papers.[37]

It was in the light of this experience that the same source argued that the party leadership had decided to abandon this press conference as the solution to the perceived problem:

> For a long time it had been thought the way to answer this media vacuum problem on the Monday is you put the Party Chairman and Basil Feldman to answer to a press conference; this was not a clever idea . . . Press conferences these days are a singularly ineffective method of getting across your message, they are the 1990s equivalent of bear baiting . . . So even if we had not known that we had Alan Howarth coming, we had decided to scrap that Monday afternoon press conference.[38]

When asked about the scrapping of the press conference, a former Party Chairman blamed the journalists:

> I didn't know that they got rid of it, I didn't know that this year. I just experienced twenty-four questions out of the twenty-five on the subject of Mark Thatcher. I think [they] brought that upon themselves. But I hadn't decided that press conference would go. Obviously Brian Mawhinney did, having decided with Hugh Colver, that instead of being on the defensive on a matter of the press's choice, we wanted to promote the conference.[39]

Egos and personal animosity

The leadership's ability to promote the planned agenda may be undermined by internal disputes between leadership actors and by poor co-ordination. Both problems were in evidence at the Conservative conference.[40] There was particularly noticeable conflict between Eurosceptics and Europhiles in the Conservative government as well as other personal rivalries, the most visible of which was the leadership challenge mounted by John Redwood in 1995. These divisions could not be disguised from journalists and led to ministers briefing journalists against each other or making direct attacks on aspects of the leadership's official policy. The divisions did not disappear at conference time and acted as a 'brake' on successful policy promotion. In response the then Party Chairman, Brian Mawhinney, tried at the 1995 and 1996 conferences, to quell disputes for the conference period and get ministers to sing from the same hymn sheet. But the response of certain ministers at being told – as they saw it – what to do was hostile; they perceived the Chairman's initiatives as an incursion. This was the case at the 1996 Conservative conference, a supposed rallying conference before the general election. Here the reaction of ministers was encapsulated by the then Chancellor's claimed remark to the Party Chairman: 'Tell your kids to get their scooters off my lawn', an impression reinforced in complaints by several ministers (Bottomley, Newton, Shephard and Hogg) that party spin doctors were briefing against them at conference.[41]

However, management tactics initiated by the Party Chairman could not prevent ministers briefing against each other during conference. As one journalist suggested: 'You can't underestimate the fair amount of incorrigible gossips around who sometimes can't stop themselves from rubbishing their opponents in the same party.'[42] Another journalist confirmed the point:

> You would've thought the rational way to go about being a party . . . is that everybody sticks to the party line and doesn't say anything to the contrary because then the media will have nothing to report. But it just amazes me that there are always people who will talk to the media and brief against their colleagues.[43]

The party managers could not prevent journalists gaining access to senior party members. Journalists at the BBC and ITN indicated in interviews that conferences provide unrivalled opportunities for reaching party actors compared to other times of the year, even though they admitted that things had been toughened-up. A senior *Channel Four News* source noted: 'It is a period of great access . . . you have access to politicians then and there which you really never get at any other time.'[44] Similarly a senior BBC source suggested that: 'You have much more access across a wider range of contacts within the party at conferences than you have any other time of the year. You . . . do inevitably have more access to the leadership and the leading lights in all the parties, you have more access to MPs.'[45] At the Conservative conferences such access amplified divisions.

Divisions are also compounded by poor co-ordination between leadership actors. Difficulties in centrally co-ordinating the dissemination of information led to various members of the leadership promoting their own particular policy areas. A Conservative admitted at the 1995 conference:

> There are all sorts of people who are not entirely under Central Office's control, who are going around briefing sometimes with authorization sometimes without. All the ministers' special advisers for example are up there and they may be pursuing their own strategy in terms of who they want to leak their stories to.[46]

The same source gave one example from the 1995 conference:

> Last weekend our intention had been that we were going to trail with some papers the 'Enterprise Centre of Europe' phrase from the Prime

Minister's speech as the big idea, now we subsequently learnt that the Foreign Secretary's team had briefed I think the *Sunday Telegraph* that he was going to be announcing in his speech on Tuesday his idea of the North Atlantic Free Trade Area. And we were a bit irritated about that because he did that without clearance.[47]

The same Conservative source noted that this was in part due to being in government rather than opposition.

When you are in government it's actually much more difficult to exercise a single ruthless centralized control over what everybody does than it is when you are in opposition. Blair is able to rule his shadow cabinet with a rod of iron and all the rest of it, not least because his shadow cabinet do not all have in addition to various political advisers a huge staff of departmental press officers working for them.[48]

In comparison the Labour leadership has been more disciplined in both opposition and government. The Labour party elite 'put a high premium on collective responsibility'[49] and while in opposition 'shades of opinion within the shadow cabinet and beyond are rarely expressed for fear of causing trouble'.[50] However, this not to say that there were not similar lapses of orchestration in their media operation. Labour's 1994 conference provides an example of such a lapse. One journalist present noted of that conference: 'I had found it difficult to work out which spin doctor was in charge.'[51] The lack of co-ordination surrounded the trailing and follow-up of Blair's first speech to conference. David Hill, Alastair Campbell and Peter Mandelson were all providing differing insights into the content of Blair's forthcoming speech, giving journalists a confusing picture of whose version was most reliable. The lack of co-ordination was underlined by a certain level of tension between the three actors on their positions and responsibility within Labour's new elite. Campbell, newly appointed to the position of Blair's press secretary, took to attacking Mandelson in his column in the *Today* newspaper, which he was still writing at the time.[52] 'Turf wars', in the form of personality conflicts and the jostle for position and power within the new Labour elite, and the inexperience of a new communications team, undermined the co-ordination and therefore the effectiveness of conference communication strategies. The Liberal Democrat communications team was not immune from similar co-ordination problems. Such conflicts and poor co-ordination undermined the leadership's ability to provide a clear message and steer journalistic attention on to the planned policy area.

Conclusion

There is little the conference managers can do to prevent critical claim-makers using the fringe and other forums as a platform to gain news coverage. In addition they cannot predict what events may occur at conferences and the impact they may have on the planned agenda. However what the party managers and spin doctors seek to do is control news coverage of these events. To achieve this they regularly implement reactive communication strategies. An idea imported from America and honed during general elections, such strategies are used to kill off or play down publicity originating from outside the leadership cadre. In highly conflict-laden debates where the leadership may be engaged in a struggle with their opponents to set the news agenda, the strategies are used to ensure that journalists give priority to their interpretations, and that their opponents' views do not dominate the news agenda or go unchallenged. In some situations the collective condemnation of an individual may be called for. Spin doctors and ministers, especially at Conservative conferences, found themselves having to denounce dissenting claim-makers and their perspectives, and keep journalists on message with threats if necessary. As this chapter also shows, reactive strategies try and minimize the attention journalists give to blunders and gaffes and external events. In these situations the spin doctors talk down the significance of the event.

Short-term responses are combined with longer-term attempts to remove the sources of such problems. As the Conservatives' conference showed, ineffective press conferences were axed and presentational arrangements rearranged. However, more serious problems could not so easily be removed. The co-ordination of the Conservatives' media operation left much to be desired but more important was the persistent infighting at the heart of the party which could not be remedied by communication strategies. Members of the leadership often had their own goals in terms of the ideas they wanted to put across, there was a fair amount of personal animosity between leadership actors and resistance to any attempts to get the leadership to sing from the same hymn sheet.

There is a limit to the extent to which each leadership can manage their conference agenda. Even using reactive strategies spin doctors ultimately cannot determine how much coverage an event receives, the nature of that coverage or the sources used; and attempts at editorial interference can be actively resisted, as the O. J. Simpson example demonstrates. As the following chapter shows, journalists frame conflictual debates involving the leadership and any gaffes and mishaps that occur in a largely negative light.

7

Manufacturing Debate

This chapter examines the contribution of both journalists and the spin doctors to coverage of conflict-laden debates. These debates are framed by broadcast journalists as a drama of diametrically opposed actors – those for, those against – irrespective of the distinct nature of the conferences. The packaging of debates differs from the packaging of the leader's speech in that journalists seek to capture party actors with differing opinions on a particular issue. Sometimes differences are already present in a timetabled debate and the journalists show this. However, not all the overtly conflictual debates have been formally timetabled; many have been prevented from being aired in the main hall by the tighter conference management. The journalists seek to circumvent this and (re)construct the debate for the viewer by juxtaposing differing opinions and reactions from protagonists in assorted conference locations. Whatever the scenario, and this chapter examines both, the broadcasters' reports further contextualize the conflict in the commentary – for instance, indicating whether the debate is a sign of wider division within the party on ideological or policy grounds or highlighting the ramifications of the divisions for the party and the leadership. The broadcasters often supplement the edited version of events with additional news items. These typically 'spin' the debate further, expanding upon the issues being debated, examining any 'informal agendas' that arise, such as the personal history of those involved, loyalty to the party leader, betrayal and other dramatic elements that are part of the debate. They also sometimes speculate about the outcome of such debates and what impact they would have on a party's electoral fortunes.

Unlike leaders' speeches, debates are more difficult to spin as events. The leadership does not benefit from the sacerdotal attitude of broadcasters; leadership actors are often not in control of developments and certainly are unable to prevent their opponents from contributing to reports. Indeed journalists have access to a vast array of relevant sources that are beyond the control of conference managers. Each leadership cannot afford to ignore the role the broadcasters play in framing these internal struggles. The party elites therefore respond – some in a more coherent manner than others – by using the communication strategies and management techniques detailed in chapter 6. The party elite has to make sure that their perspective is put across and to try and define the dominant line of interpretation within the debate. They also simultaneously have to attack their opponents and rebut their perspectives on events and even publicly repudiate them where necessary.

This chapter focuses on the following overtly conflictual debates. At the Liberal Democrats, the debates on 'Cannabis', 'the Minimum Wage', and 'the Monarchy' in 1994; at the Labour conference, the Clause Four debate in 1994; and at the Conservatives' conference, the debate between left and right of the party in 1993 and on Europe in 1994. The framing of these debates by the same six evening news bulletins that covered the leader's speech is examined, as well as the attempts by spin doctors and leadership actors to shape their coverage. The construction and representation of the debates by journalists, through the juxtaposing of perspectives surrounding those issues,[1] and the use of 'contextualizing remarks' is also investigated. The research also looks at the extent to which the bulletins 'go beyond' (Semetko *et al.*, 1991) the given agenda, extending coverage of the day's events and speculating about the likely outcome of a ballot through a series of pegged items, two-ways and interviews.

Defying Ashdown

This section examines news coverage of three debates on the first two days of the 1994 Liberal Democrat conference. The coverage on the first day in most of the bulletins focused on the debate and vote on an amendment to a policy motion on 'the use of drugs'. This amendment called for 'The decriminalization of the use and possession of cannabis in order that the police and Customs and Excise are able to target their resources on the vital battle against the use of hard drugs.'[2] The Liberal Democrat party leadership opposed the amendment, but it was carried. On the second day, coverage focused on debates around two policy motions. The first was on the employment policy paper and an amendment to that on a minimum wage, which again the party leadership opposed but lost. The second was a policy motion on the head of state, and contained an amendment which called for the 'abolition of the monarchy after the current Queen's reign'.[3] This policy amendment was defeated, in line with the leadership's wishes. These debates were fairly prominent in terms of the amount of coverage they received. On the opening day of conference seven out of ten news items focused on the drugs debate. On the second day all nine news items focused on the debates and votes surrounding the two policy motions.

News reports were not just confined to representing the cannabis debate, they also amplified the leadership's embarrassment at being defeated. This informal agenda was mainly (though not exclusively) represented within the contextual narrative of the report. On the first day of the conference the cannabis vote was one of several issues covered. Indeed, the reports from the conference on the *ITN 5.40* and the BBC *Six O'clock News* made no mention of the debate – in large part owing to the fact that the debate was still in progress when these bulletins went on air. The outcome of the debate was treated as a breaking news item by the *Six O'clock News*, who went live to their correspondent to get the result and reactions to it.

On the four other bulletins the debate was represented through the juxtaposition of party elite actors for, and delegates against. The reports used various actors who spoke either for or against the amendment. Two members of the party's leadership and two delegates were quoted a total of nine times across the bulletins. Those in favour were quoted four times and those against the amendment five times. *Channel Four News* included quotes from Beith (then Home Affairs spokesperson) and Hughes (then Environment Spokesperson), both opposed to the amendment. On the BBC *Nine O'clock News* Beith was juxtaposed with two delegates in favour and *News at Ten* also featured two delegates for the amendment. In addition both the *Nine O'clock News* and *News at Ten* also included a quote by Beith about the loss of the vote. *Newsnight* incorporated one quote from a delegate in favour of the amendment.

The contextualizing commentary in the four reports referred to the result in general terms as a 'snub' and an embarrassment for the party leadership. *Channel Four*'s report opened with the anchor suggesting that 'the party's leaders were embarrassed'. The report further suggested that 'his [Ashdown's] hopes of presenting the Liberal Democrats as the voice of moderation in a Labour coalition received a setback in the debate on drugs'. The *Nine O'clock News* anchor remarked that the 'vote went against strong opposition from the party's leadership . . . '. The report went on to suggest that 'against the wishes of the party leadership . . . there was a clear majority in favour of decriminalizing cannabis'. The correspondent went further: 'Mr Ashdown, obviously unhappy, didn't stay to hear the formal result . . . ' and concluded that 'tonight the party leadership are licking their wounds over the cannabis debate . . . it's just the kind of defeat Paddy

Ashdown could do without'. *News at Ten*'s contextualizing remarks were in a similar vein. The anchor suggested that 'Liberal Democrats defied and embarrassed their leaders today by voting for the de-criminalization of cannabis. Simon Hughes begged them to be reasonable, Alan Beith said they shouldn't do it, but they did.' The correspondent continued in a similar manner: 'MPs urged members to vote No, but the majority said yes, a snub to the leadership.' The correspondent concluded with a mention of the possibility of further defeat: 'the leadership faces further possible embarrassment here tomorrow with calls for the abolition of the monarchy.' In *Newsnight*'s report the correspondent emphasized the narrowness of the vote: 'In a piece of radicalism that will send the tabloid press into a frenzy and also embarrass the leadership, the conference narrowly voted in favour of a decriminalization of cannabis.' There were also three additional news items: a two-way on the *Six O'clock News* and two interviews – one on *Channel Four News* with the Home Secretary solicited his reaction to the vote; and the other was with Party President Charles Kennedy on *Newsnight*.

Failing to kill off cannabis

The Liberal Democrat leadership seems not to have been prepared for the outcome of the cannabis debate and there was little evidence of an organized public relations strategy, although the party elite did mount a limited reactive operation. The problem lay in part with the lack of planning for the debate and poor timetabling. A senior party source suggested they had little chance of dealing with the results of the balloted motions because of their position in the timetable. 'Last year [1994] . . . awkward votes were happening right in the middle of a news bulletin, who were going live to the correspondent who was saying this has happened. We had no chance to deal with that and that set the terms for all the coverage.'[4] In fact in the cannabis debate the leadership line was very slow in getting mobilized. The *Nine O'clock News* was the first target of the party elite, with Alan Beith establishing the leadership line that 'the overall motion was the one that mattered'. This was reiterated on *News at Ten*, and *Newsnight* made reference to the amendment being immediately disowned. But the party elite line had little impact and, as an interpretation, was not adopted in the contextualizing commentary. The reports treated the party elite's perspective as a reaction to events in the hall and not as the main interpretation of those events, which is what the party elite would have wanted to achieve.

The minimum wage and monarchy

The news items on Tuesday, 20 September were dominated by two further debates in the hall. In addition there was also a reference in all reports to the previous day's cannabis vote. The first debate was on a minimum wage and the second on the abolition of the monarchy. The *ITN 5.40* only covered the minimum wage debate owing to the late conclusion of the second debate. The party elite perspective was one of opposition to the amendments to both policy motions.

On all bulletins twenty-three sources were cited thirty-eight times. Four of those twenty-three were quoted endorsing the party elite line eight times, but a majority (twelve sources) were quoted sixteen times, arguing in favour of one or the other amendment. Four sources provided a reaction to events and three could not be placed either way. Of the thirty-eight quotes, the broadcasters took twenty from the conference proceedings and initiated a further eighteen themselves from elsewhere. All the responses by Ashdown were initiated by the correspondents door stepping him. The initiation of delegates' opinions by the correspondents was confined to reports on *Channel Four News* and *Newsnight*.

The debate again was conveyed through the juxtaposing of different perspectives on the two issues being debated. The *ITN 5.40* juxtaposed both sides of the minimum wage debate, quoting Baroness Williams and Alex Carlile MP. The *Six O'clock News* only quoted Williams for the first debate and two delegates from opposing sides for the monarchy debate. *Channel Four* again quoted Williams and a delegate in favour of a minimum wage and Alex Carlile against. In the second debate two delegates were quoted in favour and Archie Kirkwood (then Chief Whip) and one delegate against. The *Nine O'clock News* only quoted Baroness Williams in the first debate and a delegate in support in the second. *News at Ten* used actors from the second debate, quoting a delegate in favour and Kirkwood against. *Newsnight* focused on both debates: on the first debate quoting Williams for and Carlile against the motion, and in the monarchy debate including two delegates for and Kirkwood against.

The correspondents' contextualizing remarks were in general critical of the party elite. They reminded the viewers about the previous day's events, explained the current day's events and in the early evening bulletins speculated about the likely outcome of the monarchy debate. The commentary also assessed the reaction of the party elite. In addition a clear emerging informal agenda was conveyed on party management. What was particularly telling in all reports was the use of such descriptive words as 'embarrassment' (six times), 'defeat' (five) and 'snub', 'loss of authority' 'damaging reverse' (once each) in reference to Ashdown. The loss of the vote was presented as a defeat for him personally and the defeat of the second motion on the monarchy as a relief for him.

The defeat on the minimum wage was strongly linked by the early evening bulletins to the previous day's defeat on cannabis. The *ITN 5.40* in its introduction suggested that 'Ashdown has suffered a second embarrassing defeat'. The *Six O'clock News* said that Ashdown had again been 'defeated . . . it's a further embarrassment for him'. *Channel Four News* noted that the 'defeat followed last night's embarrassment'. While not mentioning the cannabis vote, the *Nine O'clock News* and *News at Ten* also referred to the previous loss of the vote as a defeat for the leadership. The *Nine O'clock News'* introduction suggested that the 'Liberal Democrat leadership had suffered its second conference defeat in two days' and the *News at Ten* introduction stated that 'Liberal Democrats went against their leader . . . again'.

The defeat of the motion calling for the abolition of the monarchy was also personalized. The *ITN 5.40* and the *Six O'clock News*, on air before the vote, speculated about the likely outcome in their introductions. The *ITN 5.40* said that 'a third potential defeat loomed . . . ' and the *Six O'clock News* that they were 'debating another topic that could end in embarrassment for Mr Ashdown'. The anchors on *Channel Four News* and the *Nine O'clock News* described the outcome in terms of relief for Ashdown; and *Newsnight* saw it as an annoyance.

The contextualizing remarks in the reports raised a further issue, namely competent conference management – that is Ashdown's and the spin doctors' ability to manage conference proceedings, and the party delegates. The *ITN 5.40* noted that the setback of the minimum wage and cannabis vote 'creates an image of a leader who has been thrown off course'. The *Six O'clock News* noted that 'Liberal Democrats are asking questions. Why did party managers fail to warn the leadership of the strength of delegates' opinions?' *Channel Four*'s report dwelt on the same theme, suggesting that 'MPs are worried that delegates are ignoring how their actions appear to the outside world.' It continued: 'Just as the media focus is turning on the Liberal Democrats as future possible power brokers, the party's grass roots might be embarking on a new unruly phase.' Further in the same report it suggested that the 'patience of peers and MPs was wearing thin; some worried about the divide that appears to be developing between MPs and the delegates, and the leader is reported to be feeling frustrated'. The *Nine O'clock News* suggested that 'old hands were still muttering that he [Ashdown] really must get a grip on the party machine', and continued: 'the leadership fear their loss of authority doesn't help the party'. *News at Ten* noted that the loss of both votes suggested a 'leadership out of touch with the party'. *Newsnight* noted that 'the leadership struggled to impose its will . . . there is almost a feeling that the parliamentary party were an irrelevant rump who certainly don't know best'. And it continued: 'some wonder whether that's a sign of Paddy Ashdown's liberalism or just a case of hellishly unprofessional party management.'

Only *Newsnight* and the *ITN 5.40* provided any additional news items – *Newsnight* in the form of two interviews, the first with a group of delegates and the second with Paddy Ashdown. *ITN 5.40* had a two-way with its correspondent, seeking an explanation of how the debate was going, and reviewing the conference proceedings of the week so far.

What no spin!

There is surprisingly little evidence of the party elite engaging in any communication strategy. One might have expected, with potential defeats looming, and on the strength of the previous day's coverage, that the party leadership would have attempted to manage news community expectations as part of a strategy aimed at minimizing the impact of a defeat. However this did not happen, neither was there any organized attempt to mobilize comment to explain away the defeats. The party elite line materialized via the correspondents door stepping Ashdown. In fact all six bulletins initiated reactions to the votes in the hall. All except *Channel Four* acquired a reaction from Ashdown. The *ITN 5.40* and the *Six O'clock News* carried his response to the vote in favour of a minimum wage; the *Nine O'clock News* and *News at Ten* his reaction to both the minimum wage and the monarchy vote; and *Newsnight* his reaction to the monarchy vote only. David Steel was quoted once supporting the leadership line by the main ITN bulletins and *Channel Four News*, and Charles Kennedy once supporting the line on the *Six O'clock News*.

In covering these three debates the broadcasters clearly demonstrated their discretion. They were able to represent the results of two of the debates as a personal defeat for the party leader and the third as only a minor relief. In the commentary they raised the issue of the failure of party management. The journalists were left almost unfettered to construct their interpretation of events. In this situation the journalists expressed a preference for the most newsworthy angle on the debates, that of the defeat for Paddy Ashdown, and his embarrassment. By the second day this interpretation had built up a head of steam with the vote on a minimum wage against the leadership's advice. While there were few additional news items, the journalists initiated many of the party elite's responses themselves and were not noticeably approached by the party spin doctors. The party leadership made no real attempt to engage an effective proactive or reactive media strategy. The outcome of these two days was that Paddy Ashdown installed in Cowley Street a Director of Strategy and Planning, charged with the overseeing of conference media management for the next two conferences.

An embarrassing start for New Labour

The debate to reaffirm the Labour party's commitment to Clause Four of the party's constitution occurred on the Thursday of the 1994 conference. The debate's significance lay in the fact that it occurred two days after Blair's speech in which he signalled that the old Clause Four was to be rewritten. The reason for a debate so soon after Blair's speech was more to do with the secrecy surrounding the announcement than with poor planning.[5] The vote narrowly went against the leadership, with the delegates voting to reaffirm the party's commitment to the old Clause Four.

In the light of the leader's speech on Tuesday, the news agenda was more than simply a debate on Clause Four. It was treated as a barometer indicating whether the party would accept the proposed reform and the New Labour project. Reporting of the debate itself was conveyed through juxtaposing the two differing perspectives: the official line in support of change and the oppositional one in favour of retaining the existing Clause Four. Across all bulletins sixteen sources were quoted a total of forty-five times. Of these, seven sources endorsed change and nine were against it. In terms of the number of times both were quoted it was fairly even, twenty-three to twenty-two respectively. Further, the broadcasters initiated the majority (nine) of the sixteen sources, only taking five from the debate itself and two from fringe meetings. The bulletins actively contributed towards the debate, quoting these sources eighteen times in addition to those taking part in the main debate in the hall. All the correspondents sought out Blair. The *Six O'clock News* initiated quotes from both an endorser and a detractor, *Channel Four News* from three endorsers, the *Nine O'clock News* two endorsers, *News at Ten* an endorser and a detractor, and *Newsnight* from three detractors and two endorsers. These additional sources were added to the juxtaposition of perspectives from the debate itself. The debate was presented in a time-linear fashion with the same five actors being juxtaposed in all the evening reports.

There was also some anticipation of events in the previous night's reports. *Channel Four News* in a two-way with its political editor discussed strategies that were being put in place by the NEC to avoid the possibility of defeat. The *Nine O'clock News* suggested that the composite motion 'awkwardly for the leadership calls for re-affirmation of Clause Four'. *News at Ten* in its report's concluding remarks noted the up-coming debate, as did *Newsnight*, which suggested that 'there could be some embarrassing headlines after tomorrow if Composite fifty seven is voted through in the morning.'

Damage limitation

The party managers and spin doctors engaged in proactive and reactive communication strategies in response to the impending result of a ballot on the motion reconfirming the old Clause Four of the party's constitution. The main team of spin doctors were Blair's press officer Alastair Campbell, David Hill, Director of Communications, Peter Mandelson, Blair's confidant, and a team of junior press and broadcasting officers, amongst whom the most notable were Tim Allan and Gordon Brown's press spokesman Charlie Whelan. The proactive strategy was aimed at managing news community expectations in three ways prior to the vote taking place. First, the leadership indicated that they expected to lose. Second, although they would lose, they expected the result to be close. A BBC correspondent suggested that 'reporters were briefed by the party's publicity staff. Their judgement was that it would be close.'[6] Calling spinning 'sophisticated playing', an ITN correspondent confirmed the same point: 'they knew the vote was going to be close.'[7] Third, the spin suggested that the 'composite' (motion for debate) supported the aims of Clause Four, not the existing wording. The same ITN correspondent suggested:

> The spin was based on the wording of the resolution, that it reaffirmed support for the aims of Clause Four, not the wording. In other words changing Clause Four was compatible with that resolution . . . So there was some pre-emptive spinning that the two were not inconsistent, which is a little bit thin, but they got away with it.[8]

The proactive strategy was followed up by an attempt to play down the result of the ballot. The same BBC correspondent noted: 'there was a pretty heavy attempt by Labour's spin doctors to play down the significance of the defeat . . . the party's spin doctors' spin was that the result was not important. It was what was known as a "snow job" – blotting out any other theories.'[9] This playing down of the significance was combined with a further interpretation that (a) the narrowness of the vote indicated how far the party had travelled towards Blair's position in a short period of time, and (b) that many of the delegates had been mandated to vote the way they had and the big unions would soon be backing Blair. An ITN correspondent noted that the spin took the following format: 'even two days after Tony announced it [Clause Four], we still get 49 per cent and that is a huge vindication and anyway the motion isn't inconsistent with what Tony tried to do.'[10] This was combined with a mobilization of comment. The leadership line was reinforced in interviews given by the leader, John Prescott (deputy leader), Kinnock (former leader) and Cook (then Shadow Foreign Secretary). There was no reference to a confusion noted by Jones (1995) about whether the rewrite should be approved in the autumn or at a special conference.[11]

Putting defeat in context

The loss of the ballot on the motion was highlighted as an embarrass-ment for the leader but also qualified in a way that Ashdown's was not. The *ITN 5.40* in the anchor's introduction suggested that Blair was 'shrugging off an embarrassing defeat' and continued that by the 'narrowest of votes the party conference had defied the Labour leader'. The *Six O'clock News* made reference to the fact that Blair had been defeated. *Channel Four News* suggested, 'Blair's attempt to remodel the Labour party suffered a major setback today. Elinor Goodman reports now on the abrupt end to Mr Blair's honeymoon period.' In the report's concluding remarks Goodman (political editor) suggested: 'Tonight he claims to be confident that next year's conference will have approved the new statement of the party's aims, but today has been a reminder he can never take his conference for granted.' On the *Nine O'clock News* the anchor suggested: 'Two days after Tony Blair talked of a new Labour party without its Clause Four the old party said no.' The political editor in the report made reference to the fact that conference had 'embarrassed their new leader by defying the platform . . . '. Similarly, *News at Ten* in its introduction referred to the loss of the vote: 'Tony Blair was defeated . . . on the party consti-tution and his plans to rewrite it.' The political editor reiterated in the report that 'Nothing could alter the fact that Tony Blair has suffered an embarrassing defeat' although he did suggest it was 'not as horrible as he'd feared.' *Newsnight*'s introduction again made reference to the embarrassment: 'what's happened here is an embarrassment but hardly a major disaster for Mr Blair.'

While the contextualizing remarks still referred to Blair's embarrass-ment the attempt to shape the interpretation of the result in favour of the leadership line met with some success. In the *ITN 5.40* report's commentary, the correspondent made reference to two elements of the party elite spin. First, 'He [Blair] says it is not a setback for his plans' and, second, that the unions' position would change: 'they'll almost

certainly be backing Tony Blair by the time he produces his blueprint.'
The leadership perspective also appeared in the introduction of the *Six
O'clock News*, with the anchor stating: 'But he [Blair] said the narrowness of today's vote indicates how far the party has travelled in the last
forty-eight hours.' Further, the correspondent's commentary insisted
that the 'leadership were adamant the review would continue. They are
convinced next year's conference will support them.' *Channel Four News*
was careful to balance the party elite's line with reference to the loss of
the vote. While mentioning that the Transport and General Workers and
other unions had been mandated, the contextualizing remarks were
slightly disdainful, making reference to the fact that Blair's supporters
'had planned carefully how to discount [the vote]'. The *Nine O'clock
News* made reference to the leadership line, stating: 'but Blair immediately said the vote made absolutely no difference to the review of
Labour's constitution' and also included two elements of leadership
spin stating that the 'leadership are insistent, the constitutional review
goes on'; and second, suggesting that 'Mr Blair with union delegations
differently mandated will get his new constitution through next year'.
News at Ten referred to the leadership perspective: 'Afterwards he
[Blair] said the defeat was of no significance.' *Newsnight*'s introduction
again made reference to the party elite line: 'Blair says it won't make any
difference to his drive for change.' The party elite's spin clearly made
an impact. All the reports accepted the line that change goes on and in
the long run the unions would come on side. All carried variations
of the party leadership's line and all made reference to the closeness of
the vote.

Expanding on the issues

Three bulletins provided two-ways in addition to reports. In the two-
ways the anchor invited the correspondent or political editor to
speculate upon and explain[12] the debate further for the audience. The
speculative questions and answers about Clause Four were in a
minority compared to non-Clause Four issues such as Prescott's speech
the next day but greater, all the same, than those that provided an explanation. However, on Clause Four the party elite's perspective came
through clearly in the journalists' answers. The *ITN 5.40* report was
followed by a two-way with political editor Michael Brunson. The
question on Clause Four sought more detail on the vote:

Anchor: I understand you have some information on how that vote was
made up?
Brunson: Yes, I'm told that Tony Blair was expecting a far worse defeat

than this . . . they are taking quite a lot of comfort from that final figure in
the leadership because they think quite a lot of delegates did decide to
switch on the basis of what they heard from Tony Blair.

The section of *Channel Four*'s two-way on Clause Four involved two
speculative questions. The first was about whether the reforms
proposed would be successful and the second about whether the debate
had caused any damage to the party. The first answer by Goodman
raised the point that a future debate may divide the party. Her second
answer suggested that the vote had 'clearly been a setback . . . but at the
end of the day we know that he, Mr Blair, will get his way next year'.
And she reinforced the point that the debate could damage the party:
'the problem for him is that voters don't trust divided parties'. The *Nine
O'clock News'* question asked if this was a setback of any significance for
Blair. While the political editor referred to the vote by conference as
'bumps and scratches rather than a deep wound', he did speculate that
success depends on 'how long and bitter the wrangle [lasts] . . . because
the public doesn't like divided parties'.

Both *Channel Four News* and *Newsnight* provided additional reports.
The Channel Four report took the vote as a peg on which to hang an
analysis of the images of division within the party past and present. The
anchor's introduction noted that the 'virtual fifty-fifty split over Clause
Four threatens once again to present an image of a divided Labour
party'. The report's commentary then dealt with the state of internal
party relations under Kinnock and how both he and Smith had
attempted to unite the party behind their reforms. *Newsnight*'s
additional pegged report was a retrospective of Tony Blair's first conference as leader. Using the metaphor of a Blackpool roller-coaster, it
referred to his speech as a high, and to the reaction of the party to the
proposed rewrite of Clause Four as a low. The first outing of what was
to be the New Labour team behind the 1997 general election campaign

Table 7.1 *The number of speculative and explanatory questions and
answers in two-ways on 6 October 1994*

	Speculation	Explanation	Non-Clause 4	Total
ITN5.40	0	1	1	2
BBC9	1	0	2	3
Ch 4	2	0	2	4
Total	3	1	5	9

(ITN5.40 = ITN News at 5.40 p.m.; BBC9 = BBC Nine O'clock News;
Ch 4 = Channel Four News. None of the other bulletins carried two-ways)

was successful despite the hiccups noted by Jones (1995) in chapter 6. The team was able to ensure that broadcast journalists carried the leadership line in a way that the Liberal Democrats could not manage a week earlier.

On the Tory fringe: creating and contextualizing debate

While journalists saw the debates in the main hall at the Conservative conference as well managed and often anodyne affairs, they saw the fringe as the site of the 'real' differences of opinion in the party on policy and other matters. *Newsnight* and *Channel Four News* and the later evening bulletins, in particular, saw the Tory fringe as an important source of dissent that was not present in the main hall, and to a large extent the fringe was contextualized in this way. Out of fifty-three reports over the four conferences, only in a small minority of the reports – six – was a debate on the fringe a news item in its own right and not included as part of a wider conference package. In the remaining forty-seven, attacks on the leadership made at fringe meetings formed part of a wider package including events in the main hall. It was a resource from which quotes from recognizable party critics could be used and juxtaposed with sources speaking in the main hall or at other fringe meetings. In other words, various recognizable critics speaking at different fringe meetings were brought together within a report to form a debate. The fringe was treated therefore as a key 'building block' (Blumler and Gurevitch, 1995) in the construction of intra-party debate on a series of issues.

Those reports which used the fringe in this manner did so in a number of ways: twelve juxtaposed the perspectives expressed on the fringe with those expressed in the main hall; thirty-three reports used the fringe as a sampling exercise in which the different views expressed in meetings served to illustrate divergent views on matters of policy, such as left versus right or pro-European versus Eurosceptic. And in two reports the fringe provided a 'professional' counter-view to that being expressed in the main hall by partisan actors. The bulletins contextualized the debates they had constructed as evidence of overt divisions within the party on particular issues. The following section focuses particularly on the framing of a speech made by former Chancellor Norman Lamont at the 1994 party conference and other debates on the fringe between the 'left' and 'right' of the party.

Stormin' Norman

Lamont's speech to a fringe meeting on the opening day of the conference, 11 October 1994, was treated in a similar manner by all the bulletins. It was timed to coincide with a speech made by the then Foreign Secretary, Douglas Hurd. Lamont's speech formed part of the lead news report on every bulletin. The speech was viewed by all bulletins as reopening existing party divisions on the European Union. The *ITN 5.40*'s introduction suggested that Lamont had: 're-opened Conservative party wounds over Europe on Day One of a party conference aimed at unity.' The *Six O'clock News* similarly noted: 'Norman Lamont has re-opened divisions over Europe.' *Channel Four News'* report noted that Lamont had 're-opened Conservative wounds over Europe'. The *Nine O'clock News'* report suggested that Lamont had 'opened up the Tories' divisions on Europe', *News at Ten*'s that divisions on Europe had been 'dramatically forced back into the open'. *Newsnight* saw the speech as opening up divisions over Europe too. *Newsnight*'s introduction used a particularly graphic metaphor: 'Europe is the scab the Conservatives cannot stop picking. At the point the party thought it had grown something of a callous over the issue, the former Chancellor Norman Lamont has opened it up again.'

The speech was also seen as a direct attack on the party leader and his policy. The *ITN 5.40* report noted: Lamont 'accused John Major of deceit . . . He declared that we should tell the European Union "Here we stand and no further" and floated the idea that Britain could withdraw totally and still be viable on its own.' The *Six O'clock News* also highlighted the attack: 'He accused the government of deceiving the British people and suggested that Britain should consider pulling out of the European Union.' *Channel Four* quoted Lamont's speech three times, calling it a 'complete demolition job on everything John Major has claimed to have achieved in Europe'. The *Nine O'clock News'* report raised Lamont's personal animosity and added that, 'He told a fringe meeting the benefits of membership had proved remarkably elusive. Britain was losing the argument over Europe, he said, and if we were not already members there wouldn't be a case for joining now.' ITN's political editor suggested that Lamont had 'directly attacked the Prime Minister, his own party leader, for his heart of Europe ideas'. The report put Lamont's speech in the wider context of the impact of the European debate on the party leader: 'Once again, just as the Prime Minister seemed to have turned the political corner, the nightmare issue which has so badly split the Tories over the years, Europe, has returned.' *Newsnight* contextualized the speech as an attack on the Prime Minister, linked to what the report called Lamont's 'downfall', and referred to his feelings about Mr Major: 'Mr Major's friends say Mr Lamont now regards his old friend as worse than Beelzebub.'

To illustrate the fact that behind the image of unity in the main hall the party was divided on the issue of European integration the reports juxtaposed Lamont's speech with that made by Douglas Hurd (the then Foreign Secretary and Europhile). *ITN 5.40*'s correspondent, after quoting Lamont suggested: 'all of that is at odds with the Foreign Secretary's conference speech which talked of Britain's positive achievements in Europe.' The *Six O'clock News* suggested: 'this view is firmly rejected by the Foreign Secretary . . . who warned against listening to siren voices speaking out against Europe.' The report further contextualized the debate in terms of an ideological drift to the right. The BBC correspondent suggested the party's strategy of 'resisting a sweep to the right suffered a serious blow this evening over Europe'. *Channel Four News* also contrasted Lamont's views with the Foreign Secretary's speech, 'telling representatives not to be defeatist or to give in to the temptation to turn their backs on the awfulness of Europe'. *Channel Four*'s political editor noted that Hurd's speech was aimed at 'Eurosceptics both in the media and his own party'. The *Nine O'clock News*' introduction also contrasted Lamont's views with Hurd's. 'Earlier the Foreign Secretary . . . warned the conference of the dangers of getting high on xenophobia.' It also suggested that Lamont had 'pitched in to the debate about . . . the party's future direction by backing right-wing calls for more clear blue water to be put between the Conservatives and Labour'. *Newsnight* contrasted Lamont's speech with Hurd's, referring to him as the *'bête noire* of the anti-European right.' But Hurd's speech was not given the prominence of Lamont's in terms of the number of times it was sampled.

In the concluding remarks the reports examined the impact of the speech on the party. The *ITN 5.40* report ended by the correspondent raising the possibility of a leadership challenge. The *Six O'clock News*' report concluded:

> This evening the debate is over Europe but the argument goes much wider than that. It is about how the Conservatives position themselves after the advent of Mr Blair . . . Should the Tories stay largely in the centre ground or should they shift to the right? And that argument will go on throughout this week.

The *Channel Four* report concluded that Mr Lamont's speech had 'spoiled the carefully choreographed image of unity which party strategists were hoping to present today'. The *Nine O'clock News*' report concluded that while dissent might have been muted from the floor, 'Mr Lamont's intervention tonight has put the focus back where the Tories didn't want it, on the eternally divisive subject of Europe'. ITN's political editor concluded: 'in fact, though, it still remains a dispirited conference, given all the Tories' present troubles, but now it risks being somewhat of a divided conference as well over the issue of Europe.'

Some of the bulletins initiated additional news items immediately after the reports. *Newsnight* and *Channel Four News* each interviewed Lamont and Hurd, and the *ITN 5.40* and the *Nine O'clock News* had a two-way. Both two-ways continued the process of assessing the impact of Lamont's speech. The anchors of both bulletins asked the political editors to speculate about the impact of the speech on the party. For the *ITN 5.40* the political editor suggested: 'Well of course it's damaging when a former Chancellor gets up and says these sort of things.' The political editor for the *Nine O'clock News* insinuated the same: 'Oh I think inevitably it is damaging. It's a direct challenge to the arguments used by Mr Major and Douglas Hurd.' He continued: 'Mr Lamont is really going much further than the Maastricht rebels have done in the past, and of course parties that look divided within their own ranks never really appeal to the public.'

The news broadcasters elected to cover the meeting because it illustrated the wider newsworthy intra-party conflict on Europe behind the image of unity that was being presented in the main hall. Using his personal resources, the fringe and adapting to the logic of the broadcasters, Lamont (with the aid of the broadcasters) was able to set the news agenda.

Attacking Lamont

The Conservative leadership engaged a reactive strategy in response to Norman Lamont's attacks from the fringe. Party spin doctors mobilized senior party figures, including the then Foreign Secretary, to repudiate Lamont and his attacks on government policy. The rebuttal operation was referenced on the main evening news reports. The leadership's criticism of Lamont featured in news items on the *ITN 5.40* and the *Nine O'clock News*. The *ITN 5.40* raised the reactions both in the report and in a live two-way. The report quoted Hurd saying: '"He's perfectly entitled to put his point of view. I think he's wrong, I think partly because he's out of date".' This view was underlined in a reference to further unsourced ministerial comment:

> "beyond the pale" was one senior back-bencher's comment. "A bitter man who always vowed to get his revenge on the Prime Minister, and he has", that was another minister's point of view. Another . . . simply said to me "Norman Lamont's barking mad" . . .

The *Nine O'clock News* similarly in its report suggested that 'many former colleagues were swift to reject his call' and then carried Lord Howe's reaction.

Speaking their minds

Debate was not only constructed using views expressed on the fringe and in the hall. Nine reports also used divergent views expressed by members of the leadership on the fringe. The most noticeable examples were reports on the *Nine O'clock News*, *News at Ten* and two on *Newsnight* on 7 October 1993. All four reports constructed the debate on the fringe through juxtaposing differing views of ministers and placing them in the context of an ideological debate between the 'left' and 'right' of the party and set this against the overall leadership aim of presenting a unified party image.

In its introduction the anchor on the *Nine O'clock News* suggested: 'Conservative party managers today appeared to succeed in fostering a show of unity between the Prime Minister and Lady Thatcher' but added: 'tonight the struggle to give the Conservative party that distinctive ideology continued with two very different speeches from cabinet ministers.' *News at Ten*'s introduction similarly highlighted the difference: 'The Prime Minister got a hand shake from his predecessor' but suggested: 'Mr Major has been pushed to the right this week.' *Newsnight*'s introduction to the first of two reports was more acerbic in unmasking the divisions: 'Almost every single speech we've heard . . . has contained some protestation that the party is united in undying loyalty to John Major as if the mere statement is enough rather than perhaps drawing attention to the fact that divisions are as deep as ever, if less visible.' The introduction to the second report followed a similar line: 'Well if the Conservatives leave this conference having succeeded in convincing themselves that the party is now united by John Major it will be quite an achievement, because despite the fact that almost everyone is now using the same language the philosophical divisions still run deep.'

In all four reports the fringe meetings were framed in the context of party unity behind the leadership of John Major. The *Nine O'clock News*, *News at Ten* and the first *Newsnight* report described the day's events in the hall, Thatcher's reception by the representatives and John Major, Clarke's pledge of support for Major, and Heseltine's first conference appearance since his heart attack. All contextualized this as an attempt to reinforce party unity in the light of the events that week. But then came the caveat. The *Nine O'clock News'* report suggested: 'But her departure did little to ease the tensions outside the conference hall.' *News at Ten*'s report said disdainfully: 'But behind the theatre of reconciliation in the conference hall a battle has been developing over the future of government policy.' *Newsnight*'s commentary ran: 'But in the last few hours two of the more thoughtful members of the supposedly united leadership have made plain the ideological chasm which separates the left from the right.' The speeches of different leadership actors, in particular Michael Portillo and Douglas Hurd, were juxtaposed in order to underline the point. *Newsnight*'s second report reinforced this angle, placing the fringe meeting as the arena for a struggle between 'left' and 'right'. The correspondent started the report: 'This was supposed to be the conference that was all about unity. In fact in the vacuum at the heart of the party, ministers are engaged in a struggle for domination.' The report then went on to juxtapose the speeches from four different fringe meetings addressed by Hurd, Portillo, Kenneth Clarke and Norman Tebbit, and John Gummer.

The 'left'/'right' debate was further highlighted in a series of two-ways on the *ITN 5.40*, *Channel Four News* and *News at Ten*. The two-way on *Nine O'clock News* focused exclusively on the Chancellor's speech.

Table 7.2 shows that just under half the questions and answers in the two-ways were on this debate on the fringe, and none of the two-ways speculated about the outcome of the debate: instead they sought to explain further the nature of the debate and who the main protagonists were. On the *ITN 5.40* the anchor enquired whether there had been a 'distinct shift to the right wing of the party.' The political editor suggested ' . . . that certainly is the sense of it, isn't it?' and after reading out trailed extracts from the forthcoming speeches by Portillo and Hurd he suggested 'the battle is on really for the soul of the party.'

The *Channel Four News* anchor similarly asked whether there was an 'ideological struggle going on, on the fringe tonight'. The political editor

Table 7.2   *The number of speculative and explanatory questions and answers in two-ways 7 October 1993*

	Speculation	Explanation	Non-debate	Total
ITN5.40	0	1	1	2
Ch 4	0	2	2	4
BBC9	0	0	2	2
ITN10	0	1	1	2
Total	0	4	6	10

(BBC9 = BBC Nine O'clock News; ITN5.40 = ITN News at 5.40 p.m.;
ITN10 = ITN News at Ten O'clock; Ch 4 = Channel Four News.)

agreed, and outlined the debate as taking place between 'those who say the Thatcherite revolution must continue and those who argue it shouldn't'. She then summarized the positions of four actors speaking on the fringe, Portillo and Tebbit representing the former, and Clarke and Hurd the latter. Asked further whether the 'bastards' (in John Major's own reported terminology) had had a good week, Goodman suggested: 'They feel in command, that they have taken the high ground.'

The theme of a shift to the right was also pursued by *News at Ten*. The anchor stated:

> The party really shifted to the right . . . and that was emphasized again today wasn't it'?
> Brunson: 'Well I asked one cabinet minister about this in this very hotel tonight. I said, "Are you shifting to the right?" He said: "Look, we've always been a right of centre party. What I think the Conservatives have realized is that there is huge concern in the country especially about something like law and order". And as another minister said to me today: "The agenda which we have tried to tackle these things on in the past has not worked and so we have now got to try (if you like) a more right-of-centre approach".' That's where all this is coming from.

Conclusion

In comparison to the leader's speech journalists play a more active role in (re)constructing newsworthy debates. They seek to capture the different views within each debate. These views are split into opposing positions and juxtaposed. In the debates analysed, a significant proportion of the sources used were gathered during follow-up gathering rather than being taken from the proceedings in the main hall. In the 'Cannabis', 'the Minimum Wage' and 'the Monarchy' debates, twenty of forty-seven quotes were media-initiated, and in Clause Four, eighteen of forty-five. All the reports on the debates acted as a common carrier for the different views. The weight given to opposing sides in a report was an indicator of the discretion held by the correspondents. A mixed picture emerged in terms of leadership line versus those opposed to it. In the Liberal Democrats' conference coverage, six actors supporting the leadership line were quoted thirteen times, while sixteen against were quoted twenty-two times. In the coverage of the Clause Four debate seven actors supporting the leadership line were quoted twenty-three times, compared to nine detractors quoted twenty-two times. In terms of the Conservative conferences the news broadcasters also played an active role in the manufacture of debate. The different views on an issue expressed in different conference locations were juxtaposed against one another to form the debate for the viewer.

The reports then amplified the issues raised in such debates, choosing which issues they would 'spotlight' and which would receive less coverage. The reports contextualized the various perspectives outlining the nature of the debate. Although the journalists far from merely reflected any actor's interpretation of events, interpretations of events favourable to or directly referenced by the party elite found their way into many of the reports, particularly during the debate on Clause Four. In some reports such an interpretation was taken at face value, while in others it was acknowledged as spin.

There was a certain amount of what has been termed disdain (Semetko *et al.*, 1991). The journalists attempted to open viewers' eyes to the divisions that exist within the party on a host of issues. At the Labour conference in 1994, amidst the launch of New Labour, there was an attempt to remind the viewers of what old Labour conferences used to be like. At the Conservative conference they sought to alert the viewer to the divisions within the party, evident on the party fringe.

Disdain was combined with an assessment of the impact of these debates on the leadership. Defeats were nearly always seen to be embarrassing for the leadership and contextualized in the language of defiance as shown by examples presented. The debates at the Liberal Democrat conference in 1994 reveal that the interpretative framework over the two days became one of leadership competence. This was due in no small part to the fact that the leadership did not enact an effective reactive communication strategy. This assessment also included a certain amount of journalistic speculation; indeed analysis of the two-ways showed a high level of speculation about the impact of the Clause Four debate, and less during the 'Cannabis', 'the Minimum Wage' and 'the Monarchy' debates.

The coverage of debates both in the main hall and on the fringe reveals divergent although overlapping interests between the news broadcasters and the different party actors. For the critical claim-makers the news bulletins are open to their views more so than at any other time. These actors, when newsworthy can therefore overcome any resource disadvantages that exist between themselves and the leadership. For the news broadcasters the overt expressions of opinion increase the newsworthiness of a particular issue and in the case of the fringe allows them to explore what they see as core issues not appearing on the formal conference agenda.

However, such coverage is at odds with the party elites' desire to publicize policy and present an image of party unity to the viewers. In these situations the spin doctors therefore need to ensure that the official line is widely referenced and to rebut the alternative perspectives, and they use public relations strategies to this end. In the examples given New Labour's communications team perhaps proved more successful in shaping the way journalists framed debates than the Liberal Democrats or Conservatives.

8

The Formation of Conference News Agendas

In the era of the permanent campaign the autumn party conferences are an important opportunity for the main political parties to set the national news agenda without the interjection of their rivals. However, as this book has shown what the audience sees on television is more than simply a reflection of spin doctors' publicity initiatives. The broadcasters also play an active role in (re)constructing events for the viewer. Television news from the party conferences is co-produced; it is the creation of a 'composite source' (Blumler and Gurevitch, 1995). Both party actors and the media personnel are involved in different ways in the construction of the final product. The parties and the broadcasters plan; the parties disseminate information; and the broadcasters gather, select and present this information. Both make an active contribution to shaping what the audience sees.

This concluding chapter seeks to highlight some key themes of the book with respect to the formation of news agendas. It begins by reflecting on the impact of the modern publicity process on party elites before examining the publicity risks and challenges they face. The chapter also examines the journalists' role in the construction of news agendas. It shows the extent to which the interests of the party elite and the broadcasters converge and diverge. Finally it situates the production of conference news within wider changes in the political and media environment.

Political parties and news agenda formation

Any attempt to understand the role of political parties in the construction of conference news needs to see them as 'polyvocal' organizations divided in numerous ways. They are made up formally of different sections – such as conference delegates, MPs, in Labour's case the trade unions, and the leadership – and informally divided along ideological grounds or on particular issues. Party conferences represent one of the few times in the year where the whole party is gathered together and all party actors can potentially shape the news agenda. The role of political elites and party communication professionals has, therefore, to be considered alongside that of these other party actors.

Earlier chapters have shown that the leadership in each party plays the dominant role in shaping their conference's coverage. The modern publicity process has driven the leadership to find more effective ways of exploiting the undivided news coverage conferences receive to promote policies to a national audience beyond the conference hall. To achieve their agenda-setting goals the leadership utilizes a wide group of actors. In the months leading up to conference, actors at party head-quarters are devoted full time to logistical planning, professionals are brought in to design the stage set, and specialist committees formulate the conference agenda and timetable. Senior party spin doctors have increasingly assumed a visible role in the planning process: they not only advise other party actors and committees on publicity matters, but also spend a great deal of time and effort planning the delivery of policy announcements and updating and formulating new strategies to ensure that the leadership can set the news agenda more effectively.

The enduring influence of these communication specialists can be seen in the way speeches made by leadership actors are now used as a launch pad for new policy announcements or the latest pronounce-ments on party reform. There has been a move, across all parties, to ensure that all leadership actors include key announcements in speeches – something the spin doctors can then promote to journalists. There is a recognition that it is easier to set the news agenda if the party message is newsworthy. The spin doctors also take advantage of journalists' sacerdotal attitude towards the leader's speech in order to gain maximum attention for party policy. Key policy announcements are saved for the speech, some being trailed the day before in the build up to it. The speech is used as a platform from which the leader sets the day's news agenda unopposed by other parties and actors within his own party. Each speech is then subject to a series of follow-up interviews.

During conference the spin doctors routinely use a series of proactive communication strategies to maximize the attention the announce-ments receive. They actively subsidize the cost of gathering information, making it easier for journalists on tight deadlines to get the story. They provide a stream of press releases and packaged background informa-tion and may offer certain journalists an exclusive insight into speeches' content ahead of their rivals. The teams of spin doctors also provide additional sources of visuals in the form of photo-opportunities and access to the leadership for interviews. In sum these communications specialists adapt conference communication efforts to the demands of the news media but in a way that benefits the leadership. They seek to provide journalists with a 'ready made' story on the issues of the leadership's choosing, combined with visuals and interviews.

Despite the planning, there is no guarantee that the television news agenda will mirror the planned leadership-endorsed agenda. There is a real fear amongst media sensitized elites that the undivided attention of the national news broadcasters will be distracted from the promotion of planned policy and instead focus on any intra-party conflicts, gaffes and mishaps that occur, projecting a negative image of the party. To prevent their four days in the limelight being overshadowed, the party managers continually try to improve conference management. All agenda committees systematically seek to prevent controversial issues getting on to the conference agenda or timetable such debates for slots where coverage is minimal. In addition, during conference, the spin doctors seek to keep journalists' attention fixed on the planned agenda. They know broadcasters driven by news values will focus on the most newsworthy events at conference whoever initiates them, and so they employ reactive strategies to coax journalists to stay on message and if necessary coerce them by bullying, intimidation or complaining.

Even with this increased emphasis on party and media management dissent still occurs. The conferences offer opportunities for other party actors outside the leadership circle to capture the news agenda. Leadership-endorsed policy inevitably has its opponents and these critical claim-makers see conferences as a chance to get their views across to a national audience. There is at each conference a certain amount of intra-party competition to set the news agenda that pits party elites against their often resource poor critics. While party elites have a competitive advantage, in terms of the resources they can mobilize in such a struggle, this does not guarantee success. During conflict-laden debates, dominance of the news agenda is not something they always automatically achieve; in some situations, described in earlier chapters, they lose control of the news agenda altogether.

Conflict-laden debates continue to be part and parcel of each conference whether in the main hall, on the fringe or in television studios. Management procedures do not prevent dissent erupting at conference but may merely displace it on to the conference fringe. The state of unity or division of the political party is not determined top down by party managers – contrary to some views. Discipline ebbs and flows and dissent finds an outlet somewhere. This was clearly illustrated in the case of the Conservative conferences during the 1990s. The Conservative leadership wanted to set the news agenda on issues of its choosing but found itself having to react to a news agenda set by 'old stars' like Norman Lamont and other Eurosceptic factions on the conference fringe at every conference from 1992 to 1997. The Labour conferences, although not riven with the same divisions in the 1990s, were still the subject of intense tussles between the leadership and certain unions over party policy on a series of issues, particularly One Member, One Vote in 1993. More recently, the leadership's attempts to set the agenda on chosen policy areas was scuttled by high-profile conflicts with the main unions on the level of the minimum wage and reinstating the link between state pensions and earnings. The greater the level of party disunity and internal dissent the greater the constraint on the leadership's ability to set the news agenda throughout the period of its conference.

Broadcasters and the construction of news agendas

The role of the news broadcasters cannot be seen solely as one of 'agenda-senders' – reflecting the planned agenda (Semetko and Canel, 1997). As this book has shown the broadcasters at conferences exercise a certain amount of 'discretionary power' (Semetko et al., 1991). While reflecting planned conference agendas they also shape and amplify agendas initiated by other actors and even initiate them themselves.

The broadcast journalists reporting the conferences are guided by organizationally derived series of attitudes. News teams still see certain events such as the leader's speech as worthy of prominent coverage largely regardless of news values. The coverage of the other events, however, is decided on their newsworthiness alone. A key element of consideration in the coverage of speeches is who is making the speech and the announcements being made, and/or the extent to which it criticizes the leadership. In terms of debates, the greater and more overt the conflict between actors the greater its attention, which further increases if the leadership is involved. In addition the news teams are attuned to unexpected newsworthy events – a gaffe, a surprise resignation or a defection, or a leadership actor who deviates from the agreed party line.

The news teams continually weigh speeches and debates on 'news value scales' (Blumler and Gurevitch, 1995), discerning the relative merit of each as a story. The planned speeches compete with debates and other events for exposure based on their newsworthiness. News teams start each day with an idea of what the main story will be but it may not fulfil their expectations. Where a speech or debate fails to live up to these expectations they reduce coverage and where they live up to or exceed expectations they give greater coverage. Their decisions are not shifted by information subsidies. News teams expect the cost of gathering all information to be subsidized and therefore by themselves subsidies do not ensure the requisite coverage. Furthermore, the news rooms in London also weigh events at conference against events happening elsewhere. Their decisions determine the size of the slot open to journalists and the subsequent position of reports in the bulletin running order. Planned party announcements are not guaranteed a prominent airing but have to compete for it. Bulletin running orders evolve throughout the day and events elsewhere may mean conference events are relegated to the end of the bulletin.

As mentioned the broadcast journalists are particularly attracted by intra-party conflict and dissent. If the animosity is part of a scheduled debate in the main hall reports reflect it. However, where these news-worthy controversial issues have been prevented from being debated in the main hall, by tighter control over the planning process, the journal-ists often seek to (re)construct debates for the viewer. They do this by juxtaposing the differing opinions and reactions from protagonists in various conference locations – usually the fringe. In other words they are prepared on some issues, because of their significance, to circum-vent party management tactics. This can be seen as an attempt, documented elsewhere (Blumler and Gurevitch, 1995), to reassert their contribution to the construction of conference agendas. As a by-product journalists enable dissenting voices within the party to achieve a momentarily national voice, which the leadership has sought to silence. To some extent the increasingly news-value driven broadcasters go some way to counter-balancing the resource advantages and manage-ment strategies of the leadership.

Once gathering is complete journalists package the speeches and debates into a report. The raw material initiated by party actors is combined with a narrative that attaches significance to events or announcements putting them in context for the viewer. When covering the leader's speech, journalists tend to adopt a 'reactive' role (Blumler et al., 1986) 'translating' the most significant passages of the leaders' speeches whether they are policy announcements or party reforms and other matters. In addition there is also a certain amount of what has been termed 'value added' (Blumler et al., 1995). The journalists take an interest in party reactions to the speeches, the response of the audience in the hall and in assessing the leader's performance. On some occasions the speeches are also contextualized historically – which was par-ticularly the case with the Labour leader's speech. In all reports the concluding remarks tended to further explain the significance of each leader's speech to the viewer in terms of a continuous process of electoral competition.

When covering highly charged debates journalists also adopt a reactive role but give equal weight to the leadership's opponents and interpreting their contribution to the debate. The journalistic input is greater than when reporting the leader's speech; the journalists not only examine the issues under debate but also speculate about the damaging consequences of such a debate for the party's electoral fortunes and whether or not this is a sign of deeper divisions within the party. With routine stage-management, reports see conflictual debates as an opportunity to open viewers' eyes to the state of party division behind the choreographed main hall. This approach was common at the Conservative conferences in the 1990s where the divisions on 'Europe' were highlighted as the true state of the party behind the show of unity in the main hall. In the case of Labour conferences there were attempts to remind audiences of the strife-ridden conferences of the 1970s and 1980s. Depending on the newsworthiness of the issue there is also a desire to expand upon the agendas initiated by the parties. The bulletins, particularly *Newsnight* and *Channel Four News*, often analyse the issues raised at conference and explore the tensions within parties through a series of additional reports.

Overall the process of news agenda formation resembles a game between players (the party and the news broadcasters) with particular aims that converge and diverge during the course of the conference week. Their aims converge around the coverage of events like the leader's speech. Here the party managers' need to maximize coverage for the planned policy announcements chimes with journalists' view that the leader's speech is the most significant event of the conference and worthy of prominent coverage. The 'reactive' approach of journalists to the leader's speech means that the leadership agenda is effectively reflected and amplified by journalists. But as we have seen, there are always momentary tensions at the heart of the game. Differences of interest inevitably arise between the leadership and the news broadcasters. While the party managers prefer that all leadership speeches receive coverage, news values mean that this is unlikely. In terms of the coverage of conflict-laden debates, party managers prefer that their views are given precedence over those of dissenting claim-makers. However, journalists want to capture the wider conflict and choose which claim-makers' views they are going to use. In addition they are also keen to reveal this as the true state of party unity and remind the viewer of the electoral consequences of such spats. In relation to gaffes, mishaps and external events, while the party managers prefer no coverage at all, journalists see them as eminently attractive, particularly in light of the increasingly managed conference environment.

So the news broadcasters reflect both what the leadership want covered and would prefer is not covered. However, because they are mutually dependent, any divergences that arise rarely lead to sustained conflict – although outbursts do occur. In this sense both sides realize that they cannot have everything they want out of this annual encounter. In the short term, both players usually reach a compromise in order to allow the attainment of their coverage goals. In the longer term however, there may be strategic manoeuvrings to gain an advantage ahead of the next encounter.

Conferences and the consequences of the modern publicity process

The quest for agenda domination by the leadership and their spin doctors leads to an emphasis on developing ever more effective ways of managing the conference and the news media in order to reduce risks. In the long term this quest may well impact on the function of conferences themselves. The Labour leadership, and to a lesser extent the Liberal Democrats, view the traditional format of their conferences – a series of plenary sessions – as inherently risky in publicity terms. The Labour leadership know only too well that such a set-up means they are hostages to fortune and that any rows or divisions will be picked up and dissected by a news-hungry media which then contextualize the occurrences in an unfavourable way. There are long-term aims by certain sections of the party to reduce these risks. Two Labour party interest groups, Labour 2000 and the Labour Co-ordinating Committee, have produced pamphlets arguing for a fundamental change in the nature of the conference. Labour 2000 called for the conference to be turned into 'a good old-fashioned, American-style convention'.[1] The Labour Co-ordinating Committee similarly suggested that the party should copy the format of the presidential conventions and 'get rid of boring and damaging debates'.[2] Margaret Hodge, who was closely connected to the Labour leadership, suggested:

> What I think we need to do is move away from the formalized posturing debate that we have at conference and allow members an opportunity to express honestly what they feel, within smaller regional policy forums across the country or in smaller discussion-based groups in conference.[3]

In a recent move the Labour party introduced private sessions where issues deemed controversial are debated without the cameras present.

While the Conservative conference has always been seen as a rally (Kavanagh, 1996; McKenzie, 1964; Whiteley *et al.*, 1994) there has been some speculation that its format may change. Pierce and Sherman note that 'Mr Hague [party leader] is being urged to scrap the traditional four-day format and replace it with a two-and-half day gathering which would end on Saturday'.[4] Although these pressures to change the existing format of conferences have not been acted upon yet, the force for change may lead to a radical overhaul in the nature of the conferences, which will feed into the content of conference news.

The continual quest for greater control affects the newsworthiness of conferences in the eyes of journalists. Some journalists already feel that conferences are more managed than in previous decades and many of the debates on key issues are prevented from being aired in the main hall. In the long term such an over-cautious approach by political elites may lead to a growing divergence of interest with journalists who are increasingly driven by news values.

In the competitive world of broadcast news both ITN and BBC attach importance to ratings (Blumler, 1991; Nossiter *et al.*, 1995). The 1990 Broadcasting Act intensified the commercial pressure on ITN to deliver an affordable, high quality and popular news service to its clients the ITV network, Channel Four and Channel Five. As a company with shareholders it has to ensure that it is profitable and this means maximizing audiences and advertising revenues. Although the BBC is funded by a licence fee, BBC News still competes with ITN for a share of the national audience. This competition has recently intensified with the move of the BBC *Nine O'clock News* to 10 p.m. and its head-to-head competition with ITN's *News at Ten*. For both news broadcasters maximizing audience size (shown in quarter-hourly ratings) is now crucial. However both networks face competition from new broadcast outlets, such as *Sky News*, CNN, CNBC and Bloomberg; in addition both ITN and the BBC have launched twenty-four hour news channels themselves.

The growth of channels means that both the BBC and ITN news on terrestrial channels now attract a smaller share of the audience than they once did. While the ratings show audiences for the main terrestrial news channels have fluctuated over the 1990s, they also show a long-term decline in their audience share. BBC television news audiences declined by eighteen per cent between 1996 and 1999 (Barnett, 2001). Audiences for live coverage on the BBC have fluctuated over the 1990s but remain low. Live coverage of the Liberal Democrats' conference attracted an average audience of 276,000 between 1992 and 1998. The audience for live coverage of Labour conferences over the same period averaged 455,000 and for the Conservatives 557,000.[5]

The pressure to maintain audience share may have two outcomes on conference coverage. First, journalists may approach the conferences in a more pragmatic way. Although tempered by a diluted sense of public service duty, there will be a stricter application of news values to events at conference and greater efforts to shape conference news agendas on behalf of their audiences. One BBC source noted in relation to conference coverage: 'There are tensions between strict commercial news judgements and the public service aspect.'[6] An ITN source concurred:

> When the public service ethic was more prominent, you had a public service obligation to go down to Brighton and broadcast half of News at Ten. We are a long way from that situation . . . , now we just do packages from the scene and there is much more news judgement . . . But I suppose we still take it for granted that we will be there.[7]

Pragmatic considerations were also raised in other interviews with news broadcasters. One senior journalist noted the possible consequences: 'Politicians are risking less and less on the floor of conference in both camps . . . If you risk less then you lay yourself open to the media hunting for more. And if they can't get it on the floor of the conference, they will get it in Cherie Blair's wardrobe'[8] or on the fringe. In addition, as the main venue becomes more and more managed, when conflicts arise, or gaffes or externally initiated events occur, they may be seen as all the more newsworthy and given greater coverage by journalists. The greater the number of media outlets covering conferences, the more coverage any altercations, gaffes and mishaps will receive when they happen. For the spin doctors this means that they need to continually think of new ways to keep journalists' attention focused on the planned policy messages.

The second outcome may be that the broadcasters will cut back on

Table 8.1 *The total amount of conference news coverage by year and bulletin, 1993–6 (in minutes)*

	ITN5.40	ITN10	BBC6	BBC9	Ch 4	NN	Total
1993	45	88	85	101	234	294	847
1994	43	70	74	77	210	263	737
1995	47	55	71	69	183	302	727
1996	44	54	49	58	168	214	587
Total	179	267	279	305	795	1073	2898

(BBC6 = BBC Six O'clock News; BBC9 = BBC Nine O'clock News; ITN5.40 = ITN News at 5.40 p.m.; ITN10 = ITN News at Ten; Ch 4 = Channel Four News; NN = Newsnight)

Table 8.2   *The average length of conference news items by year and bulletin, 1993–6 (in minutes and seconds)*

	ITN5.40	ITN10	BBC6	BBC9	Ch 4	NN	Av.
1993	1.47	3.01	2.45	3.05	4.52	5.20	3.28
1994	1.52	2.47	2.32	2.51	4.34	4.52	3.15
1995	2.47	2.55	2.58	2.54	4.28	8.38	4.06
1996	2.13	2.54	3.05	3.27	4.41	4.45	3.30
Av.	2.10	2.54	2.50	3.04	4.39	5.54	3.35

(BBC6 = BBC Six O'clock News; BBC9 = BBC Nine O'clock News;
ITN5.40 = ITN News at 5.40 p.m.; ITN10 = ITN News at Ten O'clock;
Ch 4 = Channel Four News; NN = Newsnight)

coverage. Table 8.1 shows that the overall amount of conference news coverage by the major terrestrial network bulletins strongly declined between 1993 and 1996. There was a particularly noticeable decline in the coverage provided by *Channel Four News* and *Newsnight*, and also substantial declines in the coverage on *News at Ten* and the BBC *Six O'clock News* and *Nine O'clock News*, although coverage on *ITN 5.40* fluctuated. Commenting on the decline of news coverage one ITN source admitted:

> We have cut back. In the old days we had Sandy Gall (Anchor) in the studio and Alastair Burnet (Anchor) down in Brighton and the whole of the first half of *News at Ten* would be reporting the conferences. We used to have a cast of thousands literally.[9]

While the amount of coverage declined this could not be attributed to a shortening of report lengths. Table 8.2 shows that there was no corresponding yearly decline in the average length of news items across all bulletins – instead, it remained almost constant, but with an upward blip in 1995.

Table 8.3 shows that the decline in coverage can be accounted for by a fall in the number of news items produced by the news bulletins. The number of news items produced by *Channel Four News*, *News at Ten*, the BBC *Six O'clock* and *Nine O'clock News* declined steadily, although those produced by *ITN 5.40* and *Newsnight* fluctuated slightly but also fell back. One source highlighted an annual debate over *Channel Four News'* commitment to covering the conferences.

> Every year we do have a serious debate about whether we should go [and] would the money be better spent some other way. I suspect if there were a different presenter, who didn't particularly want to go, they (*Channel*

Table 8.3   *The total number of conference news items by year and bulletin, 1993–6*

	ITN5.40	ITN10	BBC6	BBC9	Ch 4	NN	Total
1993	25	29	31	33	48	55	221
1994	23	25	29	27	46	54	204
1995	17	19	24	20	41	35	156
1996	20	19	16	17	36	45	153
Total	85	92	100	97	171	189	734

(BBC6 = BBC Six O'clock News; BBC9 = BBC Nine O'clock News;
ITN5.40 = ITN News at 5.40 p.m.; ITN10 = ITN News at Ten O'clock;
Ch 4 = Channel Four News; NN = Newsnight)

Four News) might be happy to settle for not going and just have a correspondent up there. And that would reduce the emphasis we give to it. If we retreated, would *Newsnight*?[10]

It is difficult to say with certainty from the available data whether the decline of news coverage is part of a longer-term trend across all bulletins. However, data is available for twenty-six years of live gavel-to-gavel conference coverage. Figure 8.1 shows an overall decline in live coverage. Although ITV's live output was lower than the BBC's, the commercial network stopped covering the conferences live in 1982. Channel Four matched the BBC's live output from 1983 to 1985 before cutting back and only covering the leaders' speeches live. The BBC's coverage rose from around 3,500 minutes in 1972 to a peak of over 5,000 minutes in 1986, before declining steadily to 2,500 minutes in 1998. From the high point of the mid-1980s live coverage – an outward sign of the BBC's conference commitment – has been in decline.[11]

However, this book provides evidence that could be construed as contradictory. If overall coverage is declining, then one would expect the presence of the broadcasters at the conference, including the numbers of journalists and technicians who attend, to be declining also. But there is an increased demand for new camera angles and for space in the conference venue, driven by a greater number of broadcasters, including breakfast and satellite TV plus radio, which now attend the conferences. Indeed Franklin (1996) and Gaber (1998) argue that there has been a 'rapid increase in the market for political news . . . [with] the advent of round-the-clock radio and television news outlets plus the growth in political programmes on both the BBC and commercial channels'.[12] At conferences what seems to be happening is that total coverage across all media has increased because there are more media outlets

Figure 8.1 *Live coverage of the annual autumn party conferences, 1972–98*

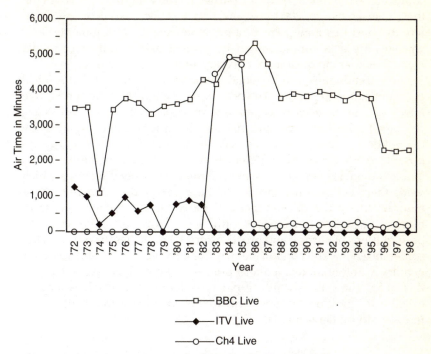

Source: Author, compiled from the *Radio Times, TV Times, The Times* and the *Financial Times*

present, although the coverage that each outlet provides remains small and has declined. Conference coverage is becoming more fragmented across an increasing number of channels.[13] One could argue that the process of fragmentation will continue with the digitalization of broadcasting and the advent of Internet news services.

The impact of digital multi-channel broadcasting and Internet technologies will inevitably have both negative and positive implications for conference coverage. More outlets covering the conferences may not mean more in-depth coverage, only greater coverage of conference highlights, such as speeches by party 'luminaries' or overt intra-party conflicts. However, the potential remains for conferences to be covered in the same way that Parliament is, with a channel devoted to gavel-to-gavel live coverage, which existing broadcasters cannot provide because of time and commercial restrictions. Indeed, the Parliament Channel provides such coverage at the moment and there is potential for coverage to be produced by the parties themselves. Conference websites, first produced in 1995, have become increasingly sophisticated. While none of the parties has as yet talked of producing their own coverage, 2000 saw the first live webcasts from the conferences and this may point to a potential future development. Party websites are also supplemented by an increasing number of media websites widening traditional coverage to include fringe meetings.

These trends raise fundamental challenges for students of political communication to ponder. The possibility remains that the cumulative effect of the long-term hegemony of broadcast media priorities, combined with the development of systematic counter-responses by the political parties themselves, will be the production of a set of supposedly media-oriented conferences which attract progressively less and less media coverage – because all the uncontrolled features which made them newsworthy in the past have been either stamped out or neutralized by the development of party elites' management techniques. Such an outcome is still some way off. The complex permutations of parties' and broadcasters' complicities in co-producing conference news still contain elements of creative tension and space for genuinely autonomous media responses and dissident voices. Despite this space, the future health of party conferences themselves may be called into question by long-term trends towards a fragmented and more apolitical news media.

Appendix: Research Methods

The research for this book involved a combination of interviews with parties and media actors, observations at the conferences and content analysis of news output. A total of twenty-five interviews were conducted, some face-to-face and others on the phone – all were taped and on the record. The interviews lasted on average one hour ten minutes and were then fully transcribed. The interviews were all semi-structured and investigative in nature, and based around particular themes. The use of such interviews allowed these different themes, some of which arose in the interview, to be investigated more thoroughly than with the alternative, structured interviews. Such techniques also allowed the establishment of confidence and rapport with the interviewee; this is essential in order to obtain more in-depth answers to particular questions. The questions on particular themes were open-ended, designed to get the interviewee to talk in detail on an issue. Of course there were tangential comments, but in some cases they provided additional information that had not been previously considered. There was a particular effort when interviewing journalists and spin doctors to get them to discuss particular examples from conference news coverage. The interviews were analysed thematically, with the issues raised by interviewees being cross referenced to provide as complete a picture as possible. While interviews with those involved in the pre-conference planning occurred at different times throughout a three-year period, some of the interviews, particularly those with journalists and political actors, were conducted in the months immediately after the conferences, when events were still fairly fresh in their minds. Although I tried to interview as wide a cross section of people as possible, the main problem I faced was getting access for interviews. Many requests were never replied to, even though I sent each subject several reminders.

It has become standard practice in news media research to conduct observational studies, and there have been many of news broadcasters (see for instance Gans, 1979; Schlesinger, 1987; Tuchman, 1978). I attended all three party conferences over a three-year period. For the duration of the conferences I carried out a daily observation of journalistic and party activities in the press room and made a series of field notes. The press room was chosen because it was a key space in which journalists, press teams and spin doctors interacted. It was a particularly important venue to observe spinning in action. The observation was carried out for set periods of time, chosen to coincide with key moments of the day, such as when journalists returned to the press room after major speeches and debates or for press conferences. The periods of observation also involved eavesdropping on the spin doctors at work and journalists talking amongst themselves. This was made possible by the group nature of both occurrences. On occasions, it also involved talking to journalists and gauging their reactions to the spin. In addition I attended all press conferences given during the day.

There have been numerous definitions of content analysis, which have evolved and shifted over time (Berelson, 1971; Holsti, 1969; Krippendorf, 1980; Weber, 1990). Content analysis cannot be regarded as an objective quantified exercise. The researcher's values and predispositions inevitably influence the selection of categories, and the categories in turn influence the findings of the research. However, it is still a useful method for the analysis of news coverage.

The content analysis focused on the output of six evening terrestrial news bulletins ITN News at 5.40 p.m. on ITV, the BBC *Six O'clock News*, *Channel Four News*, the BBC *Nine O'clock News*, ITN *News at Ten* on ITV and *Newsnight*. This mix was chosen as it included both the 'regular' and 'serious' news output and because the bulletins, despite the advent of satellite, still attracted the largest audiences (for instance the BBC *Nine O'clock News* and *News at Ten* regularly had over 4 million viewers each). The aim of the content analysis was to examine four years of news output year by year on these six bulletins. A coding sheet was developed designed to gather information on certain elements of news coverage. The coding sheet focused on two main areas. First, the framing of the conferences by the different news bulletins and, second, evidence of the use of media strategies by the political parties.

The content analysis was combined with a textual analysis of the news transcripts. I directly transcribed all main news reports, some pegged items, all two-ways between anchors and correspondents and some interviews. Transcribing from video, it has been argued, provides greater accuracy. Indeed, Philo notes interestingly when comparing Glasgow University Media Group's content analysis with that of Harrison's (1985): 'When we compared these transcripts with the video tapes of the news programmes in our research archive we found that there were serious material differences between them and what ITN had actually broadcast.'[1] The aim of the textual analysis was to provide a more detailed analysis of the packaging of particular debates and speeches. The transcripts of reports and pegged items were used to analyse the journalists' contextualizing remarks and the evaluations made in the reports' conclusions. The transcripts of two-ways between anchor and correspondent were examined for their use of speculative and explanatory questions and answers.

I alone was responsible for carrying out the content and textual analysis. As most of the variables in the content analysis were fairly clear-cut in their application the absence of reliability coding does not qualify the conclusions drawn. Intercoder reliability, though, was an important consideration in establishing the trustworthiness of subjective variables. However, it was difficult within the time, and with available resources, to find anyone else to carry out the content analysis as well. Certain variables were therefore defined as specifically and exclusively as possible and tested on a small sample of news items with a colleague.

Finally as part of my research I also referred to *The Daily Telegraph*, *The Times*, *The Guardian* and *The Independent*, *The Sunday Telegraph*, *The Observer*, *The Sunday Times*, and *The Independent on Sunday* over the period of the study for their conference coverage and to keep abreast of developments within the political parties. I also used the British Newspaper Library to examine TV programme guides in order reliably to construct data on the amount of live conference coverage from 1972 to 1998.

Notes

Introduction: The News from Blackpool, Bournemouth and Brighton

1 Rosenbaum (1997, p. 140) notes: 'Following a series of approaches from the BBC to both parties, the Conservatives agreed to their conference being televised in 1954. Labour however . . . refused to let the TV cameras in. Nevertheless, the coverage of the Conservative conference was regarded as such a success that Labour was reluctantly forced to follow suit the following year'. Cockerell (1989, p. 41) concurs: 'In autumn 1955, the BBC for the first time had cameras at both main party conferences.' An authoritative source noted when interviewed that Granada provided the first coverage of the TUC conference in 1957 for ITV, followed by the Liberal Assembly in 1959 and Labour and Conservative conferences in 1960, and ITV continued to cover the three main party conferences live until 1982. Live coverage continued on Channel Four until 1985, including the SDP conference. Now Channel Four only covers the leaders' speeches live. The BBC still covers the party conferences live but the amount of air time has been reduced. Interestingly in the US, according to Fant (1980), television coverage of presidential conventions began in 1948 and extensive coverage started in 1952, only two years before Britain.

2 Party conferences are not a true media event by Dayan and Katz's (1992, pp. 5–7) definition. They suggest media events are 'transmitted and occur in real time . . . The organizers typically are public bodies with whom the media co-operate . . . There may well be collusion between the broadcasters and organizers . . . The events are pre-planned, announced and advertised in advance . . . These broadcast events are presented with reverence and ceremony . . . These ceremonials electrify very large audiences.' Party conferences clearly fit some of these criteria but not all. They are certainly not presented with reverence nor do they electrify the audience. Dayan and Katz argue that 'an event that fails to excite the public or one that is not presented with reverence by the broadcasters . . . does not qualify according to the definition, but they are particularly interesting because they suggest a pathology of media events, of which the former is an event "manqué" and the latter an event "denied" by the broadcasters' (p. 10).

3 McNair, 1995, p. 111.

4 Blumler defines it as: 'a competitive struggle to influence and control

popular perceptions of key political events and issues through the major mass media' (1990, p. 103).

5 Bruce (1992, p. 136) notes: 'The concept was invented in the US and developed as part of the process whereby the briefers fought to claim victory in the Ford–Carter debates.' Kerbal (1994, p. 45) calls them 'campaign operatives who vehemently attempt to get reporters to accept their version of the story'. Routledge (1995, p. 3) notes that 'a spin doctor according to Brewer's definition is a campaign official or public relations expert attached to a party or a candidate whose task is to channel the facts to the media which put the best possible construction on events . . . This is certainly one way of describing it, but it misses out the threats and cajolery, the screeching of obscenities, the threats to get people sacked.'

6 For the Liberal Democrats, who usually attract significantly less news attention than the Government or the Opposition (Semetko, 1989), their autumn conference is an especially welcome chance to boost the profile of their policies.

7 McNair (1995, pp. 118–19), using Boorstin's concept, notes that a 'pseudo event' is a 'happening which bears only a tenuous relationship to political reality. It has meaning in and of itself, primarily as a media event. It lacks authenticity and rationality . . . Closer perhaps to the "pure" pseudo event are occasions such as party conferences'.

8 Thompson (1995, p. 134) argues: 'If Foucault had considered the role of the communications media more carefully, he might have seen that they establish a relationship between power and visibility that is quite different from that implicit in the model of the Panopticon. Whereas the Panopticon renders many people visible to a few and enables power to be exercised over the many by subjecting them to a state of permanent visibility, the development of communications media provides a means by which many people can gather information about a few and, at the same time, a few can appear before the many. Thanks to the media, it is primarily those who exercise power rather than those over whom power is exercised, who are subjected to a certain kind of visibility.'

9 Blumler *et al.*, 1995, p. 76.

10 See Schlesinger, 1990, p. 79.

11 Blumler, 1990, pp. 107–8.

12 Blumler, 1990, p. 107.

13 The broadcast times of the ITN news bulletins on ITV have changed since 1999. The *News at 5.40* p.m. is now scheduled at 6.30 p.m. and *News at Ten* after a brief spell at eleven o'clock has returned to ten o'clock on at least three nights a week. The broadcast time of the BBC *Nine O'clock News* changed to ten p.m. from 2000.

1 Creating the 'Good' Conference

1 Minkin, 1978, p. 133.

2 Kavanagh, 1996, p. 29.

3 The Liberal Democrats' Conference and Events Office may be considered

too small to count as a machine bureaucracy in the sense that Mintzberg (1983) intended. A party source noted: 'At the present I have one full-time assistant [who] is paid by me three days a week and my other assistant is a volunteer and works two days a week and I do the whole lot with that staff' (interview with Penny McCormack). But it was nevertheless part of a wider bureaucratic machine with devolved responsibilities specifically for conference planning.

4   Following William Hague's reforms of the party's structure after the 1997 general election defeat the National Union has been replaced by the National Conservative Convention, whose board fulfils the same function as the National Union Executive Committee in terms of organizing the annual conference.

5   Although their roles were similar, there were some differences in their structure. The FCC was a partially elected body consisting of 26 members, of whom 11 were elected each year by the conference and 15 were appointed. The CAC consisted of 7 members, 5 of whom were elected directly by the conference and the remaining 2 by the constituency parties. The Conference Agenda Subcommittee was a wholly-appointed subcommittee of the National Union Executive Committee. Its replacement since 1997, a standing committee, is appointed by the National Conservative Convention.

6   Interview with Larry Whitty, September 1996. Former General Secretary of the Labour Party under leaders Neil Kinnock and John Smith.

7   Shaw notes (1994, p. 127), 'In the past, party conferences tended to be sources of political embarrassment and poor publicity. The control the leadership now wielded over conference . . . enabled Labour strategists to convert it into a media event. The whole operation was aimed at securing maximum favourable media coverage; in Mandelson's words: "Totally unashamedly, we have used the conference to project the party, to make an impact on the public".'

8   Labour Party, 1997, p. 14.

9   Interview with Larry Whitty, September 1996.

10 One controversial issue in 1995 which the Labour leadership wanted to minimize broadcast coverage of through timetabling it on the same day as the leader's speech was the deselection of Labour Prospective Parliamentary Candidate Liz Davies. When asked if the agenda committee was involved in the timetabling decision, a source replied: 'Totally involved, but I would say in reality it is the Chair and the secretary... that are the political operators.'

11 Interview with Derek Gladwin, January 1996. Former Chairman of Labour's Conference Arrangements Committee under leaders Neil Kinnock and John Smith.

12 Interview with Sally Morgan, January 1996. Former Secretary to the CAC under leaders Neil Kinnock and John Smith.

13 Interview with Larry Whitty, September 1996.

14 Quoted in Grice, 1998, p. 4. Grice, (1998, p. 4) also notes 'The NEC which

meets on Tuesday (28 July) will approve the private sessions . . . The sessions on welfare reform, health, crime and Europe will take place behind closed doors, with the media excluded. Party officials are adamant that the lock out will be enforced.' Grice (1998, p. 4) further notes 'Blair's people were getting very twitchy about the question-and-answer session; they didn't want the TV coverage dominated by delegates attacking ministers or asking difficult questions.'

15 Interview with Alan Leaman, July 1995. The Liberal Democrats' Director of Strategy and Planning during the mid-1990s.

16 Interview with Alan Sherwell, June 1996. The Chair of the Liberal Democrats' Federal Conference Committee during the mid-1990s.

17 Interview with Penny McCormack, February 1996. The Liberal Democrat Conference Organizer.

18 Ibid.

19 Interview with Alan Sherwell, June 1996.

20 Kelly, 1989, p. 139.

21 Interview with Chris Poole, August 1995. The Secretary of the National Union of Conservative and Unionist Associations in the mid-1990s.

22 Ball, 1996, p. 4.

23 Ibid., p. 5. Ball also provides a detailed account of the submission of Euro-sceptical motions to the Conservatives' conference between 1992 and 1995.

24 Interview with Chris Poole, August 1995.

25 In the Labour Party there has been some disquiet about the downgrading of the policy formulating role of conference. In particular, changes proposed in 'Party in Power' to limit the say of delegates on policy matters caused a backlash. More than 100 motions critical of the reforms or calling for delay had been submitted by the constituencies and unions for the 1997 annual conference (Wintour, 1997, p. 2).

26 The Labour Party have a rolling policy programme with key subjects reviewed over a two-year cycle by a 175-strong National Policy Forum. It is elected for two years and includes 30 trade unionists, 54 constituency members and representatives from the regions.

27 Interview with Larry Whitty, September 1996.

28 Interview with Alan Sherwell, June 1996.

29 Ibid.

30 Interview with Penny McCormack, February 1996.

31 Interview with Larry Whitty, September 1996.

32 Interview with Alan Sherwell, June 1996.

33 Former Party Chairman Norman Tebbit took credit for introducing themes after the 1985 Conservative conference (1988, p. 244). However, one Conservative source, when interviewed, did raise some problems with sticking to themes. 'If you wanted to do an economy theme-day in the years when Michael Heseltine was Secretary of State for Trade and Industry you couldn't do it because you couldn't have him and the Chancellor speaking on the same day. Yet to say that one day is an economy theme-day when

the Chancellor isn't speaking or the President of the Board of Trade . . . simply won't work' (interview with Tim Collins, October 1995).

34 Interview with Larry Whitty, September 1996.
35 Ibid.
36 Wintour, 1995b, p. 25.
37 Grice, 1996, p. 7.
38 Interview with Alan Sherwell, June 1996.
39 Interview with Tim Collins, October 1995. Special Media Advisor and former Director of Communications for the Conservative Party 1992–5.
40 Ibid.
41 This has not always been the case. Kelly (1994, p. 228) notes of the Conservative conference: 'Prior to 1965 the leader's speech was scheduled to take place after the conference's formal cessation, as if to demonstrate that the leadership was not directly affected by its events.'
42 Clifton, 1997, p. 23.
43 Interview with Jeremy Hanley, November 1995. Former Conservative Party Chairman 1994–5.
44 Interview with Penny McCormack, February 1996.
45 Interview with Alan Sherwell, June 1996.
46 Interview with Tim Collins, October 1995.
47 Ibid.
48 Interview with Jeremy Hanley, November 1995.
49 Interview with Tim Collins, October 1995.
50 Interview with Joyce Gould, June 1996. Former Director of Development and Organization at the Labour party under leaders Neil Kinnock and John Smith.
51 Interview with Tim Collins, October 1995.
52 Ibid.
53 Interview with Alan Leaman, July 1995.
54 Ibid.
55 Interview with Tim Collins, October 1995.
56 Interview with Alan Leaman, July 1995.
57 Interview with Chris Poole, August 1995.
58 Interview with Tim Collins, October 1995.
59 A firm called 'Moving Experiences' had the contract in the late 1990s.
60 Interview with Alan Leaman, July 1995.
61 Morris, 1994, p. 43.
62 Landale, 1996, p. 10.
63 Interview with Chris Poole, August 1995.
64 Rosenbaum (1997, p. 142) notes: 'In the 1960s and 1970s, the average platform consisted of politicians crowded onto a serried row of tables draped in cloth and cluttered with microphones, carafes and papers.'
65 Rosenbaum (1997, p. 145) notes: 'The first time that Labour had a custom-built set for the platform . . . was at Brighton in 1983. Kinnock wanted a proper set for what would be his first conference as leader. Labour's publicity team had no idea who to get to build it. So . . . they phoned

Conservative central office to obtain the details of the company that had constructed the Tory conference set in Brighton the previous year.'

66 Interview with Alan Leaman, July 1995.
67 Interview with Chris Poole, August 1995.
68 Interview with Jeremy Hanley, November 1995. Rosenbaum (1997, p. 143) notes of the same innovation: 'This reinforces his image as an accessible "man of the people" rather than a grand and aloof figure.'
69 Interview with Jeremy Hanley, November 1995.
70 Interview with Alan Leaman, July 1995.
71 Interview with Chris Poole, August 1995.
72 Wintour, 1996, p. 7.
73 Interview with Penny McCormack, February 1996.
74 Maguire, 2000b, p. 6.
75 The slogans for the twelve conferences in the period of study were:

1993. Liberal Democrats: 'Facing up to the Future'; Labour: 'Building for the Future'; Conservatives: 'Building on the Recovery'.
1994. Liberal Democrats: (no slogan); Labour: 'New Labour New Britain'; Conservatives: 'Britain Growing Stronger'.
1995. Liberal Democrats: 'Britain's People Britain's Future'; Labour: 'New Labour New Britain: Lasting Prosperity'; Conservatives: 'Our Nation's Future: Conservative'.
1996. Liberal Democrats: 'Take Courage for the Future'; Labour: 'New Labour New Life for Britain'; Conservatives: 'Opportunity for All'.

76 Interview with Jeremy Hanley, November 1995.
77 Hogg and Hill, 1995, p. 128.
78 Bradshaw, 1991, p. 17.
79 Scammell, 1995, p. 101.
80 Fant (1980, p. 132) notes: 'During recent US Presidential conventions the parties have virtually forced the networks to televise their films by dimming the house lights, thus discouraging coverage of asides.'
81 Cockerell, 1989, p. 21.
82 See Scammell, 1995, p. 101.
83 Rosenbaum (1997, pp. 142–3) notes that Thomas 'Managed to create a separate speaker's rostrum as a visual focal point and to clear the area around and directly behind this to provide a cleaner TV image.'
84 Interview with Chris Poole, August 1995.
85 Ibid.
86 Ibid.
87 This trend seems set to continue. A confidential Labour National Executive Committee report leaked to the *Sunday Times* noted: 'The [1998] conference will be more stage managed than ever. The platform set and hall will be designed to provide a "united look". While the aisles will be carpeted to make everyone feel part of the proceedings. "Presentation needs to be both physically and visually egalitarian and inclusive" . . . ' (Grice, 1998, p. 4).

2 Negotiating Coverage

1   Waltzer in his study of the US presidential conventions makes a similar point: 'Political parties and television networks cannot separately plan national conventions or coverage of them' (1966, p. 36).
2   Interview with Linda Parker, August 1995. The BBC Conference Unit Manager.
3   Ibid.
4   Interview with Ric Bailey, February 1996. Editor, BBC Political News.
5   Interview with Martin Smith, August 1996. The ITN Resource Manager.
6   Interview with Bill Bush, July 1995. The head of BBC Political Research Unit.
7   Interview with Linda Parker, August 1995.
8   Interview with Martin Smith, August 1996.
9   Ibid.
10   Ibid.
11   Interview with Linda Parker, August 1995.
12   Ibid.
13   Interview with Roy Graham, January 1996. Architect responsible for designing conference layout.
14   Ibid.
15   Ibid.
16   An agenda was drawn up for the meetings with points for discussion on: conference sessions, accreditation, entrances and security, stage, lighting, cameras and commentary positions, sound, radio broadcasters, media facilities, media technical vehicles, TV sets, hotel and other matters. There are striking similarities with Waltzer's study of the conventions. He notes: 'Network representatives attend meetings of the conventions sites committees to explain television's needs . . . The networks and the parties consulted about the physical appearances, programs, and schedules of the conventions. Lighting was left largely to the determination of the television networks' (1966, p. 36).
17   Interview with Penny McCormack, February 1996. Liberal Democrat Conference Organizer.
18   Interview with Chris Poole, August 1995. The Secretary of the National Union of Conservative and Unionist Associations.
19   Interview with Martin Smith, August 1996.
20   Interview with Bill Bush, July 1995.
21   Interview with Linda Parker, August 1995.
22   Ibid.
23   Walker, 1996, p. 15.
24   Campbell, 1996, p. 6.
25   Interview with Linda Parker, August 1995.
26   Ibid.
27   Interview with Martin Smith, August 1996.
28   Interview with Bob Oliver, May 1996. The Organizational Manager for Sky News.

29   Interview with Martin Smith, August 1996.
30   Interview with Roy Graham, January 1996.
31   Interview with Linda Parker, August 1995.
32   Interview with Roy Graham, January 1996.
33   Ibid.
34   Interview with Chris Poole, August 1995.
35   Ibid.
36   A written reply by Judith Fryer. The Liberal Democrat Head of Press and Broadcasting.
37   Interview with Penny McCormack, February 1996.
38   Interview with Chris Poole, August 1995.
39   Interview with Steve White, April 1996. News Engineer in charge of outside broadcast planning at ITN.
40   Interview with Bob Oliver, May 1996.
41   Interview with Roy Graham, January 1996.
42   Interview with Bob Oliver, May 1996.
43   Waltzer (1966, p. 36) notes a similar occurrence in planning the coverage of the conventions. 'To avoid possible allegations of preferential treatment . . . the parties made over-all bloc assignments to the television networks and other media, and delegated to them the task of dividing [it] among themselves.'
44   Interview with Bob Oliver, May 1996.
45   Interview with Martin Smith, August 1996.
46   Ibid.
47   Ibid.
48   Ibid.
49   Rosenbaum (1997, p. 140) notes of early conference coverage: 'One down side of televising was that it subjected those sitting on the platform to the intense and uncomfortable glare of early TV lighting. Many Labour politicians in particular (even including party leader Hugh Gaitskell) responded by wearing dark glasses, making this political assembly look more like a convention of gangsters.'
50   Interview with Roy Graham, January 1996.
51   Interview with Penny McCormack, February 1996.
52   Interview with Linda Parker, August 1996.
53   A source noted: 'I get a cost from Geoff Taylor [BBC] and say can you tell me how much it is going to cost to scaffold and light all these various places. He will then say if I were you I would charge 25 per cent to ITN, 10 per cent to Sky or something like that' (interview with Linda Parker).
54   Interview with Steve White, April 1996.

3 The Broadcasters by the Seaside

1   Parker, 1994 , pp. 5–8.
2   Interview with Ric Bailey, February 1996. Editor, BBC Political News.
3   Interview with Gary Gibbon, August 1995. Political Correspondent, *Channel Four News*.

4   Interview with Ric Bailey, February 1996.
5   Interview with Gary Gibbon, August 1995.
6   Interview with Hugh Pym, November 1996. Political Correspondent, ITN.
7   Interview with Gary Gibbon, August 1995.
8   Blumler and Gurevitch, 1995, p. 50.
9   Ibid., p. 89.
10 Ibid., p. 56.
11 Interview with Gary Gibbon, August 1995.
12 Interview with Hugh Pym, November 1996.
13 Blumler and Gurevitch, 1995, p. 89.
14 Interview with Gary Gibbon, August 1995.
15 Interview with Hugh Pym, November 1996.
16 This was the case with Norman Lamont. Lamont made a speech attacking government policy to fringe meetings at the 1993 and 1994 Conservative conferences which received widespread attention (see chapter 7). Similar speeches in 1995 and 1996 received hardly a mention on any of the bulletins.
17 Interview with Ric Bailey, February 1996.
18 Interview with Jon Snow, August 1995. Presenter, *Channel Four News*.
19 Interview with Gary Gibbon, August 1995.
20 Interview with Jon Snow, August 1995.
21 Interview with Ric Bailey, February 1996.
22 McNair, 1995, p. 76.
23 Speculation in this case is understood to mean a series of conjectures about the consequences of a particular event at some future point in time; and explanation to mean the interpretation of events so as to aid the audience's understanding.
24 Interview with Jon Snow, August 1995.
25 The observations were made at fringe venues, the conference hotels and press rooms at the Liberal Democrat, Labour and Conservative Conferences.
26 Baker, 1993, p. 295.
27 Interview with Ric Bailey, February 1996.
28 Interview with Gary Gibbon, August 1995.
29 Interview with Jon Snow, August 1995.
30 Sigal, 1973, p. 39.
31 Interview with Hugh Pym, November 1996.
32 Interview with Gary Gibbon, August 1995.
33 Interview with Jon Snow, August 1995.
34 Jones (1995, p. 123) suggests that: 'journalists were often desperate to speak to authoritative sources capable of giving them an instant interpretation of what happened and also the background guidance on the likely consequences.'
35 Interview with Hugh Pym, November 1996.
36 There was particular interest in finding out the Press Association's line.
37 Interview with Hugh Pym, November 1996.
38 Interview with Jon Snow, August 1995.

39   Interview with Hugh Pym, November 1996.
40   Interview with Ric Bailey, February 1996.
41   Interview with Gary Gibbon, August 1995.
42   Ibid.
43   Ibid.
44   Interview with Hugh Pym, November 1996.
45   Interview with Jon Snow, August 1995.
46   Franklin, 1994, p. 19.
47   Interview with Gary Gibbon, August 1995.
48   Ibid.
49   Interview with Ric Bailey, February 1996.
50   Letter from Nick Jones, January 1995. Political Correspondent, BBC News.
51   Interview with Hugh Pym, November 1996.
52   Interview with Ric Bailey, February 1996.
53   Ibid.
54   Ibid.
55   Ibid.
56   Ibid.
57   For a fuller exposition of the O. J. Simpson trial verdict and the Labour conference, see chapter 6.
58   Interview with Gary Gibbon, August 1995.

4 Spinning on the Conference Circuit

1   This division is based loosely on Ericson *et al.*'s (1989) binary of front and back regions within news sources.
2   Interview with Alan Leaman, July 1995. The Liberal Democrats' Director of Strategy and Planning during the mid-1990s.
3   Peter Mandelson became a central part of Labour's 'strategy-making community' (Shaw, 1994) under Neil Kinnock in the mid-eighties. While Smith's period as leader (1992 to 1994) marked Mandelson's absence from the leadership, he returned to a key strategy making role with the election of Tony Blair as Labour leader in 1994. Richards (1995b, p. 17) notes: 'Whereas Smith was relatively indifferent about political coverage, Blair placed the projection of his party and himself at the top of his priorities and therefore Mandelson with his experience and expertise was central to achieving these aims. Mandelson played a central co-ordinating role, displacing the role of Director of Media, Campaigns and Elections and masterminding Labour's 1997 general election victory. However Mandelson has lost this central strategic role in the party with his final departure from government in January 2001 (see also Appleyard, 1995; Howard, 1990).
4   Grice, 1996, p. 7.
5   Brooke, 1996, p. 23.
6   Interview with Tim Collins, October 1995. Special Media Advisor and former Director of Communications for the Conservative party from 1992 to 1995.

7 Bruce (1992, p. 133) argues that their main task was to be the 'public voice of the principal; to fill in the background facts; to provide a context for events and issues for the day; to correct misconceptions and factual errors; and to act as a liaison for media "bids" . . . '

8 Between 1994 and 1996 the number of press officers increased from 16 to 18.

9 In all different forms, at the 1995 conferences, the Liberal Democrats' press office produced a total of 42 press releases, Labour's 41 and the Conservatives' 38. The actual total number of press releases produced by all party actors was impossible to calculate accurately.

10 At Labour's conference the leadership produced a document entitled 'Proposed Action on Composites and Resolutions on the Conference Timetable' listing the attitude of Labour's National Executive Committee to each composite and resolution. The Liberal Democrats' conference committee provided daily announcement sheets carrying information about amendments to resolutions.

11 At the Liberal Democrats' conferences the press office issues a daily document, called 'Daily Press Focus', which is a timetable indicating where the leadership will be throughout the day.

12 The term 'perspective' refers to a 'set of views, arguments, explanations and policy suggestions . . . ' (Schlesinger *et al.*, 1983, p. 2).

13 *Channel Four News*, 6 October, 1995 noted: 'Before delegates go to conference they were asked to attend briefing sessions around the country – 85 per cent did. While they chatted and socialized their sympathies were noted. The end result is that when speakers are selected the officials can with reasonable accuracy predict their views.'

14 Interview with Tim Collins, October 1995.

15 Ibid.

16 Watt, 2000, p. 2.

17 McNair, 1995, p. 107.

18 Interview with Tim Collins, October 1995.

19 Ibid.

20 Ibid.

21 Ibid.

22 Ibid.

23 At their 1994, 1995 and 1996 conferences they held two press conferences daily. Each one involved their Head of Press and Broadcasting reading the agenda for the morning and afternoon and the National Executive Committee's responses to the various amendments and composites. At the 1995 conference, as the week progressed the attendance by journalists declined rapidly until the Friday morning when there were only five journalists present. From my observations, none of the journalists asked any direct questions. There seemed to be a tacit understanding between journalists and the spin doctors about the role of these press conferences. There were also rather few post-speech press conferences held by the party

elite, despite the fact that Labour had built a rather grand stage-set in the press room for press conferences.

24 Interview with Gary Gibbon, August 1995. Political Correspondent, *Channel Four News*. Jones (1995, pp. 127–8) also notes the use of similar tactics by Peter Mandelson.

25 Interview with Jon Snow, August 1995. Presenter, *Channel Four News*.

26 Interview with Tim Collins, October 1995.

27 Former journalists Hugh Colver and Charles Lewington at Conservative Central Office had built strong contacts in the media in their previous roles as has their replacement Amanda Platell. Similarly, for the Liberal Democrats Jane Bonham-Carter and previously Olly Grender, and for Labour Joy Johnson before her resignation and Alastair Campbell.

28 Interview with Tim Collins, October 1995.

29 Interview with Alan Leaman, July 1995.

30 Schlesinger, 1987, p. 91 and p. 128.

31 Interview with Alan Leaman, July 1995.

32 Bruce (1992, p. 159) notes that photo-opportunities are regulated by certain rules: 'First, the cameras must not obstruct the principal's path; secondly, they must be stationary some yards away; thirdly, some physical means (e.g. crash barriers), need to be employed to restrain the camera crews; fourth, minders have to be present to brief the crews on the timing of the interviewee's appearance; fifth, the minders must scan the background "in frame" . . . to remove or conceal extraneous distractions or embarrassments; and lastly the interviewee must rehearse . . . ' During my observation at the conferences, the first five of these were regularly applied to the arrival of the party leaders at the conference hotel and the main conference hall, and at other occasions such as the tour by the party leaders of the conference exhibition stalls.

33 Interview with Alan Leaman, July 1995.

34 Interview with Hugh Pym, November 1996. Political Correspondent, ITN.

35 Ibid.

36 Interview with Gary Gibbon, August 1995.

37 Interview with Ric Bailey, February 1996. Editor, BBC Political News.

38 Interview with Gary Gibbon, August 1995.

39 Jones, 1995, p. 168. Jones details such an occurrence at the 1994 Labour party conference.

40 Interview with Gary Gibbon, August 1995.

41 Interview with Ric Bailey, February 1996.

42 McSmith, 2000, p. 9.

43 Interview with Tim Collins, October 1995.

44 Ibid.

45 Interview with Hugh Pym, November 1996.

46 Ibid.

5 Packaging the Leader's Speech

1   Scammell and Semetko (1998, p. 14) suggest that contextualizing comments 'refer to the way reporters' remarks surround or set the scene for party activities and statements'. Such comments could be 'non-directional (straight/descriptive), reinforcing or deflating of the activities and statements of politicians'. For the purposes of the leaders' speeches it was important to see the wider application of the notion of contextualizing commentary. Non-directional comments were value-laden with references to the audience and the symbolic or visionary nature of the speech, amongst other things. Their content and not simply their direction was of importance, particularly in gaining an understanding of the journalists' contribution to contextualizing the speeches.

2   These are question and answer sessions between anchor in the studio and the journalist in the field.

3   The strategy of maintaining the middle ground in policy terms between Labour and the Conservative parties and being prepared to co-operate with either should there be an inconclusive general election result.

4   The length of each passage varied between reports. For the sake of analysis the fullest possible version of the passage is quoted.

5   The 'Liberal Democrat Guarantee' policy document, which was launched at this conference, was in addition only mentioned in reports on the BBC *Six O'clock News* and *Newsnight*.

6   Only those remarks directly referring to the leader's speech were coded as reactive comments on the content analysis sheet. A positive reaction was defined as one which praised the leader and endorsed his reforms or policy announcements. A negative reaction was defined as one which was hostile toward and critical of the leader's speech. A neutral reaction was neither endorsing nor critical of the speech but mainly descriptive.

6 Off Message: the Limits of Agenda Management

1   Throughout the period of the study there were two opinion polls commissioned, both by *Newsnight* – one on the Labour party in 1993 and the other on the Liberal Democrats in 1994. The findings of both polls formed the content of two programmes.

2   Norton, 1996, p. 12.

3   Stanyer and Scammell, 1996, p. 1.

4   Interview with Gary Gibbon, August 1995. Political Correspondent, *Channel Four News*.

5   Kelly (1994, p. 253) notes: 'After 1979 the fringe acquired a new dimension as it came to provide a platform from which sacked ministers such as Gilmour (in 1981) and Pym (in 1985) ventured criticism of government policy.'

6   Interview with Hugh Pym, November 1996. Political Correspondent, ITN.

7   Interview with Gary Gibbon, August 1995.

8   Jones, 1995, p. 146.

9   Routledge, 1995, p. 3.
10 The inter-party nature of rebuttal did not disappear: the three parties continued to respond to developments at each other's conferences through phoning the journalists directly or faxing them. Jones notes that the spin doctors 'obtain the telephone numbers of the temporary news rooms established by the radio and television services during the party conferences. Labour's response to a development at a Conservative conference can then be communicated directly to the relevant political correspondent' (Jones, 1990, p. 25).
11 An example of this occurred at an evening event at the 1999 Labour conference. Frank Dobson's (former Health Secretary) spin doctor Joe McCrea confronted *Channel Four News* correspondent Victoria MacDonald over a complaint about his activity to his boss. McCrea verbally reduced her to tears before the situation was eventually calmed down (see Milne, 1999).
12 Jones, 1995, p. 124.
13 There were numerous cases where the parties sought to influence news coverage or to complain. These include the then Chairman Chris Patten's call for Conservative representatives to complain to the BBC about their coverage of the 1991 conference (see Dovkants, 1991; Franklin, 1994) and Labour's attack on the BBC for delaying the *One O'clock News* in order to cover the Conservative Party Chairman's speech at the 1995 Conservative conference (see Thynne, 1995).
14 Interview with Alan Leaman, July 1995. The Liberal Democrats' Director of Strategy and Planning during the mid-1990s.
15 Jones, 1995, p. 132.
16 Interview with Alan Leaman, July 1995.
17 Interview with Chris Poole, August 1995. The Secretary of the National Union of Conservative and Unionist Associations in the mid-1990s.
18 Ibid.
19 Staff Reporters, 1994, p. 11.
20 Maguire, 2000, p. 7.
21 Interview with Hugh Pym, November 1996.
22 Ibid.
23 Ibid.
24 Ibid.
25 Interview with Tim Collins, October 1995. Special Media Advisor and former Director of Communications for the Conservative party from 1992 to 1995.
26 Ibid.
27 Jones, 1995, p. 123.
28 Webster, 1995, p. 1.
29 Johnston, 1995, p. 2.
30 Ibid., p. 2.
31 Webster, 1995, p. 1.
32 Culf, 1995, p. 1.
33 Ibid., p. 1.

34   Interview with Tim Collins, October 1995.
35   Interview with Jeremy Hanley, November 1995. Former Conservative Party Chairman 1994–5.
36   Interview with Chris Poole, August 1995.
37   Interview with Tim Collins, October 1995.
38   Ibid. Former Conservative spin doctor Brendan Bruce also notes: 'News conferences have a dreadful tendency to go wrong . . . ' (1992, p. 169).
39   Interview with Jeremy Hanley.
40   Kelly (1998) argues that disputes have a long history of erupting at Conservative conferences.
41   Smithers (1996, p. 3) notes: 'Ministerial aides admitted that the problem had reached a head around the time of the party conference in October; one official said: "Of course there are always disputes behind the scenes, but this was getting out of control. Mrs Gillian Shephard, for example, was extremely unhappy. She confronted Dr Mawhinney over this . . . when she thought he was trying to suggest she should be sacked" . . . What really got ministers' backs up, it seems, is the Chairman's meddling in policy.'
42   Interview with Gary Gibbon, August 1995.
43   Interview with Hugh Pym, November 1996.
44   Interview with Jon Snow, August 1995. Presenter, *Channel Four News*.
45   Interview with Ric Bailey, February 1996. Editor, BBC Political News.
46   Interview with Tim Collins, October 1995.
47   Ibid.
48   Ibid.
49   Richards, 1995, p. 15.
50   Ibid., p. 15.
51   Jones, 1995, p. 168.
52   See ibid., p. 168.

7 Manufacturing Debate

1   Paletz and Elson (1976, pp. 121–2) note of journalists, in their study of news coverage of the US presidential conventions: 'Their aim seemed to be to find people who would present opposing views on the major themes with which coverage was concerned. This process tended to emphasize divisiveness . . . It was most apparent in the way NBC interviewed people who opposed McGovern, alternating them with McGovern supporters. The juxtaposition of their comments and classifications created the impression of hostility and disunity among participants.'
2   Liberal Democrats, 1994, p. 17.
3   Ibid., p. 28.
4   Interview with Alan Leaman, July 1995. The Liberal Democrats' Director of Strategy and Planning during the mid-1990s.
5   Wintour and Harper note: 'It had been agreed weeks ago by the conference arrangements committee . . . [they] could have been persuaded to say there was no need for a debate on the issue at this year's conference. But the provisional agenda was agreed many weeks ago, before Mr Blair had

decided to propose the re-writing of Clause Four, similarly it had been agreed weeks ago that [the] debate would be staged on Thursday . . . Mr Blair's team . . . felt they could not go to the CAC . . . and ask for re-timetabling to Monday without raising suspicions' (1994, p. 7).

6   Letter from Nick Jones, January 1995. Political Correspondent, BBC News.
7   Interview with Hugh Pym, November 1996. Political Correspondent, ITN.
8   Ibid.
9   Letter from Nick Jones, January 1995.
10 Interview with Hugh Pym, November 1996.
11 Jones (1995, p. 169) notes: 'Mandelson gave a prerecorded interview for the "World at One" in which he suggested that if a consensus developed behind a move to re-write Labour's constitution then the issue would be resolved quickly so that the debate over Clause Four did not dominate the 1995 autumn conference . . . Prescott immediately rejected this suggestion on *Conference Live*, "a special conference" he said "would not be necessary".'
12 Speculative questions and answers were those in which the anchor asked about and the journalist actually commented upon the likely future outcome of a vote or the possible impacts of such a debate on the parties' electoral fortunes. Explanatory questions and answers sought to further illuminate events or provide background to the issues.

8 The Formation of Conference News Agendas

1   Grice, 1996, p. 7.
2   *Newsnight*, 1 October, 1996.
3   *Newsnight*, 1 October, 1996.
4   Pierce and Sherman, 1997, p. 2.
5   The average audience viewing figures are calculated from data obtained from BARB.
6   Interview with Ric Bailey, February 1996. Editor, BBC Political News.
7   Interview with Hugh Pym, November 1996. Political Correspondent, ITN.
8   Interview with Jon Snow, August 1995. Presenter, *Channel Four News*.
     Indeed there were several short news stories on the dress sense and role of Norma Major and Cherie Blair on ITN. Also see Junor (1993) for news media reporting of Norma Major's purchase of a dress at the 1992 Conservative party conference.
9   Interview with Hugh Pym, November 1996.
10 Interview with Jon Snow, August 1995.
11 If we look to the US TV coverage of the presidential conventions as a possible future scenario, it is one where coverage has radically declined. Hames notes: 'Less than twenty years ago they lasted for four whole days and were devoted to the internal means of the party organization. The entire platform, often 100,000 words long, would be read to delegates for their approval. The evening sessions were devoted to speeches of thirty minutes or more by senior figures who spoke by right of their position no matter how dreadful their oratory. The whole occasion, every minute, was

covered by all three major networks. Starting in the 1980s, responding to ratings, the stations cut back their coverage. This year (1996) little more than an hour a day is live, and that punctuated by commercials and commentary' (1996, p. 11). In Britain this scenario is starting to occur. The BBC declared in 1999 that in the future most of its live coverage would be broadcast not on terrestrial channels but on the cable Parliament channel.

12 Gaber, 1998, p. 1.

13 Franklin (1996, pp. 312–13) notes that there has been a proliferation of broadcast media outlets reporting on Parliament and these have impacted on 'what was a previously very stable system of broadcast and print media' leading to a 'highly competitive environment, prompting market driven efficiencies . . . and market imperative to generate low cost popular programming'.

Appendix

1 Philo, 1987, p. 398.

Bibliography

Altheide, D. L. and Snow, R. P. 1979: *Media Logic*. Sage Library of Social Research, Vol. 89, Beverley Hills, CA: Sage.

Appleyard, B. 1995: The Third Man: Labour's Peter Mandelson. *The Sunday Times Magazine*, 1 October, pp. 16–22.

Baker, K. 1993: *The Turbulent Years: My Life in Politics*. London: Faber and Faber.

Ball, M. 1996: *The Conservative Conference and Euro-Sceptical Motions 1992–95*. Bruges Group Occasional Paper No 23.

Barnes, J. 1994: Ideology and Factions. In A. Seldon and S. Ball (eds), *Conservative Century: The Conservative Party Since 1900*, Oxford: Oxford University Press.

Barnett, S. 2001: Here's a Shock Headline You Won't See Elsewhere: Auntie Gets it Right. *The Observer*, Business, 20 May, p. 5.

Barnett, S. and Seymour, E. 2000: You Cannot be Serious. *The Guardian*, G2, 10 July, pp. 2–3.

Bennett, W. Lance. 1990: Toward a Theory of Press–State Relations in the United States. *Journal of Communication* 40 (2), 103–25.

——. 1996: *News: The Politics of Illusion*. Third Edition, White Plains, NY: Longman.

Bennett, W. Lance, Gressett, L. A. and Haltom, W. 1985: Repairing the News: A Case Study of the News Paradigm. *Journal of Communication* 35 (3), 50–86.

Berelson, B. 1971: *Content Analysis in Communications Research*, reprinted, New York: Hafner.

Blumenthal, S. 1982: *The Permanent Campaign*. New York: Simon and Schuster.

Blumler, J. G. 1990: Elections, the Media and the Modern Publicity Process. In M. Ferguson (ed.), *Public Communication the New Imperatives: Future Directions for Media Research*, London and Newbury Park, CA: Sage.

——. 1991: The New Television Market Place: Imperatives, Implications, Issues. In J. Curran and M. Gurevitch (eds), *Mass Media and Society*, London: Edward Arnold.

——. 1996: Introduction to Political Communication. *Centre for Mass Communication Research MA Handbook* 1 (2), 4–42.

Blumler, J. G. and Gurevitch, M. 1995: *The Crisis of Public Communication*. London: Routledge.

——. 1998: Change in the Air: Campaign Journalism at the BBC, 1997. In

I. Crewe, B. Gosschalk and J. Bartle (eds), *Political Communications: Why Labour Won the General Election of 1997*, London: Frank Cass.

——. 2000: Rethinking the Study of Political Communication. In J. Curran and M. Gurevitch (eds), *Mass Media and Society*, Third Edition, London: Arnold.

Blumler, J. G., Dayan, D. and Wolton, D. 1990: West European Perspectives on Political Communications: Structures and Dynamics. *European Journal of Communication* 5 (2), 261–84.

Blumler, J. G., Gurevitch, M. and Nossiter, T. J. 1986: Setting the Television News Agenda: Campaign Observation at the BBC. In I. Crewe and M. Harrop (eds), *Political Communications: The General Election Campaign of 1983*, Cambridge: Cambridge University Press.

——. 1989: The Earnest vs. the Determined: Election News Making at the BBC, 1987. In I. Crewe and M. Harrop (eds), *Political Communications: The General Election Campaign of 1987*, Cambridge: Cambridge University Press.

——. 1995: Struggles For Meaningful Election Communication: Television Journalism at the BBC, 1992. In I. Crewe and B. Gosschalk (eds), *Political Communications: The General Election Campaign of 1992*, Cambridge: Cambridge University Press.

Blumler, J. G., Kavanagh, D. and Nossiter, T. J. 1996: Modern Communications versus Traditional Politics in Britain: An Unstable Marriage of Convenience. In D. Swanson and P. Mancini (eds) 1996: *Politics, Media and Modern Democracy*, Westport, CN: Praeger.

Boorstin. D. J. 1961: *The Image: Or What Happened to the American Dream*. London: Weidenfeld & Nicolson.

Bradshaw, D. 1991: Just who was that Woman? *The Conference Guide 1991*. London: The Labour Party, p. 17.

Brooke, S. 1996: Meet the Specialists in Party-speak. *The Times*, 9 October, p. 23.

Bruce, B. 1992: *Images of Power: How the Image Makers Shape Our Leaders*. London: Kogan Page.

Butler, D. and Kavanagh, D. 1997: *The British General Election of 1997*. Basingstoke: Macmillan.

Campbell, A. 1996: Auntie's Spinners. *The Sunday Times News Review*, 22 September, p. 6.

Clifton, D. 1997: Crafting Blair's Speech. *The Times*, 1 October, p. 23.

Cockerell, M. 1989: *Live From Number 10: The Inside Story of Prime Ministers and Television*. London: Faber and Faber.

Cosgrave, P. 1978: *Margaret Thatcher: A Tory and Her Party*. London: Hutchinson.

Culf, A. 1995: BBC Denies Blair Camp Dictated News Priorities. *The Guardian*, 5 October, p. 2.

——. 1995b: BBC to Log Political Pressure. *The Guardian*, 9 October, p. 6.

Curran, J. 1990: The New Revisionism in Mass Communication Research: A Reappraisal. *European Journal of Communication* 5 (1), 135–64.

——. 1990b: Culturalist Perspectives of News Organisations: A Reappraisal and a Case Study. In M. Ferguson (ed.), *Public Communication the New Imperatives: Future Directions for Media Research*, London and Newbury Park, CA: Sage.

Curran, J., Gurevitch, M. and Woollacott, J. 1982: The Study of the Media:

Theoretical Approaches. In M. Gurevitch, T. Bennett, J. Curran and J. Woollacott (eds), *Culture, Society and the Media*, London: Methuen.

Davies, A. J. 1995:*We the Nation: The Conservative Party and the Pursuit of Power*. London: Little Brown & Co.

Dayan, D. and Katz, E. 1992: *Media Events: The Live Broadcasting of History*. Cambridge, Mass.: Harvard University Press.

Deacon, D. 1996: The Voluntary Sector in the Changing Communication Environment. *European Journal of Communication* 11 (2), 173–99.

Dovkants, K. 1991: The Truth About Those Four Minutes That Shook the BBC. *The Evening Standard*, 24 October, p. 15.

Dunleavy, P. and O'Leary, B. 1987: *Theories of the State: The Politics of Liberal Democracy*. Basingstoke: Macmillan.

Ericson, R., Baranek, P. and Chan, J. 1989: *Negotiating Control: A Study of News Sources*. Milton Keynes: Open University Press.

Fant, C. H. 1980: Televising Presidential Conventions, 1952–1980. *Journal of Communication* 30 (4), 130–9.

Faucher, F. 1998: *Is there Room for Democratic Debates at British Labour Party Conferences*. A conference paper delivered at the Political Studies Association Conference, Keele University, 7–9 April.

Fowler, N. 1991: *Ministers Decide: A Personal Memoir of the Thatcher Years*. London: Chapmans.

Franklin, B. 1992: Televising the British House of Commons. In B. Franklin (ed.), *Televising Democracies*, London: Routledge.

——. 1994: *Packaging Politics: Political Communications in Britain's Media Democracy*. London: Edward Arnold.

——. 1996: Keeping it "Bright, Light and Trite": Changing Newspaper Reporting of Parliament. *Parliamentary Affairs* 49 (2), 298–315.

——. 1997: *Newszak and News Media*. London: Arnold.

Gaber, I. 1995: *Driving the News or Spinning out of Control: Politicians, the Media and the Battle for the News Agenda*. A conference paper delivered at the Elections, Parties and Opinion Polls (EPOP) Group Conference, London, 15 September.

——. 1998: *New Labour and the New Information Order: The View from the Television Newsroom*. A conference paper delivered at the Political Studies Association Conference, University of Keele, 7–9 April.

Gandy, O. 1982: *Beyond Agenda Setting: Information Subsidies and Public Policy*. Norwood, NJ: Ablex.

Gans, H. J. 1979: *Deciding What's News: A Study of CBS Evening News, NBC Nightly News, Newsweek and Time*. New York: Pantheon Books.

Goddard, P., Scammell, M. and Semetko, H. 1998: Too Much of a Good Thing? Television in the 1997 Election Campaign. In I. Crewe, B. Gosschalk and J. Bartle (eds), *Political Communications: Why Labour Won the General Election of 1997*, London: Frank Cass.

Golding, P. and Elliott, P. 1979: *Making the News*. Harlow, Essex: Longman.

Greenslade, R. 1995: The Light Blue Touchpaper. *The Guardian*, G2, 26 June, p. 14.

Grice, A. 1996: Nothing Left to Chance for Blair's Babes. *The Sunday Times*, 29 September, p. 7.

——. 1998: Secrecy on the Road to Blackpool Pier. *The Sunday Times*, News Review, 28 July, p. 4.

Griffin, M. 1992: Looking at News: Strategies for Research. *Communication* 13 (1), 121–41.

Gurevitch, M. and Blumler, J. G. 1977: Linkages Between the Mass Media and Politics. In J. Curran, M. Gurevitch and J. Woollacott (eds), *Mass Communication and Society*, London: Edward Arnold.

Hall, S., Critcher, C., Jefferson, T., Clarke, J. and Roberts, B. 1978: *Policing the Crisis: Mugging, the State and Law and Order*. Basingstoke: Macmillan.

Hallin, D. C. 1992: Sound Bite News: Television Coverage of Elections. *Journal of Communication* 42 (2), 5–24.

Hames, T. 1996: Dissenters Silenced as Republican Image-makers Massage the Media. *The Times*, 16 August, p. 11.

Harris, P. and Lock, A. 1995: *Sleaze or Clear Blue Water: The growth of strategic corporate business and pressure group interests at the major UK party conferences: Blackpool, Bournemouth and Brighton, 1994 an explanatory study and proposed research agenda*. A conference paper delivered at the British Academy of Management Conference, Sheffield, 11–13 September.

Harrison, M. 1985: *TV News: Whose Bias?* London: Policy Journals.

——. 1992: Politics on the Air. In D. Butler and D. Kavanagh (eds), *The British General Election of 1992*, Basingstoke: Macmillan.

——. 1997: Politics on the Air. In D. Butler and D. Kavanagh (eds), *The British General Election of 1997*, Basingstoke: Macmillan.

Harrop, M. 1990: Political Marketing. *Parliamentary Affairs* 43 (3), 277–91.

Heffernan, R. and Marqusee, M. 1992: *Defeat from the Jaws of Victory: Inside Kinnock's Labour Party*. London: Verso.

Heffernan, R. and Stanyer, J. 1997: The Enhancement of Leadership Power: The Labour Party and the Impact of Political Communications. In C. Pattie, D. Denver, J. Fisher and S. Ludlam (eds), *British Elections and Parties Review Vol. 7*, London: Frank Cass.

Helm, T. 1995: Cracks in the High Command. *The Sunday Telegraph*, 17 September, p. 20.

Heritage, J. and Greatbatch, D. 1986: Generating Applause: A Study of Rhetoric and Response at Party Political Conferences. *American Journal of Sociology* 92 (1), 110–57.

Hibbs, J. 1995: A Helping Hand from the Media's Mates. *The Daily Telegraph*, 11 October, p. 9.

Hogg, S. and Hill, J. 1995: *Too Close To Call: Power and Politics – John Major in No. 10*. London: Little Brown & Co.

Hoggart, S. 1994: Mild Party Agrees to Differ in the War of Conjunctions. *The Guardian*, 20 September, p. 6.

Holsti, O. R. 1969: *Content Analysis for the Social Sciences and Humanities*. New York: Addison-Wesley.

Howard, A. 1990: The Gospel According to Peter. *The Independent on Sunday*, 7 October, p. 4.

Hughes, C. and Wintour, P. 1990: *Labour Rebuilt: The New Model Party*. London: Fourth Estate.

Ingle, S. 1987: *The British Party System*. Oxford: Basil Blackwell.

Johnston, P. 1995: Blair Aide Pleaded with BBC Not to Lead News on OJ. *The Daily Telegraph*, 5 October, p. 2.

Jones, B. 1993: The Pitiless Probing Eye: Politicians and the Broadcast Political Interview. *Parliamentary Affairs* 46 (1), 66–90.

Jones, E. 1994: *Neil Kinnock*. London: Robert Hale.

Jones, N. 1990: The Spin-Doctors in Battle. *British Journalism Review* 1 (2), 23–7.

——. 1994: Warrior of Words. *The Guardian*, G2, 12 September, p. 14.

——. 1995: *Soundbites and Spin Doctors: How Politicians Manipulate the Media and Vice Versa*. London: Cassell.

——. 1995b: Taking Tony to the People. *The Guardian*, G2, 5 June, p. 14.

——. 1995c: Doctors in the House. *The Guardian*, G2, 18 September, p. 16.

——. 1997: *Campaign 1997: How the General Election was Won and Lost*. London: Indigo.

——. 1999: *The Sultans of Spin: The Media and the New Labour Government*. London: Orion.

Junor, P. 1993: *The Major Enigma*. London: Michael Joseph.

Katz, R. and Mair, P. 1995: Changing Models of Party Organization and Party Democracy. *Party Politics* 1 (1), 5–28.

Kavanagh, D. 1995: *Election Campaigning: The New Marketing of Politics*. Oxford: Blackwell.

——. 1996: British Party Conferences and the Political Rhetoric of the 1990s. *Government and Opposition* 31 (1), 27–44.

Kelly, R. N. 1989: *Conservative Party Conferences: The Hidden System*. Manchester: Manchester University Press.

——. 1994: The Party Conferences. In A. Seldon and S. Ball (eds), *Conservative Century: The Conservative Party Since 1900*, Oxford: Oxford University Press.

——. 1994b: Power and Leadership in the Major Parties. In L. Robins, H. Blackmore and R. Pyper (eds), *Britain's Changing Party System*, Leicester: Leicester University Press.

——. 1998: It'll be a Punch-Up. It always is. *New Statesman*, 2 October, p. 17.

Kelly, R. N. and Foster, S. 1990: Power in the Parties: McKenzie Revisited. *Contemporary Record* 3 (3), 18–22.

Kerbal, M. R. 1994: *Edited for Television: CNN, ABC and the 1992 Presidential Campaign*. Boulder, CO: Westview Press.

Kirkbride, J. and Hibbs, J. 1995: Good News Tories Get Early Slots to Rally Conference. *The Daily Telegraph*, 5 August, p. 10.

Krippendorf, K. 1980: *Content Analysis*. Beverley Hills, CA: Sage.

Kumar, K. 1977: Holding the Middle Ground: The BBC, the Public and Professional Broadcaster. In J. Curran, M. Gurevitch and J. Woollacott (eds), *Mass Communication and Society*, London: Edward Arnold.

Labour Party. 1997: *Labour into Power: A Framework for Partnership*. London: Labour Party.

Landale, J. 1996: Presenting Policy in a Good Light. *The Times*, 3 October, p. 10.

Liberal Democrats. 1994: *Conference Agenda: Liberal Democrat Autumn Conference*. Yeovil: Castle Carey Press.

Livingstone, S. and Lunt, P. 1994: *Talk on Television: Audience Participation and Public Debate*. London: Routledge.

McKenzie, R. 1964: *British Political Parties: The Distribution of Power within the Conservative and Labour Parties*. London: Heinemann.

——. 1982: Power in the Labour Party: The Issue of "Intra Party Democracy". In D. Kavanagh (ed.), *The Politics of the Labour Party*, London: George Allen & Unwin.

McNair, B. 1994: *News and Journalism in the UK*. London: Routledge.

——. 1995: *An Introduction to Political Communication*. London: Routledge.

McQuail, D. and Windahl, S. 1993: *Communication Models, for the Study of Mass Communications*. Second Edition, Harlow, Essex: Longman.

McSmith, A. 2000: Hague Spurns BBC Interviews. *The Daily Telegraph*, 5 October, p. 9.

Maguire, K. 2000: Heat Turned on Spinners as they Try to Explain. *The Guardian*, 27 September, p. 7.

——. 2000b: Conference Diary. *The Guardian*, 2 October, p. 6.

Mancini, P. 1993: Between Trust and Suspicion: How Political Journalists Solve the Dilemma. *European Journal of Communication* 8 (1), 33–51.

Midgley, C. 1996: Meet the Specialists in Party Speak. *The Times*, 9 October, p. 23.

Milne, S. 1999: Conference Diary. *The Guardian*, 30 September, p. 7.

Minkin, L. 1978: *The Labour Party Conference: A Study in the Politics of Intra-Party Democracy*. Manchester: Manchester University Press.

——. 1986: Against the Tide: Trade Unions, Political Communication and the 1983 General Election. In I. Crewe and M. Harrop (eds), *Political Communications: The General Election Campaign of 1983*, Cambridge: Cambridge University Press.

Mintzberg, H. 1983: *Structure in Fives: Designing Effective Organizations*. London: Prentice Hall International.

Molotch, H. and Lester, M. 1974: News as Purposive Behaviour: On the Strategic Use of Routine Events, Accidents, and Scandals. *American Sociological Review* 39 (1), 101–12.

Morris, R. 1994: Quite an Event: Labour's New Commercial Operations Department. *The Conference Guide 1994*, London: The Labour Party, p. 43.

Morrow, J. D. 1994: *Game Theory for Political Scientists*. Princeton, NJ: Princeton University Press.

Negrine, R. 1996: *The Communication of Politics*. London and Thousand Oaks, CA: Sage.

——. 1998: *Parliament and the Media: A study of Britain, Germany and France*. London: Pinter.

Norris, P. 1998: The Battle for the Campaign Agenda. In A. King (ed.), *New Labour Triumphs: Britain at the Polls*, Chatham, NJ: Chatham House.

Norris, P., Curtice, J., Sanders, D., Scammell, M. and Semetko, H. 1999: *On Message: Communicating the Campaign*. London: Sage.

Norton, P. 1996: A Cut Above the Average Fringe. *The House Magazine*. 21 (732), 23 September, p. 12.

Nossiter, T. J., Scammell, M. and Semetko, H. 1995: Old Values Versus News Values: the British General Election Campaign on Television. In I. Crewe and B. Gosschalk (eds), *Political Communications: The General Election Campaign of 1992*, Cambridge: Cambridge University Press.

Osbourne, M. J. and Rubinstein, A. 1994: *A Course in Game Theory*. Cambridge, Mass.: MIT Press.

Paletz, D. and Elson, M. 1976: Television Coverage of Presidential Conventions: Now You See it, Now You Don't. *Political Science Quarterly* 91 (1), 109–31.

Panebianco, A. 1988: *Political Parties: Organization and Power*. Cambridge: Cambridge University Press.

Parker, L. 1994: *BBC Conference Unit Fact Finder*. BBC pamphlet.

Parkinson, C. 1992: *Right at the Centre*. London: Weidenfeld & Nicolson.

Peele, G. 1990: British Political Parties in the 1980s. In A. Seldon (ed.), *UK Political Parties Since 1945*. London: Philip Allen.

Philo, G. 1987: Whose News? *Media Culture and Society* 9 (4), 397–406.

Pierce, A. and Sherman, J. 1997: Hague Facing Revolt by MPs Over Reform. *The Times*, 13 October, p. 2.

Prior, J. 1986: *Balance of Power*. London: Hamish Hamilton.

Prosser, T. 1993: Public Service Broadcasting and Deregulation in the UK. *European Journal of Communication* 7 (1), 173–93.

Rawnsley, A. 1993: Tribes and Tribulations. *The Conference Guide 1993*, London: The Labour Party, pp. 7–9.

Reese, D., Grant, A. and Danielian, L. 1994: The Structure of News Sources on Television: A Network Analysis of "CBS," "Nightline," "MacNeil/Lehrer," and "This Week with David Brinkley" *Journal of Communication* 44 (2), 84–107.

Rentoul, J. 1995: *Tony Blair*. London: Little Brown & Co.

Richards, S. 1994: Mugged by the Media. *The Guardian*, G2, 12 December, p. 14.

——. 1995: Silence of the Lambs. *The Guardian*, G2, 17 March, p. 15.

——. 1995b: Spinning a New Line. *The Guardian*, G2, 8 May, p. 15.

Rosenbaum, M. 1997: *From Soap Box to Soundbite: Party Political Campaigning in Britain since 1945*, Basingstoke: Macmillan.

Routledge, P. 1995: Will the Screeching Doctors Win With the Spin. *The Independent on Sunday*, 15 October, p. 3.

Scammell, M. 1995: *Designer Politics: How Elections are Won*. New York: St Martins.

Scammell, M. and Semetko, H. 1998: *The Campaign in the News: Media and Party Agendas in the 1997 General Election*. A conference paper delivered at the Political Studies Association Conference, Keele University, 7–9 April.

Schlesinger, P. 1987: *Putting "Reality" Together: BBC News*. Second Edition, London: Routledge.

——. 1990: Rethinking the Sociology of Journalism: Source Strategies and the Limits of Media-Centrism. In M. Ferguson (ed.), *Public Communication the New*

Imperatives: Future Directions for Media Research. London and Newbury Park, CA: Sage.

Schlesinger, P. and Tumber, H. 1994: *Reporting Crime: The Media Politics of Criminal Justice*. Oxford: Clarendon Press.

Schlesinger, P., Murdock, G. and Elliott, P. 1983: *Televising Terrorism: Political Violence in Popular Culture*. London: Comedia Publishing Group.

Semetko, H. 1989: Television News and the "Third Force" in British Politics: A Case Study of Election Communication. *European Journal of Communication* 4 (4), 453–79.

Semetko, H. and Canel, M. J. 1997: Agenda-Senders Versus Agenda-Setters: Television in Spain's 1996 Election Campaign. *Political Communication* 14 (4), 459–79.

Semetko, H., Blumler, J. G., Gurevitch, M. and Weaver, D. H. 1991: *The Formation of Campaign Agendas: A Comparative Analysis of Party and Media Roles in Recent American and British Elections*. New Jersey: L. E. Arnold.

Seyd, P. 1999: New Parties/New Politics? A Case Study of the British Labour Party. *Party Politics* 5 (3), 383–405.

Seyd, P. and Whiteley, P. 1992: *Labour's Grass Roots: The Politics of Party Membership*. Oxford: Clarendon Press.

Seymour-Ure, C. 1989: Prime Ministers' Reactions to Television. *Media, Culture and Society* 11 (3), 307–25.

——. 1991: *The British Press and Broadcasting Since 1945*. Oxford: Basil Blackwell.

——. 1996: Leaders. In J. Seaton and B. Pimlott (eds), *The Media in British Politics*, reprinted, Aldershot: Dartmouth.

Shaw, E. 1994: *The Labour Party Since 1979: Crisis and Transformation*. London: Routledge.

Shoemaker, P. 1991: *Gatekeeping*. Newbury Park, CA: Sage.

Sigal, L. V. 1973: *Reporters and Officials: The Organization and Politics of News Making*. Lexington, Mass.: D. C. Heath & Co.

Smithers, R. 1996: Party's Mr Nasty Scores Another Own Goal. *The Guardian*, 30 November, p. 3.

Sowemimo, M. 1996: The Conservative Party and European Integration 1988–95. *Party Politics* 2 (1), 77–97.

Spector, M. and Kitsuse, J. I. 1987: *Constructing Social Problems*. New York: Aldine de Gruyter.

Staff Reporters. 1994: Tory Celebrities Face Photo Call-off. *The Times*, 11 October, p. 11.

Stanyer, J. 1997: The 1996 British Party Conferences as News Events: Assessing the Contribution of the Broadcasters to Conference News Agendas. In Jeffrey Stanyer and G. Stoker (eds) *Contemporary Political Studies: Vol 1*. Oxford: Blackwells.

Stanyer, J. and Scammell, M. 1996: *On the Fringe: The Changing Nature of the Party Conference Fringe and its coverage by the Media*. A conference paper delivered at the Political Studies Association Conference, Glasgow University, 10–12 April.

Swanson, D. and Mancini, P. 1996: Patterns of Modern Electoral Campaigning and Their Consequences. In D. Swanson and P. Mancini (eds), *Politics, Media and Modern Democracy*, Westport, CN: Praeger.

Tebbit, N. 1988: *Upwardly Mobile*. London: Weidenfeld & Nicolson.

Thomas, H. 1989: *Making an Impact*. Newton Abbot: David and Charles.

Thompson, J. B. 1995: *The Media and Modernity: A Social Theory of the Media*. Cambridge: Polity.

Thynne, J. 1995: Labour Row Over BBC News Delay. *The Daily Telegraph*, 11 October, p. 9.

Tiffen, R. 1989: *News and Power*. Sydney: Allen and Unwin.

Timmins, N. 1991: The Prince of Darkness Casts Shadow Over Labour. *The Independent*, 25 May, p. 11.

Toolis, K. 1998: The Enforcer. *The Guardian*, Weekend Section, 4 April, pp. 29–36.

Tracey, M. 1977: *The Production of Political Television*. London: Routledge and Kegan Paul.

Tuchman, G. 1978: *Making News: A Study in the Construction of Reality*, New York: The Free Press.

Tunstall, J. 1970: *The Westminster Lobby Correspondents: A Sociological Study of National Political Journalism*. London: Routledge and Kegan Paul.

Tunstall, J. 1971: *Journalists at Work: Specialist Correspondents, their News Organizations, News Sources and Competitor Colleagues*. London: Constable.

Tutt, B. 1992: Televising the Commons: A Full, Balanced and Fair Account of the Work of the House. In B. Franklin (ed.), *Televising Democracies*, London: Routledge.

Walker, D. 1996: From Our Own 500 Correspondents. *The Independent*, 1 October, p. 15.

Waltzer, H. 1966: In the Magic Lantern: Television Coverage of the 1964 National Conventions. *Public Opinion Quarterly* 30 (1), 35–53.

Watt, N. 2000: Hague Orders Gag on Thatcher to Stop Her Stealing Tory Show. *The Guardian*, 22 July, p. 2.

Webb, D. 1994: Party Organizational Change in Britain: The Iron Law of Centralization? In R. Katz and P. Mair (eds), *How Parties Organize: Change and Adaptation in Party Organizations in Western Democracies*, London and Newbury Park, CA: Sage.

Weber, R. P. 1990: *Basic Content Analysis*. London and Newbury Park, CA: Sage.

Webster, P. 1995: BBC was Implored to Give Leader's Speech Priority. *The Times*, 4 October, p. 1.

White, L. 1994: Blair's Head Boy. *The Sunday Times Magazine*, 11 December, pp. 58–64.

Whiteley, P., Seyd, P. and Richardson, J. 1994: *True Blues: The Politics of Conservative Party Membership*. Oxford: Clarendon Press.

Wilson, M. 1977: Grass Roots Conservatism: Motions to the Party Conference. In N. Nugent and R. King (eds), *The British Right: Rightwing Politics in Britain*, London: Saxon House.

Wintour, P. 1990: The Rise of the Red Rinse Conference. *The Guardian*, 6 October, p. 6.

——. 1991: Kinnock Tries to End Propaganda Feud. *The Guardian*, 30 May, p. 2.

——. 1994: Hanley Deputy Adds to Gaffes. *The Guardian*, 11 October, p. 6.

——. 1994b: Ashdown to Recruit Key Strategy Chief. *The Guardian*, 30 December, p. 14.

——. 1995: Tories Revive Unit to Check Media Bias. *The Guardian*, 9 May, p. 3.

——. 1995b: How the Party Fixed the Show. *The Guardian*, 7 October, p. 25.

——. 1996: Labour Changes Colour to Suit TV. *The Guardian*, 26 January, p. 7.

——. 1997: Blair Rethink Over "Emasculating" Party. *The Guardian*, 27 July, p. 2.

Wintour, P. and Harper, K. 1994: Defeat Raises Questions Over Blair Team's Conference Management. *The Guardian*, 7 October, p. 7.

Wring, D. 1998: The Media and Intra-Party Democracy: New Labour and the Clause Four Debate in Britain. *Democratization* 5, (2), 42–61.

Index

Page numbers in bold type indicate a main reference. Use of *passim* indicates that a number of references to a topic are scattered throughout the immediately preceding page range. Where identically numbered endnotes are found on the same page, the relevant chapter number is given in brackets to aid identification.